The King's Royal Rifle Corps
... the 60th Rifles

A Brief History: 1755–1965

John Tweed's Bronze Statue of a First World War Rifleman

The bronze statue of a First World War Rifleman by John Tweed (above) stands atop the Regimental War Memorial opposite the West Door of Winchester Cathedral. The Memorial, which was paid for by regimental subscription, was unveiled on 24 May 1922 by HRH Prince Henry, later The Duke of Gloucester and an officer in the Regiment from 1919-21. Originally dedicated as a memorial to all those who died in the service of The King's Royal Rifle Corps in the First World War, it now serves as the Regimental War Memorial to all those who died in the service of The King's Royal Rifle Corps in both World Wars and other conflicts.

The King's Royal Rifle Corps ... the 60th Rifles

A Brief History: 1755–1965

From Royal Americans to Royal Green Jackets

by
Lieutenant-General Sir Christopher Wallace
KBE DL

Published by
The Royal Green Jackets Museum Trust

Maps drawn by Bob Thorn
Designed by Columns Design Limited, Caversham, Reading, Berkshire
Printed and bound by Cromwell Press Limited, Trowbridge, Wiltshire

Contents

Illustrations

Note: Every effort has been made to trace the origin and give attribution to illustrations that are not sourced from within the Regiment. Where thanks are due, they are readily given.

Illustrations

MAPS

HM Queen Elizabeth II, Colonel-in-Chief 1953–65, wearing her King's Royal Rifle Corps regimental brooch

The King's Royal Rifle Corps

Titles of the Regiment

1755	62nd or Royal American Regiment of Foot
1756	60th or Royal American Regiment of Foot
1824	60th Regiment, The Duke of York's Own Rifle Corps
1830	The 60th, The King's Royal Rifle Corps
1881	The King's Royal Rifle Corps
1958	2nd Green Jackets, The King's Royal Rifle Corps

Motto

Celer et Audax
(Swift and Bold)

Colonels-in-Chief

1755-7	Lieutenant-General the Earl of Loudoun
1757-8	Major-General James Abercromby
1758-68	Lieutenant-General Sir Jeffery Amherst
1768	Major-General Thomas Gage
1768-97	Field Marshal Lord Amherst
1797-1827	HRH Prince Frederick, Duke of York
1827-50	HRH Prince Adolphus, Duke of Cambridge
1850-2	HRH Prince Albert, the Prince Consort
1852-3	General Viscount Beresford
1854-69	Field Marshal Viscount Gough
1869-1904	HRH Prince George, Duke of Cambridge
1904-36	HRH The Prince of Wales (From 1910: HM King George V)
1937-52	HM King George VI
1953-65	HM Queen Elizabeth II

Field Marshals of the Regiment

Field Marshal Sir John Forster Fitzgerald GCB
Field Marshal Lord Clyde GCB KSI
Field Marshal the Rt. Hon. Lord Grenfell GCB GCMG PC
Field Marshal Sir Roland Gibbs GCB CBE DSO MC
Field Marshal Lord Bramall KG GCB OBE MC

Battle Honours

1756–1902

Louisburg   Quebec, 1759   Martinique, 1762   Havannah
North America, 1763–64   Rolica   Vimiera   Martinique, 1809   Talavera
Busaco   Fuentes d'Onor   Albuhera   Ciudad Rodrigo   Badajoz
Salamanca   Vittoria   Pyrenees   Nivelle   Nive   Orthes   Toulouse
Peninsula   Mooltan   Goojerat   Punjaub   South Africa, 1851-53
Delhi, 1857   Taku Forts   Pekin, 1860   South Africa, 1879   Ahmad Khel
Kandahar, 1880   Afghanistan, 1878–80   Tel-el-Kebir   Egypt, 1882, 1884
Chitral   Defence of Ladysmith   Relief of Ladysmith
South Africa, 1899–1902

The First World War

Mons   Retreat from Mons   Marne, 1914   Aisne, 1914
Ypres, 1914, '15, '17, '18   Langemarck, 1914, '17   Gheluvelt
Nonne Bosschen   Givenchy, 1914   Gravenstafel   St Julien   Frezenberg
Bellewaarde   Aubers   Festubert, 1915   Hooge, 1915   Loos
Somme, 1916, '18   Albert, 1916, '18   Bazentin   Delville Wood   Pozieres
Guillemont   Flers-Courcelette   Morval   Le Transloy   Ancre Heights
Ancre, 1916, '18   Arras, 1917, '18   Scarpe, 1917   Arleux
Messines, 1917, '18   Pilckem   Menin Road   Polygon Wood
Broodseinde   Poelcappelle   Passchendaele   Cambrai, 1917, '18   St Quentin
Rosieres   Avre   Lys   Bailleul   Kemmel   Béthune   Bapaume, 1918
Drocourt-Quéant   Hindenburg Line   Havrincourt   Epéhy   Canal du Nord
St Quentin Canal   Beaurevoir   Courtrai   Selle   Sambre
France and Flanders, 1914–18   Italy, 1917–18   Macedonia, 1916–18

The Second World War

Calais, 1940   Mont Pincon   Falaise   Roer   Rhineland   Cleve   Goch
Hochwald   Rhine   Dreirwalde   Aller   North-West Europe, 1940, '44–45
Egyptian Frontier, 1940   Sidi Barrani   Derna Aerodrome   Tobruk, 1941
Sidi Rezegh, 1941   Gazala   Bir Hacheim   Knightsbridge
Defence of Alamein Line   Ruweisat   Fuka Airfield   Alam el Haifa
El Alamein   Capture of Halfaya Pass   Nofilia   Tebaga Gap
Argoub el Megas   Tunis   North Africa, 1940–43   Sangro   Arezzo
Coriano   Lamone Crossing   Argenta Gap   Italy, 1943-45   Veve
Greece, 1941, '44–45   Crete   Middle East, 1941

The Battle Honours printed in **bold** type are those the Regiment is entitled to bear on its Appointments

x

For Valour

Twenty-four Victoria Crosses were awarded to members of the Regular, Service and Territorial battalions of The King's Royal Rifle Corps

Rifleman	S. Turner	Delhi, 1857
Colour Sergeant	S. Garvin	Delhi, 1857
Lieutenant	A.S. Heathcote[e]	Delhi, 1857
Colour Sergeant	G. Waller[e]	Delhi, 1957
Rifleman	J. Thompson[e]	Delhi, 1857
Rifleman	J. Divane[e]	Delhi, 1857
Bugler	W. Sutton[e]	Delhi, 1857
Ensign	E.A. Lisle Phillipps[†]	Delhi, 1857
Rifleman	V. Bambrick	India, 1858
Brevet Lieutenant-Colonel	R.H. Buller	Zululand, 1879
Rifleman	F. Corbett	Egypt, 1882
Lieutenant	P.S. Marling	Sudan, 1884
Lieutenant	The Hon. F.H.S. Roberts[†]	South Africa, 1899
Lieutenant	L.A.E. Price-Davies DSO	South Africa, 1901
Lieutenant	J.H.S. Dimmer	Belgium, 1914
Lieutenant	J.F.P. Butler	West Africa, 1914
Second Lieutenant	G.H. Woolley (QVR)	Belgium, 1915
Rifleman	W. Mariner	France, 1915
Rifleman	G.S. Peachment[†]	France, 1915
Sergeant	A. Gill[†]	France, 1916
Sergeant	E. Cooper	Belgium, 1917
Rifleman	A.E. Shepherd	France, 1917
Lance-Corporal	J.A. Christie (Finsbury Rifles)	Palestine, 1917
Rifleman	J. Beeley[†]	North Africa, 1941

e = Elected by Ballot   † = Posthumous

Notes:
1. Ranks and decorations were those held at the time of the act of gallantry for which the Victoria Cross was awarded.
2. Privates were known as Riflemen, although the rank was not formally approved until 1923.

xi

Key Events in the History of the Regiment

Note: Battalions involved in Key Events are listed in brackets. Years in which the Title of the Regiment and its Colonels-in-Chief changed are shown on page ix. Years in which battalions were disbanded and, in some cases, re-formed are recorded at Appendix B.

25 Dec 1755	Lord Loudon appointed Colonel-in-Chief
	Regimental Birthday
1756	1st, 2nd, 3rd and 4th Battalion raised
1756–63	Seven Years War & Conquest of Canada
	(1st, 2nd, 3rd & 4th)
	26 Jul 1758 Capture of Louisbourg (2nd and 3rd)
	13 Sep 1759 Battle of Quebec (2nd and 3rd)
	27 Jan 1762 Capture of Martinique (3rd)
	13 Aug 1762 Capture of Havana (3rd)
1763–4	Pontiac's Rebellion & War with the Indians (1st)
	5/6 Aug 1763 Battle of Bushy Run (1st)
1775–83	American War of Independence (2nd, 3rd and 4th)
	Oct 1779 Defence of Savannah (4th)
1793–1802	French Revolutionary Wars (3rd and 4th)
Dec 1797	Act of Parliament raising 5th Battalion
Jul 1799	Act of Parliament raising 6th Battalion
1803–10	Napoleonic Wars – West Indies (3rd, 4th and 6th)
	24 Feb 1809 Capture of Martinique (3rd and 4th)
1808–14	Napoleonic Wars – Peninsula (2nd and 5th)
	(*See page 46*)
1813	Act of Parliament raising 7th and 8th Battalion
1812–15	War against the United States (7th)
1816–19	Reduction from Eight to Two battalions
1848–9	Second Sikh War (1st)
	Dec 1848 to Jan 1849 Siege of Mooltan (1st)
	21 Feb 1849 Battle of Goojerat (1st)
1849–50	North-West Frontier (1st)
1850–3	War in South Africa (2nd)
26 Feb 1852	HM Troopship *Birkenhead* wrecked (2nd)
1857–9	Indian Mutiny (1st and 2nd)
	Jun to Sep 1857 Relief and Capture of Delhi (1st)
	1858 Campaigns in Rohilkund and Oudh (1st)

KRRC BRIEF HISTORY – ERRATA

Page vi, Line 14. Page 57, Heading; Para 2, Line 8; Caption to Picture. Index, Page 263. It has come to light since the History was printed that the huge elephant that carried the pole of the Officers Mess marquee on the march to Goojerat (1849) was called Gullala and not Tullala. Please amend where shown.

Page xi, Line 6   Amend the date alongside Colour Sergeant Waller to read 1857 not 1957.

Page xii, Line 3 of Note at top of page   Amend Appendix B to read Appendix A.

Page xiii, Line 9   Amend the date of the First Boer War to read 1881 not 1880.

Page 89, Line 5   Amend 1881 to read 1891.

Page 207, Line 4 under *Borneo, 1965*   Delete "previously" as Brunei remained a British protectorate until 1984.

If readers of this Brief History spot any other errors and can verify the facts, please be sure to let me know c/o The Royal Green Jackets Museum, Winchester, SO23 8TS.   Thank you.

Christopher Wallace

1858	Rifle Depot established at Winchester
1860	Second China War (2nd)
	21 Aug 1860 Capture of Taku Forts (2nd)
1870	Red River Expedition, Canada (1st)
1878-80	Second Afghan War (2nd)
	9-31 Aug 1880 March from Kabul to Kandahar (2nd)
1879	Zulu War (3rd)
	2 Apr 1879 Action at Ginghilovo (3rd)
1880	First Boer War (3rd)
	8 Feb 1881 Action on the Ingogo River (3rd)
1882	Egypt (3rd)
	13 Sep 1882 Battle of Tel-el-Kebir (3rd)
1884-5	Egypt and Sudan (3rd)
	29 Feb 1884 Battle of El Teb (3rd)
	13 Mar 1884 Battle of Tamaai (3rd)
1891-2	Manipur and Burma (4th)
1891-5	North-West Frontier (1st)
	Apr 1895 Chitral Relief Expedition (1st)
14 Jan 1897	RIMS *Warren Hastings* wrecked (1st)
1899-1902	South African War (1st, 2nd, 3rd and 4th)
	20 Oct 1899 Battle of Talana Hill (1st)
	30 Oct 1899 to 28 Feb 1900 Defence and Relief of
	Ladysmith (1st, 2nd and 3rd)
	15 Dec 1899 Battle of Colenso (3rd)
	24 Jan and 5-7 Feb 1900 Twin Peaks and Vaal
	Krantz (3rd)
1914-18	First World War (All)
	(See Chapter 6)
1936-7	Palestine (2nd)
1939-45	Second World War (All)
	22-26 May 1940 Defence of Calais (2nd and 1 QVR)
	21/22 Nov 1941 Sidi Rezegh (1st)
	23 Oct to 3 Nov 1942 Battle of El Alamein
	(1st, 2nd and 11th)
	Jun 1944 Normandy (2nd and 12th)
1946-8	Palestine (2nd)
1958	Green Jackets Brigade formed
1965	Malaysia (Borneo) (2 GJ)
1 Jan 1966	Regiment merged into The Royal Green Jackets

Introduction

This Brief History of The King's Royal Rifle Corps has been written to coincide with the 250th Anniversary of the founding of the Regiment in North America in 1755 – a Regiment that was titled the Royal Americans and was the first in the British Army to wear green jackets instead of red coats and to be issued with rifles instead of muskets.

This volume replaces and expands upon three earlier editions, published in 1912, 1917 and 1948. Mindful that the Regiment ceased to form a part of the British Army's order of battle at midnight on 31 December 1965, and that nearly all the surviving members are now aged over sixty, I anticipate that it will be the last. I have, therefore, endeavoured to make it a useful source of quick reference for historians in the future; hence it traces the history of the Regiment chronologically and is full of facts. I have also tried to write it in a manner, which those with only limited or no previous knowledge of the Regiment will find easy to read and informative.

Space dictates that this Brief History is what it is – a brief history. It reduces the content of 2,500 pages in seven volumes of Regimental *Annals* to one-tenth of their original length. I am conscious, therefore, that some may be disappointed that I have excluded mention of an event or individual, maybe a relative, of particular matter to them. I am also conscious that this is not an original work. It is culled almost entirely from the content of the *Annals*, supplemented by other material in the Regimental Archives, including the *Chronicles* from 1901 to 1965. Additionally, I have drawn upon Osprey Publishing's admirable series of *Essential Histories* for background information on the wars and campaigns in which the Regiment was involved. Where quoted material is not sourced in the text, it will be from the *Annals*.

It is an admission on my part that, despite being commissioned into the Regiment in 1962, I had not previously read the *Annals* prior to offering to write this Brief History. Only now do I realize how excellent they are, and the huge debt of gratitude that the Regiment owes the authors. During my research the occasional error of fact was identified, which I have corrected. Equally, I make no claim that all errors of fact have been eliminated from this volume; indeed, one thing I have learned as a student of military history is that errors of fact have a habit of being perpetuated by those who choose to rely on other people's work.

I have looked upon it as my role in writing this Brief History to focus on the facts rather than offer personal comment or opinion. I have also recorded events as they occurred, reporting on the good and the bad, the successes and the failures. I have sought to avoid eulogizing. In my view, the facts speak for themselves. For those who wish for more information than is included in this Brief History, some further reading is listed at Appendix G.

I end this Introduction by thanking a number of people who have helped to produce this Brief History, especially Roy Trustram Eve, whose idea it was, and who has devoted enormous time and effort to its publication. I am also extremely grateful to Andrew Ayling for compiling the Index and to Giles Mills, author of the last two volumes of the *Annals*, whose advice I have often sought and whose knowledge of Regimental history is second to none. Others who have made significant contributions (in alphabetical order) are Dwin Bramall, Ron Cassidy, Richard Frost, Roly Guy, Patrick Maclure and Ian McCausland. I also thank the Museum staff – Ken Gray, Stuart Morris and Christine Radford. I am particularly grateful to Bob Thorn for drawing the maps and for the assistance given to him by Richard Bunel. Columns Design and Cromwell Press have been extremely helpful in providing expert advice. Above all, very special thanks are due to the Directors of RAB Capital plc, a hedge fund quoted on the Alternative Investment Market, who at the outset contributed handsomely towards underwriting the costs of publication of this Brief History, thus enabling more of the sale proceeds to accrue to The Royal Green Jackets Museum. To all who have contributed, whether mentioned by name or not, thank you; and to all who read this Brief History, I hope you will find it of interest. I dedicate it to the Regiment.

Christopher Wallace
President, The King's Royal Rifle Corps Association

Winchester, July 2005

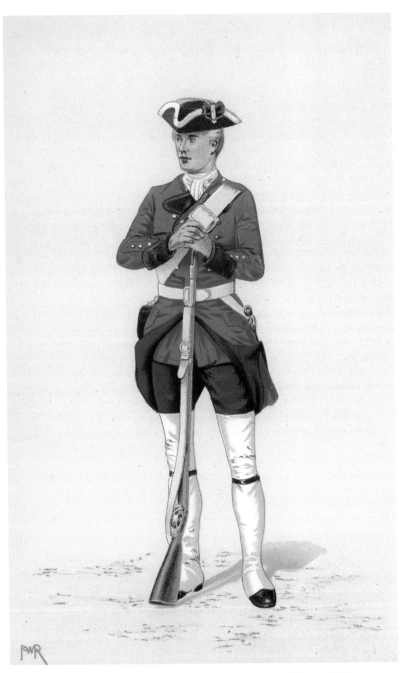

Private, 60th or Royal American Regiment of Foot, 1758

Chapter 1

1755–83: The Royal Americans

The Origins of the Regiment

In 1755 storm clouds were brewing over Europe as open and undisguised hostilities between France and Great Britain threatened the start of what was later to be known as the Seven Years War (1756–63). These hostilities extended to North America where the settlers from both countries competed for territory and trade with the native Indians.

On 9 July 1755, on the Monongahela River, a numerically inferior force of French and Indians routed two regiments of the British Army sent from England under the command of Major General Edward Braddock to displace the French from Fort Duquesne (now Pittsburgh). The British redcoats, trained to conform to the ways of European warfare, proved no match for their more cunning and elusive opponents in the broken and afforested terrain of western Pennsylvania. Recognising the shortcomings of his force and of their tactics, and as he lay dying from wounds sustained during the battle, General Braddock uttered the immortal words for which he will always be remembered: 'Who would have thought it? We shall know better next time how to do it' – words whose meaning was not lost on those who were soon to play a central role in the creation and training of the Royal Americans.[1]

General Braddock's unexpected defeat heightened the need for the British Government to make better provision for the defence of its Thirteen Colonies in North America.[2] Those looking for ideas may well have heard of the very creditable behaviour during the battle of a group of Virginian militia under the command of Colonel George Washington,[3] whose actions showed that an abundance of good irregular troops was to be found in America and that the British needed only to learn from their enemies to defeat them.[4]

Such thoughts, no doubt, had crossed the mind of James (Jacques) Prevost, a Swiss, who arrived in London in October 1755 with a proposal that a regular regiment of the British Army should be raised in America, and that it should be manned largely by German and Swiss settlers from Pennsylvania, with a mix of foreign officers and some non-commissioned officers (NCOs) from Europe, including English, Scottish and Irish, under a British colonel-in-chief.[5] This proposal quickly found favour with The Duke of Cumberland, Commander-in-Chief of the British Army, and with the King, George II, who, before Christmas 1755, advanced £2,500 to Prevost to initiate the recruitment of suitable officers and NCOs.

Weak government under the Prime Minister, the Duke of Newcastle, and opposition from William Pitt[6] delayed receipt of the necessary Parliamentary approval. Indeed, it was not until 4 March 1756 that an Act of Parliament was passed authorising the establishment of a regiment of four battalions, to be known as the 62nd or Royal American Regiment of Foot. £81,000 was voted for the purpose. Additionally, Parliament agreed to legislation 'to enable His Majesty to grant commissions to a certain number of foreign Protestants, who have served abroad as officers or engineers, to act and rank as officers or engineers in America *only*, under certain restrictions and regulations'. The restrictions included limiting the number of foreign officers to fifty and the number of engineers to twenty, and barring their promotion above the rank of lieutenant-colonel.

To ensure proper supervision and administration of the Regiment in America, Lieutenant-General John Campbell, the Earl of Loudoun, Commander-in-Chief (Designate) in North America, was appointed the first Colonel-in-Chief of the Regiment, a title granted to the head of no other regiment at the time. Under him, a colonel-commandant was appointed to each battalion.[7] The title 'Royal Americans' was also most probably conferred with intent, not only as a sign of the King's favour, but as a means by which to associate the Regiment with the Colonies from which it was largely to recruit, and to bind its members, *ab initio*, to the British Crown.[8]

By the time the Act received Royal Assent on 9 March 1756, James Prevost had already gathered together some ninety officers and NCOs to join the Regiment, amongst whom were Henry (Henri) Bouquet and Frederick Haldimand, Swiss officers of known ability serving in the bodyguard of the Prince of Orange. Prevost also recruited his brothers, Augustin and Jean-Marc, and a contingent of Germans, including Baron Dietrich von Münster and a number of NCOs and soldiers. Half the officers were volunteers from other regiments in the British Army.[9]

Appointments were backdated, many to late December, including the appointment of Lord Loudoun as Colonel-in-Chief, which was dated 25 December 1755, the date adopted as the Regiment's birthday.

The Seven Years War in North America and the Caribbean

1756: Raising the Regiment

The raising of the Regiment coincided with the start of the Seven Years War on 18 May 1756. The uneasy peace that had in name existed in North America was now formally at an end.

Organization of the Regiment

In 1756 the establishment of each battalion of the Regiment allowed for ten companies, each of four sergeants, four corporals, two drummers and 100 privates. As the highest regimental rank for which pay could be drawn was that of captain, every colonel-commandant, lieutenant-colonel and major was nominally appointed to command of a company, although, in practice, command was exercised by captains and lieutenants.

While it was the intention that the battalions of the Regiment should adopt the tactics most suited to the environment, they were equipped in the manner of an infantry regiment of the line, with red coats, muskets and Colours. The only concession to bush warfare was that the uniforms were to be made devoid of lace.

Bouquet and Haldimand, appointed to command the 1st and 2nd Battalion respectively, were among the first to sail for America, arriving on 15 June 1756. Lord Loudoun followed, arriving in New York on 23 July.

On 13 March 1756 instructions had been forwarded to reserve the province of Pennsylvania as a recruiting ground for the Royal Americans. However, recruiting in the towns and more thickly populated districts was not easy. Greater success was achieved among the western settlements and backwoodsmen, mainly English, Swiss, Tyrolese and Germans – 'a strong and hardy race accustomed to the country and inured to the climate; from their conditions and habits of life well adapted to oppose the enemy, whether French or Red Indians; and of the very material to carry on frontier warfare, accustomed as they were to the use of the rifle'.[10]

Difficulty in recruiting prevailed.[11] On 3 October 1756, Lord Loudoun wrote: 'Three battalions of the Royal Americans are still to raise, desertion is beyond all bounds; I have lost 30 deserters of the Royal Americans since they came to Albany.'[12] Quartering, too, was a problem with the Colonists happy to accept the protection of the Army but not to pay the price. Smallpox took its toll. Notwithstanding, numbers gradually increased, although it was not until early 1758 that the battalions neared their established strengths.

Meanwhile, in August 1756, further disaster struck when the French overwhelmed the garrison of Fort Oswego, resulting in the 50th and 51st Regiment of Foot being disbanded and the 62nd or Royal American Regiment of Foot being renumbered the 60th. Some of those formerly in the 50th and 51st joined the 60th.

1757: Initial Deployments

On 16 May 1757 five companies of the 1st Battalion, weak in numbers and under command of Bouquet, sailed to Charleston on the Regiment's first operational deployment, to form part of a force to defend the frontiers of the Southern Colonies from the French in Louisiana. In the

---

Renumbering of the 62nd to the 60th

In 1745 two regiments of Provincials engaged in capturing Louisbourg from the French were taken into the British Army as the 50th (Shirley's) and 51st (Pepperrell's) Regiment of Foot. Following the Peace of Aix-la-Chapelle (1748), which brought the War of Austrian Succession to an end, the Regiments were disbanded. In September 1754 they were reinstated for service in North America.

In January 1756, anticipating war and fearing invasion from France, the British Government agreed to the creation of ten new infantry regiments of the line, numbered from 52 to 61. In March 1756 the 62nd or Royal American Regiment of Foot was added. Appointments in the regiments were backdated to December 1755, the month and year in which all are listed as being founded.

In August 1756, the 50th and 51st Regiment were severely mauled during the capture of Fort Oswego by the French. On 22 December 1756 both regiments were struck off the Army List resulting in those regiments numbered 52 to 62 being renumbered 50 to 60. Thus, the 62nd became the 60th or Royal American Regiment of Foot.

---

event, the deployment proved needless. Smallpox reappeared and, after five months in the Carolinas, Bouquet had only 300 men fit for duty. Meanwhile, under his direction and training the men improved rapidly. In March 1758, Bouquet's five companies were recalled to New York.

The Regiment's other battalions were also engaged in 1757. In mid-year the 2nd and 4th Battalion formed part of a force that sailed to Halifax with the intention of attacking Louisbourg (Louisburg), an attack that was later aborted. Subsequently, in August, 200 men of the 3rd Battalion, under their commanding officer, Lieutenant-Colonel John Young, were ordered to reinforce the British garrison at Fort William Henry which, after a brave defence, was obliged to surrender to a much larger French and Indian force. The Indians then massacred a number of prisoners, with the small group from the 3rd Battalion suffering a total loss of about eighty men from death, disease and wounds – the first casualties to be sustained in action by the Regiment.

The year 1757 marked a low point in the fortunes of the British. In December Lord Loudoun was recalled to London, to be replaced as Commander-in-Chief in North America by Major-General James Abercromby. At the same time Abercromby became the Regiment's second Colonel-in-Chief.

1758: The Conquest of Canada (Year One)

Before his departure, Lord Loudoun had decided to launch a campaign in 1758 centred on three distinct operations: first, to capture Louisbourg; secondly, to invade Canada by way of Lake Champlain; thirdly, to seize Fort Duquesne.

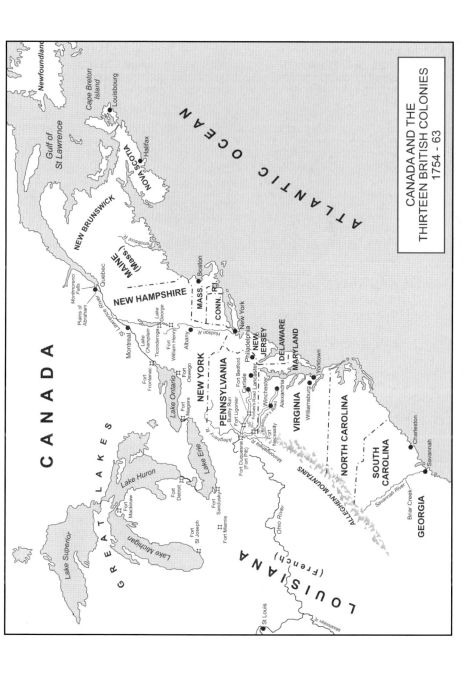

CANADA AND THE
THIRTEEN BRITISH COLONIES
1754 - 63

Capture of Louisbourg, 26 July 1758
The landing on the tricky Cape Breton coastline and the siege and capture of Louisbourg by the British, under the command of Major-General Jeffery Amherst,[13] involved a substantial force of 11,000 men, including both the 2nd and 3rd Battalion. Each was at close to full strength, the former under command of Colonel Robert Monckton, Colonel Commandant of the 2nd Battalion, and the latter under John Young.

Some 550 marksmen from the overall force, including some 70–80 from the 2nd and 3rd Battalion, were drafted to form light troops, under the title of Light Infantry. These men were chosen 'out of the most active, resolute men from all the battalions of Regulars; dressed some in blue, some in green jackets and drawers, for the easier brushing through the woods; with ruffs of black bear skin round their necks; ... Their arms were a Fusil (or Rifle) Cartouche box and a Powder Horn.'[14] Each battalion also provided a grenadier company, to be grouped with other grenadier companies, as required.

After landing on 8 June, it was not until 26 July, after a prolonged siege, that the French garrison surrendered. Losses amongst the Royal Americans were just over eighty killed and wounded. The prize, however, was great as the British now commanded the entrance to the St Lawrence and passage for ships to Quebec and Montreal. It was, however, too late in the year to exploit such opportunity, with both battalions spending the winter in Halifax, Nova Scotia. 'Louisburg' was subsequently granted as the Regiment's first Battle Honour.

Defeat at Ticonderoga, 8 July 1758
The route chosen to invade Canada involved capturing Fort Ticonderoga at the northern extreme of Lake George and south of Lake Champlain. In June, General Abercromby mustered a force of nearly 15,000, including six companies of the 1st Battalion and the whole of the 4th Battalion, the latter under command of Haldimand.[15] On 5 July the force set off by boat with Lord Howe, formerly Colonel-Commandant of the 3rd Battalion, at its head. On the following day the leading elements were in contact with the French and Lord Howe was killed.[16] On 8 July a major assault was launched against the 3,600 French troops defending Fort Ticonderoga. The outcome was disastrous. Although bravely fought, the attack failed and the British withdrew, their invasion route blocked. The British losses were heavy, nearly 2,000 men, including 50 Royal Americans killed and 230 wounded.

Seizure of Fort Frontenac, 27 August 1758
Wishing to resume the offensive, Lieutenant-Colonel Bradstreet of the 60th,[17] who had distinguished himself at Ticonderoga, persuaded Abercromby to allow him to launch an expedition to seize Fort Frontenac (now Kingston), an important post on the north bank of the strait connecting Lake Ontario with the St Lawrence. On 22 August

Bradstreet set out in a flotilla of boats on Lake Ontario with 3,000 men, including two companies of the 1st Battalion. On 27 August the French commander at Frontenac, with only 110 men at his disposal, surrendered. The blow struck was second only to the capture of Louisbourg. Fort Duquesne and the chain of French forts to the south and west were isolated.

Seizure of Fort Duquesne, 25 November 1758

The third objective in 1758 was the seizure of Fort Duquesne. Command was assigned to Brigadier-General Forbes with a force of 6,000, including, under Bouquet, the four companies of the 1st Battalion which had not been at Ticonderoga and whose task since returning from the Carolinas in the spring had been to defend the western frontiers of British territory.[18]

Forbes and Bouquet shared original ideas about the training and equipment of troops for forest warfare. Mindful of Braddock's defeat in 1755, Forbes wrote to Bouquet: 'We must learn the art of war from the Indians.' But Bouquet did not stop at mere matters of dress, for he obtained sixteen rifle-barrelled 'fusils' (rifles) for his battalion, thus turning a part of the 60th into riflemen before their time.[19]

In July 1758, with Bouquet leading,[20] Forbes's force started to cut a new 100-mile route through the forest to reach Fort Duquesne. Progress was slow and the conditions atrocious. However, without hope of reinforcement and with the British approaching, the French destroyed the fort and withdrew northwards, abandoning a key position in the Ohio valley to the British. On 25 November Forbes's exhausted troops occupied the position and started to build a new fort, named Fort Pitt (hence Pittsburgh). A garrison of 200 Provincials was left to defend the fort, while the remainder of Forbes's force returned to Pennsylvania.

1759: The Conquest of Canada (Year Two)

In September 1758, General Abercromby was recalled to England and promoted. In his place, General Amherst, victor at Louisbourg, aged 40, was appointed Commander-in-Chief in North America and became the Regiment's third Colonel-in-Chief in as many years.

Amherst's campaign plan for 1759 centred upon the conduct of a number of separate operations to achieve the conquest of Canada. These were: first, to capture Quebec; secondly, to advance upon Montreal via Ticonderoga; thirdly, to seize Fort Niagara at the south-west corner of Lake Ontario; fourthly, to relieve the garrison at Fort Pitt and capture the French forts between Forts Pitt and Niagara.

Battle of Quebec, 13 September 1759

Amherst appointed General Wolfe to command the attack upon Quebec, placing ten battalions under his command for the task, including the 2nd and 3rd Battalion of the Royal Americans, the former under command of Captain Thomas Oswald and the latter still under command of John Young. The light infantry troops and grenadier companies of both battalions were grouped centrally, as they had been at Louisbourg.

Setting sail from Louisbourg in early June, the British force moved up the St Lawrence River arriving off Quebec towards the end of the month. Various raids were conducted ashore, including an attempt on 31 July to storm the heights above Montmorenci Falls, during which the participating grenadier companies of the 60th and 200 men of the 2nd Battalion suffered severely. Such was the behaviour of the assaulting troops in the face of overwhelming odds - a heady mix of gallantry, bravado and irrationality - that General Wolfe felt obliged to comment: 'Such impetuous, irregular and unsoldierlike proceedings destroy all order, and put it out of the General's power to execute his plan.'[21]

It must then have been very welcome to the Regiment when, in a subsequent action in early August, the two grenadier companies of the 60th so impressed General Wolfe with their 'spirited conduct, alertness and intrepidity on all occasions' that he conferred upon them the motto *Celer et Audax* (See Appendix B).

Eventually General Wolfe identified a weakness in the French defences and during the night of 12 September launched the British assault on Quebec with a surprise landing by boats at the foot of the formidable Heights of Abraham. Scaling the cliffs under cover of darkness, with the light infantry troops of the 2nd Battalion seizing a key post at the top, the British amassed sufficient forces on the Plain above by early morning on 13 September to force the French into a decisive battle. At 10 a.m. the French advanced, to be met at short range by a withering volley from the British line from which the French never properly recovered. By afternoon they were in retreat leaving only a small force to defend the city, which surrendered on 18 August. Wolfe, at the age of 32, and the French commander, Montcalm, lay dying, while Monckton, Colonel-Commandant of the 2nd Battalion and one of Wolfe's brigade commanders, was seriously wounded.[22]

During the battle the 2nd Battalion, which became heavily engaged on the left flank, lost nearly 100 killed and wounded. The 3rd, which provided force protection between the landing site and the Plain above, were more fortunate, suffering only two wounded. The grenadier companies were in the centre of the line. The Regiment had won its second Battle Honour.[23]

Following the battle, representatives from the Battalions were present when the British ensign was raised over the Citadel. Subsequently, a substantial British garrison of 7,500, including seven companies from each of the 2nd and 3rd Battalion, was left to winter in Quebec under the command of another of Wolfe's brigade commanders, General James

Murray, who assumed Monckton's appointment as Colonel-Commandant of the 2nd Battalion in October. The remaining companies of both battalions retired to Nova Scotia.

Overland Expeditions, 1759

To achieve the British campaign plan in 1759, General Amherst assigned Brigadier-General Prideaux the task of seizing Fort Niagara and Brigadier-General Stanwix, Colonel-Commandant of the 1st Battalion, the task of relieving Fort Pitt. He reserved for himself command of the force to advance on Montreal.

On 15 June, Prideaux set off for Fort Niagara with a force of 5,000, including the 4th Battalion under Haldimand. After besieging Niagara for several weeks, on 24 July a relieving French and Indian force was routed and the garrison surrendered. During the advance the 4th Battalion remained at Oswego providing protection to Prideaux's lines of communication and stayed there throughout the winter.

Meanwhile Stanwix, with Bouquet appointed to be his Deputy Adjutant General, had set off for Fort Pitt at the end of May with a force of 5,000, including the 1st Battalion under command of Major John Tullikens. The route again proved to be arduous, with the 1st Battalion frequently in contact with 'skulking Indians'. Because progress was so slow, the Battalion was required at the end of July to press ahead of the column and beyond Fort Pitt, participating, with Prideaux's force, in the seizure of the French forts between Forts Pitt and Niagara. By the end of the year the whole of the upper reaches of the Ohio valley had been cleared of French with their posts further to the west hopelessly cut off from the rest of French Canada.

Amherst himself did not begin his advance upon Montreal until 21 July, seizing Ticonderoga on its evacuation by the French on 26 July. He was subsequently prevented in advancing further north by a small French naval force on Lake Champlain and was obliged to halt for many months while he built ships of his own. By then winter had set in and Montreal remained in French hands.

1760: The Conquest of Canada Completed

Winter for the companies of the 2nd and 3rd Battalion in Quebec was cold and unpleasant. Meanwhile, the French, isolated in Montreal to the west, no doubt considered it essential to recover the city.

Battle of Sainte Foy, 27 April 1760

On 20 April 1760, after the ice on the St Lawrence had melted, the French set out from Montreal with a force some 9,000 strong. After landing close to Quebec, on 27 April battle was joined with a weakened force of 3,000 British under General Murray at Sainte Foy on the outskirts of the city. The British were forced by overwhelming numbers to withdraw back into the city, which they then defended. On 17 May, with their lines of communication on the St Lawrence threatened by the arrival of a Royal Navy squadron, the French returned to Montreal.

The French action demonstrated just how insecure British tenure in Quebec was. The city was saved only by the bravery of its garrison and by the sea power of Britain. Once again the two battalions of the Royal Americans paid a price in blood with just over seventy men killed and wounded. So long as Montreal remained in the hands of the French, the conquest of Canada was incomplete.

Surrender of Montreal, 8 September 1760
With French fortunes in Canada waning, Amherst prepared for the final and decisive campaign: a simultaneous advance on Montreal from east, west and south.

General Murray in Quebec was the first to move, embarking a picked force of 2,500 men on 14 July to sail upstream on the St Lawrence to Montreal. Some 170 men of the 2nd Battalion, with an equal number from the 43rd, formed a composite battalion under command of Major Oswald. Men from the 3rd Battalion and the 35th[24] formed another composite battalion, while the grenadier companies from all the available battalions generated two further battalions. Sailing slowly, Murray's troops arrived just short of Montreal on 27 August and encamped to await the arrival of the British forces from the west and south.

On 29 August the force from the south, under Brigadier-General William Haviland,[25] having passed all the French posts between Lake Champlain and Montreal, arrived within easy marching distance of the city.

Meanwhile Amherst was assembling an army of 11,000 at Oswego, including the 4th Battalion under Colonel Haldimand and some from the 1st Battalion. Embarking on 10 August to sail down the St Lawrence, and overcoming French posts en route, Amherst's force descended upon Montreal from the west. On 6 September the force disembarked nine miles short of the city. Recognizing resistance to be hopeless, on 8 September the French surrendered. Haldimand was appointed to take possession of the city and act as Military Governor, proving in the process to be an excellent administrator.[26]

French Canada was now effectively in the hands of the British, with Colonel Bouquet and his 1st Battalion assigned to guard the western frontiers of British territory from the Indians.

1761–2: 3rd Battalion in the West Indies

The British had not long been masters of Canada, when a part of Amherst's army was required to make further conquests, this time in the West Indies.

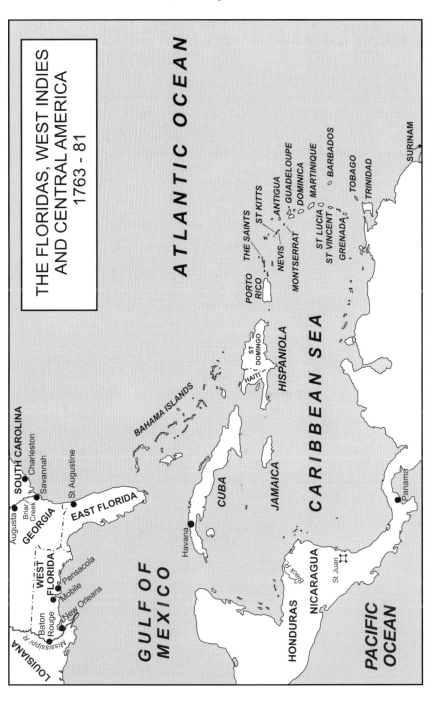

THE FLORIDAS, WEST INDIES
AND CENTRAL AMERICA
1763 - 81

Capture of Martinique, 27 January 1762

In 1761 a force of 6,000 men, under General Monckton, set sail from America to rendezvous with others at Barbados before setting out to capture the French territory of Martinique. The troops included the 3rd Battalion, under command of the newly-appointed Lieutenant-Colonel Augustin Prevost, with General Haviland, Colonel-Commandant of the 3rd Battalion, commanding a brigade.

Arriving in Barbados on Christmas Eve 1761, the force landed on Martinique in January 1762 and, after various trials and tribulations, including the difficulties of climate and terrain, and despite being afflicted by disease, captured Martinique on 27 January 1762. Detachments were then sent without delay to capture St Lucia, St Vincent and Grenada.

The exact part played in these events by the 3rd Battalion is not recorded in the Regiment's *Annals,* although at least fifty were killed or wounded in the fighting on Martinique on 24 and 27 January. 'Martinique, 1762' became the Regiment's third Battle Honour.

Capture of Havana, 13 August 1762

As Monckton was contemplating what to do next, news arrived from England that war had been declared against Spain and that an expedition, under command of Lieutenant-General Lord Albemarle, was being sent to capture Havana (Havannah), capital of the Spanish island of Cuba. A brigade from Monckton's force, under General Haviland, which included the 3rd Battalion, now numbering some 600 all ranks, was ordered to join Albemarle's expedition, which collected them from Martinique on 25 April.

Albermarle's army landed near Havana on 7 June. After a lengthy siege of the two forts at the entrance to Havana's harbour, both were captured, with the city's garrison surrendering on 13 August 1762.

During this campaign the Battalion suffered less from disease than others, but still lost fifteen men. A further 100 were killed, wounded or posted as missing. The Regiment had won its fourth Battle Honour.

In the autumn of 1762 peace with Spain was restored. Havana was returned to the Spanish and by 6 July 1763 the last British soldier had left the island.

1763: The End of the Seven Years War

On 10 February 1763 the Treaty of Paris was signed. The Seven Years War was ended. France had been defeated and was required to surrender to Britain the whole of her possessions in North America with the exception of New Orleans and the neighbouring territory.

With war over, the British no longer felt a need for four battalions of Royal Americans. In 1763 the 4th Battalion was recalled from Montreal and sent to England to be disbanded. In 1764 the 3rd, which had returned from Havana, via Pensacola, to New York, was also disbanded. Meanwhile, the strength of both the 1st and 2nd Battalion was halved.

Pontiac's Rebellion and War with the Indians, 1763–4

The Conquest of Canada and the surrender of the French at Montreal in September 1760 resulted in considerable unrest among the Indian tribes inhabiting the shores of the Great Lakes and the upper reaches of the Ohio valley. Responsibility for dealing with these problems fell largely to Bouquet and the 1st Battalion, who, by early 1763, were occupying fifteen forts stretching from Lake Michigan in the west, to Fort Bedford in the east and Fort Mackinaw (Michilimackinac) in the north. The area covered thousands of square miles of forests and lakes, with the forts garrisoned, often in small numbers, almost exclusively by the men from five companies of the 1st Battalion. The rest of the Battalion was quartered at Lancaster.

In May 1763, the Indian tribes, incited by Pontiac, Chief of the Ottawas, rebelled. Using a mixture of surprise and cunning, they attacked most of the forts, horribly murdering the occupants of some and beleaguering others. Nine were abandoned. Of those remaining, Fort Detroit and Fort Pitt, each gallantly defended, were strategically the most important.

Hearing the news, Bouquet immediately decided to launch a relief force by boat from Fort Niagara to Fort Detroit, while he led an expedition overland from Lancaster, via Carlisle, to Fort Pitt.

Battle of Bushy Run, 5/6 August 1763
By the end of June, Bouquet was on his way with a mixed force of around 500 men, including the Highlanders of the 42nd at greatly reduced strength[27] and some 150 men from the 1st Battalion. Relieving the garrisons at Fort Bedford and Ligonier en route, by 5 August the column had reached Bushy Run, a defile twenty miles short of Fort Pitt and not far from the scene of Braddock's defeat in 1755, when it was attacked by a similar number of Indians. After two days of desperate battle Bouquet's excellence as a leader achieved a brilliant victory. Learning from the ruses practised by the Indians, he feigned withdrawal, tricking the Indians to move forward in the open and be subject to simultaneous counter-attack from the front and flanks. The trick worked and the Indians were completely routed – but at a price. Amongst the 120 killed and wounded (25% of the force), the Highlanders suffered most, while the 1st Battalion's losses amounted to only twelve. Later, the American historian, Parkman, pronounced the battle to have been 'the best contested action ever fought between white men and Indians'.

On 10 August the garrison at Fort Pitt was relieved. Bouquet's march of 324 miles from Lancaster was at an end. Exhausted, and short of men and supplies, he decided to make provision for winter. Meanwhile the Indian tribes, fearing retribution, tired of their siege of Fort Detroit, although, following a series of mishaps, it was not until the following August that the fort was re-provisioned and the garrison replaced.

The Indians, however, continued to terrorise the frontier settlements. Following the resignation of Amherst and his replacement as Commander-in-Chief by Major-General Thomas Gage in March 1764,[28] it was decided that Bouquet should lead a further expedition, advancing from Fort Pitt into and beyond the Ohio valley, to enforce obedience on the recalcitrant Indian tribes. Bradstreet was to lead a similar expedition from Fort Niagara.

Much to Bouquet's irritation, Bradstreet was quick to grant the Indians generous concessions in exchange for peace, which Bouquet considered unjustified. Bouquet, on the other hand, was determined to take a more robust line. Departing from Fort Pitt on 2 October with 1,500 men, including his own Battalion and the 42nd, he advanced 100 miles into the heart of Indian country with a show of force that swiftly achieved the desired outcome. The Indians were obliged to hand back their prisoners. By 28 November Bouquet's men were back at Fort Pitt. After eight years of campaigning on the frontiers of North America, the British had finally broken French influence and native Indian power in the west.

Despite the Act of Parliament forbidding it, Bouquet was soon rewarded with promotion to Brigadier-General, being despatched shortly afterwards to assume command of all the troops in the Southern Colonies. There he contracted fever and died at his headquarters at Pensacola, Florida, on 2 September 1765.

From Canada to the Caribbean, 1765–74

In 1765, the 2nd Battalion, which had been in Canada since its conquest in 1760, relieved the 1st of its responsibility for garrisoning the forts in and around the Great Lakes. The 1st Battalion recovered to New York, with three companies on detachment in the Carolinas and five in Quebec. In 1767 it moved to Jamaica where it remained until 1786. In 1772 the 2nd Battalion moved to Antigua, despatching six companies in the following year to St Vincent to quell an insurrection by the Caribs. Meanwhile in 1770, benefiting from the lessons learned from the use of light troops at Louisbourg, Quebec and in other engagements against the French and Indians, each line regiment and battalion in the Army was directed to form a light company.

Despite the appalling conditions in the West Indies, where disease ran rife, sending both battalions of the Royal Americans to the Caribbean was not quite as malevolent an act as it might first appear. On the

Henry Bouquet

Henry Bouquet

Henry Bouquet was born in Switzerland in 1719 and was, like his close friend, Frederick Haldimand, a typical soldier of fortune. He was also well educated, proficient in English and excellent in mathematics.

He first served with the Dutch, then in the Sardinian Army and, from 1748, as a captain-commandant (lieutenant-colonel) in the Swiss Guard of the Prince of Orange. He joined the 62nd or Royal American Regiment on 3 January 1756, the day before Haldimand. After nine years in command of the 1st Battalion, he was promoted Brigadier-General in early 1765 and appointed to command all the troops in the Southern Colonies of British America. He died from an attack of fever at Pensacola, Florida, on 2 September 1765, aged 47.

Arriving in New York in June 1756, nearly a year after Braddock's defeat on the banks of the Monongahela, Bouquet quickly determined that the tactics, dress and equipment of the British redcoat were quite unsuited to fighting native Indians in the dense woods of North America. Instead, he decreed that in the field his men should wear short jackets of brown cloth, a strong tanned shirt, leggings and moccasins; carry a knapsack and oil surtout against the rain; and brown their shining gun-barrels. He also introduced and left a legacy of written instructions about new drills and tactics better suited to the circumstances of forest warfare, emphasising the importance of training, marksmanship and fieldcraft. His men quickly learned from him and thus rapidly became better able to combat their nimble foe successfully, with his ideas being copied and developed by others including, forty years later, de Rottenburg, Coote Manningham, William Stewart and Sir John Moore.

Of all those in the service of the Royal Americans in their early years, none played a more important role in determining the nature and character of the Regiment and in shaping its future than Henry Bouquet, and none lamented his passing more than his close friend, Frederick Haldimand.

Reference: Lieutenant-General Sir Edward Hutton, *Colonel Henry Bouquet: A Biographical Sketch* (Winchester: Warren, 1911).

contrary, defeat of the French and subduing the Indians served primarily to free the Thirteen Colonies from their fears and to excite the aspirations of some for independence from Great Britain. Bitter disputes and a growing rift resulted. Blood was first shed at Lexington on 19 April 1775, to be followed on 4 July 1776 by the Declaration of Independence. In these circumstances, and for some years previously, although no want of loyalty had ever been shown, the Regiment was so thoroughly American in thought, habit and association, 'that it would have been unfair to put it in the field against the colonists'.[29] This, in turn, led to an Act of Parliament being passed, prior to the 1st Battalion's move to Jamaica in 1767, decreeing, in amplification of the 1756 Act of Parliament limiting the service of the Royal Americans to 'North America only',[30] that the West Indies formed a part of North America!

The American War of Independence, 1775–83

This Brief History neither permits a detailed account of the American War of Independence nor was the Regiment greatly involved. However, one of the consequences was the re-formation of the 3rd and 4th Battalion with men recruited principally from England and Hanover. After assembly on the Isle of Wight, both battalions were sent in 1776 to Florida where they were joined by detachments from the 1st and 2nd Battalion. In February 1778 France entered the war on the side of the Americans.

At the end of the same year Augustin Prevost, Colonel-Commandant of the 4th Battalion and commander of the forces in East Florida, was ordered to march upon Savannah in Georgia with all available troops. His brother, Jean-Marc, from the 2nd Battalion, was appointed his second-in-command. Twenty officers and 400 men from the 2nd, 3rd and 4th Battalion formed a part of the group. In January 1779, after joining a larger British expedition that had captured Savannah before him, Augustin Prevost assumed command of a combined force of 4–5,000 men and was soon thereafter promoted to the rank of major-general.

Battle of Briar Creek, 3 March 1779
On 3 March 1779 J.-M. Prevost with a small force of 900 men cleverly executed an attack on a much larger American force at Briar Creek, fifty-three miles up river from Savannah, in which the grenadier companies of the 2nd, 3rd and 4th Battalions were involved. Over 500 Americans were killed, captured or drowned and their guns and baggage seized, for the loss of only sixteen men killed and wounded. In this and subsequent operations, J.-M. Prevost showed great enterprise by initiating the use of mounted infantry to cover ground quicker and thus surprise the enemy – a practice first advocated by Bouquet and which the Regiment was later to adopt on a larger scale in the 1880s.

Major-General Augustin Prevost

Defence of Savannah, October 1779

In October 1779 General Prevost, threatened by greater forces from the north and with the French fleet dominating the sea approaches, was forced into defending Savannah. After refusing an offer to surrender, on 9 October the garrison of 3,700, of whom only 2,000 men were fit for duty, was assaulted by a combined French and American force of 10,000 men. Bitter fighting ensued before the attack was called off and Savannah saved. In an action which cost the French and American forces over 1,000 men killed, wounded or captured, the British lost only fifty-five. During the defence the Royal Americans present, principally from the 4th Battalion, fought with great distinction, capturing the Colour of the 2nd South Carolina Regiment. The historian Stedman later wrote: 'The cool, steady, prudent and firm conduct of General Prevost … rank the successful defence of Savannah amongst the most brilliant achievements of the war.'[31]

Loss of St Vincent, 12 June 1779

On entry into the War, France was soon busy among the British possessions in the West Indies, capturing Dominica in 1778 and forcing the surrender of St Vincent on 12 June 1779. This latter island was garrisoned by seven companies of the 2nd Battalion whose commander, Lieutenant-Colonel George Etherington, although his signature did not appear on the instrument of capitulation, was later court-martialled for failing to offer resistance to an invading force of no more than 450. Etherington, who had served with distinction on other occasions, including during Pontiac's rebellion, was acquitted.

Surrender at Baton Rouge, 24 September 1779, and Mobile, 14 March 1780

In June 1779, Spain joined with America and France in the war against Great Britain. In anticipation of war, the British Government ordered an attack on New Orleans as soon as war was declared. In the event, the Spanish were quicker off the mark, forcing the capitulation, on 24 September 1779, of a British garrison, including three companies of the 3rd Battalion, at a fort on the Mississippi called Baton Rouge. On 14 March 1780, a second garrison, including four weak companies of the 4th Battalion, was forced into surrender at the coastal town of Mobile.

Black River Expedition, Nicaragua, 1780

In January 1780 the Governor of Jamaica, Major-General Dalling, Colonel-Commandant of the 3rd Battalion, launched a singularly ill-conceived attack on the Spanish settlements in the Black and St Juan River regions of Nicaragua. Although the expedition, which included companies from the 1st Battalion, was successful in capturing the Spanish fort at St Juan, it was ravaged by disease. By September only 300 out of a total force of around 1,400 survived. In November General Dalling recalled the handful that was left. The Royal American contingent, however, maintained the reputation of the Regiment and was said to have provided the only good troops on the expedition.[32]

Loss of Pensacola, May 1781

On 2 May 1781 the Spanish began an attack on Pensacola, which was defended by a garrison of some 800 men, including 125 men from the 3rd Battalion. For a week the garrison held out, but was eventually forced into surrender.

West Florida was now in the hands of the Spanish and, although the remnants of the 3rd and 4th Battalion remained for a time in East Florida before being sent back to New York, the Regiment took no further part in the War. In June 1783 the 3rd and 4th were disbanded. On 3 September 1783, under the terms of the Peace of Versailles, the United States gained their independence. Although the title 'Royal Americans' lived on until 1824, the service of the Regiment in the Country in which it was raised was ended.

Governor's Island, New York

Governor's Island lies approximately half a mile off the tip of Manhattan in New York Bay. Troops were stationed on the island for the first time in 1755. The 62nd/60th or Royal American Regiment used the island as its Regimental headquarters and depot for one or more of its battalions from 1756 until the 3rd and 4th Battalion moved through on disbandment in 1783.

In April 1776, at the time of the American War of Independence, the island was seized from the British but was evacuated in August shortly before the British re-occupied New York. Although the battalions of the Regiment served in Florida and the West Indies during the War, the Band remained on Governor's Island giving concerts to the Loyalists in the city. In November 1783, in accordance with the terms of the Peace of Versailles signed on 3 September 1783, the island passed permanently into the hands of the United States of America.

Chapter 2:

1784–1815: From Red Coats to Green Jackets

At the beginning of 1784 the establishment of both battalions of the 60th or Royal American Regiment of Foot was set at eight companies. The 1st Battalion was in Jamaica, from where it moved in 1786, after twenty years' service on the island, to Halifax, Nova Scotia. The 2nd, having departed Antigua in 1781, was in Barbados. It went to Montreal in 1787. The 1st remained quietly in Canada until 1797 and the 2nd likewise until 1800.

In October 1787, with the Government temporarily fearing a resurgence of conflict with France, the 3rd and 4th Battalion were reformed at Chatham with recruits from England and abroad. Among those to join was John (later Sir John) Moore, who secured a majority in the Regiment on 16 January 1788, but never left Chatham before exchanging into the 51st Regiment[1] on 1 October. Following reformation, the 3rd and 4th Battalion were despatched to the West Indies where it increasingly became the practice to send deserters from regiments at home.

The French Revolutionary Wars, 1793–1802

During the French Revolutionary Wars the Regiment's involvement in action was confined almost exclusively to the West Indies, where, in 1793, the 3rd Battalion was stationed in Antigua and the 4th in Barbados. In particular, the West Indies was of great commercial and strategic value to Great Britain, providing 25% of Britain's import trade, especially sugar. It was therefore important that the British presence in the West Indies should not only remain unchallenged but that the French should be expelled, particularly from their possessions in the Windward Islands, namely, Martinique, Tobago, Guadeloupe and St Lucia.

1793–7: The 3rd and 4th Battalion in the West Indies

On 12 April 1793, only two months after Britain and France declared war, the British landed in Tobago with a force of some 500 men, including 320 from the 4th Battalion, under Major William Gordon. On 15 April, in a courageous action led by Gordon, they stormed at bayonet point the fort guarding the capital, Scarborough, obliging the French Governor to surrender the island. Soon afterwards an assault on Martinique was aborted for want of sufficient men.

In early 1794 the men of the 3rd Battalion, less the grenadier and light companies, were posted to the 4th. Its headquarters staff was then despatched to the Channel Islands to recruit fresh numbers, including ex-soldiers from France and Holland who, unwilling to serve their Republican Governments, provided a welcome source of quality and experience in place of drafts of deserters. Meanwhile, all the grenadier and light companies of the battalions in the West Indies were grouped into grenadier and light infantry battalions, the latter under Brigadier-General Dundas, who was instructed to train them to the standard of 'perfection of light infantry that was attained during the American war'.[2]

The success of this reorganization quickly bore fruit when, between early February and the end of April 1794, the British successively seized Martinique, St Lucia and Guadeloupe in well-conducted operations involving, predominantly, the newly-created grenadier and light infantry battalions. However, by the middle of the year the tide began to turn, with the French re-emerging and inciting the islanders to oppose the British with the promise of equal privileges for blacks and whites. Outnumbered, exhausted by battle and with disease taking its toll, the British, including the remnants of the 4th Battalion, abandoned Guadeloupe at the end of 1794. In March of the following year, in St Vincent, the Caribs rose in insurrection, driving the garrison, including the invalids of the 4th, into the capital. Similar problems arose in Martinique and Grenada. In June 1795 the British evacuated St Lucia.

Meanwhile, the 3rd Battalion, having been restored to strength in the Channel Islands, returned to Barbados. In June 1795 it was sent with others to recover St Vincent. All did not go well as the force suffered a series of setbacks, leading the author of the *Annals* to write:

> *Misfortunes such as these will infallibly occur when a regiment, as in the present instance, is filled up with men of the lowest character, unused to discipline, devoid even of the tie of national feeling, or the opportunity of becoming imbued with the training and spirit of the corps in which they were enlisted.*[3]

Although the British retained a tenuous presence in St Vincent, the state of affairs in the West Indies was clearly serious. A force of nearly 18,000 men, under Sir Ralph Abercromby, with Brigadier-General John Moore serving as a brigade commander, was despatched from Britain to recover the situation. In May 1796 St Lucia was recaptured and in June the insurrection in St Vincent was effectively quelled. This time it was the turn of the 4th Battalion to be sent to the Channel Islands to reconstitute, from where the Battalion returned to the West Indies in 1797. The 3rd, meanwhile, occupied quarters in St Vincent and Tobago.

In October 1796 Spain entered the War in alliance with France. Immediately Abercromby was instructed to capture the Spanish possessions of Trinidad and Porto (Puerto) Rico. Concentrating a force of 4,000 men at Barbados, including four companies of the 3rd Battalion, he set sail for Trinidad on 15 February 1797. Two days later he landed there and on the following day the Spanish Governor surrendered the island to the British. However, an attempt to seize Porto Rico was aborted.

Thereafter, relative quiet prevailed in the West Indies pending conclusion of the War in 1802.

1793–1802: The Other Battalions

Between 1793 and 1797 the 1st and 2nd Battalion remained in Canada. In 1794 a battalion of the Regiment – there is some uncertainty as to whether it was the 1st or the 4th – was officially armed with the rifle. Although a small number of Bouquet's battalion had previously been equipped with rifles as early as 1758, and some officers and men in the Regiment habitually carried rifles when engaged in frontier warfare, this issue was the first made on a large scale, by official order, to a regiment of the British Army.[4] At or about the same time a rifle company was formed in each of the Regiment's battalions.

During this period it is probable that numbers in the 1st and 2nd Battalion fell for, in June 1797, the 1st was drafted into the 2nd at Quebec and its headquarters staff despatched to Guernsey to recruit. By November the Battalion was re-formed and sent to Portsmouth where it remained until transferring to Barbados in 1799. The 2nd moved from Canada to Barbados in 1800.

In December 1797 an Act of Parliament was passed to enable a fifth battalion to be formed. The story of the 5th Battalion, famous for its actions in the Peninsular War, follows shortly.

In July 1799 a further Act of Parliament provided for the creation of a sixth battalion. This latter Act had to some extent been anticipated for, as early as February, a company had been formed which, like the 5th Battalion before it, was armed with rifles and dressed in green.[5] At the end of September 1799 this company joined an expedition to Holland, known as the Expedition to Helder, commanded by The Duke of York, which was shortly thereafter aborted, with the company suffering seventeen killed, wounded and missing. In November 1800 the new 6th Battalion embarked for Kingston, Jamaica, arriving in March 1801.

1802: Peace of Amiens

In March 1802 the French Revolutionary Wars concluded with the Peace of Amiens, which restored all French possessions in the Windward Islands at the outset of the war to France. Coincidentally, but unsurprisingly given that the Regiment was formed for service in America (including the West Indies), all six battalions were stationed there: the 1st, 4th and 6th in Jamaica; the 2nd in Barbados; the 3rd in Grenada; and the newly-formed 5th, having arrived in Surinam in time to participate in the Dutch surrender in 1799, about to move to Trinidad.

During the War the lion's share of the action had fallen to the 3rd and 4th Battalion, who were frequently the recipients of drafts of condemned men, prisoners of war and others impressed into service against their will. In such circumstances the wonder, to quote Fortescue, is 'not that these 3rd and 4th Battalions of the 60th on occasion did badly, but that on the whole they did so well'.[6]

Continuing with Fortescue:

Service in the West Indies was loathed to an extent which is hardly credible in these days; and this was only natural, for there was no glory to be won, no profit to be gained; the work was most difficult and dangerous, the hardships very great, the climate deadly and unwholesome, the arrangements for clothing chaotic, the organisation of the hospitals abominable, and lastly the Government's ideas of carrying on war were hopelessly imbecile.

Origins and Early Service of the 5th Battalion, 1797–1808

In 1793, Lord Amherst, the Regiment's Colonel-in-Chief since 1758, bar a two-month interval in 1768, became Commander-in-Chief of the British Army. He was an advocate of the rifle and knew from his experience in North America of the value of equipping and training men in its use as marksmen and skirmishers; indeed, the French Revolutionary Wars soon resulted in French, German and Austrian émigré units, trained, armed and dressed as chasseurs and jäger entering the service of the British Crown. Amherst was keen that the British Army should have similar units integral to its order of battle. Initially he saw to it in 1794 that a battalion of his own Regiment should be the first to be equipped with rifles and that a rifle company should be formed in each of the Regiment's battalions. In 1795, however, he resigned as Commander-in-Chief to be replaced by HRH Prince Frederick, Duke of York, who also succeeded him as Colonel-in-Chief of the Regiment when Amherst died on 23 August 1797.[7]

It was left to The Duke of York, as Commander-in-Chief, to take the next step. As mentioned earlier, in December 1797 an Act of Parliament was passed to enable a fifth battalion to be formed in the Regiment. The Act, like the Act of 1756 establishing the Regiment, decreed that the Battalion was to be confined to service in North America (including the West Indies) where, ironically, it was later to spend only two of the twenty years of its existence. On 12 January 1798 an order was issued for the 5th Battalion to be armed with rifles and dressed in green.

The 5th had an interesting birth being raised in two wings and in two places from the manpower of two émigré regiments, Löwenstein's Chasseurs in Barbados and Ferdinand von Hompesch's Regiment, which was newly forming on the Isle of Wight. Initially the two wings had separate identities and did not unite until 1799.

Robert ('Black Bob') Craufurd

Robert Craufurd

Lieutenant-Colonel (later Major-General) Robert Craufurd, who was to earn both fame and notoriety commanding the Light Division in the Peninsular War, was among those who transferred from Hompesch's Regiment to the 60th on 30 December 1797. It was originally intended that he should command the 1st Battalion reconstituting in Guernsey, but was instead appointed Deputy Quartermaster General on the staff of Sir Ralph Abercomby, who, having returned from the West Indies, was Commander-in-Chief in Ireland. Craufurd, who went on to other staff appointments after service in Ireland, remained on the Regimental roll of officers until early 1802.

Francis, Baron de Rottenburg (Rothenburg) commanded the wing of 400 men of Hompesch's Regiment. Prior to service in the 5th Battalion, he had written a manual of instruction entitled *Regulations for the Exercise of Riflemen and Light Infantry*, covering the drill, manoeuvre and duties of light troops and outposts in the field. This was translated into English in 1798 and was later adopted as the textbook on the subject by Sir John Moore, after he had formed the Light Brigade at Shorncliffe in 1803. In August 1805, in a letter to the commanding officer of the 52nd, Moore wrote: 'I mean to make de Rottenburg the groundwork. ... In reading over his book attentively I perceive much good in it. It only requires to be properly applied.'[8] Many of the bugle calls of the present day also owe their origin to the book, Sir John Moore stating in November 1805 that those used by the 52nd and 95th – and, of course, the 60th – were those of de Rottenburg.

The rifle with which the Battalion was armed was not the Baker rifle, which was first issued to the Experimental Corps of Riflemen (the 95th Rifles) in 1800. It was of a different and uncertain pattern. The green uniforms that the Battalion adopted, with red facings, were almost identical to those of Hompesch's Regiment. The officers wore a black cross-belt with lion, whistle and cross, and a sword with black leather sling. All ranks had an embryo scarlet 'cherry' (rosette) on their caps. The cap badge was a silver bugle. Additionally, the riflemen were issued 'with a sword [bayonet][9] and equipped with a black belt, cartridge box and brown leather bag, worn slanting over the shoulder, in place of the ordinary knapsack. Officers and men wore moustaches; an innovation, which in conjunction with the green jacket proved so startling that on its first appearance in England the country people are said to have run away, terrified by what they believed to be a foreign invader!'[10]

1798: Rebellion in Ireland

In April 1798, de Rottenburg's wing of the 5th Battalion, consisting of 17 officers and 361 other ranks, was despatched to Cork in Ireland, where the Catholic majority, incensed by the treatment meted out to them by the Protestant minority and encouraged by the promise of support from France, were about to rebel. De Rottenburg remained in England, delegating command of the wing to Major de Verna.

The wing consisted of three rifle companies, two of which were deployed under command of Brigadier-General John Moore[11] and the third under command of General Lake, who had succeeded General Abercromby as Commander-in-Chief in Ireland.[12] On 19 June Moore's force routed a group of rebels, with up to seventy of them being killed in the pursuit by de Rottenburg's riflemen, 'deplorable though it be that the first employment of a Rifle Battalion in the British Army should have been against British subjects'.[13] On the following day, another sharp encounter followed at Foulkes's Mill, during which the rebels were again dispersed, with two Riflemen,[14] Ernst Klitzman and Gerard Osting, becoming the first Riflemen in a rifle battalion of the 60th to be killed in action. The day after, Sergeant Degenhardt was killed when the main body of 15,000 rebels was defeated at Vinegar Hill.

On 20 July de Rottenburg arrived. On 27 August a small French force of 1,100 men landed in Ireland. On 8 September it surrendered: 'thus ended this squalid and inglorious yet indispensable campaign.'[15] By the end of the year de Rottenburg's wing was back at Cork.

1799–1807: Service on Three Continents

In February 1799 de Rottenburg's wing of the 5th Battalion sailed for Martinique where, on arrival in April, it merged, under de Rottenburg's command, with the wing from Löwenstein's Chasseurs. In May the Battalion strength was 54 officers and 1,086 other ranks. Soon after, in August, an expedition of 1,300 men, including 860 from the 5th Battalion, was despatched to Surinam (Dutch Guiana), which, after a few brief skirmishes, capitulated on 20 August. A portion of the garrison, consisting of Germans, Austrians and Hungarians, was drafted into the Battalion, which General Trigg, the commander of the expedition, shortly afterwards described as 'a very fine body of men, and in every way a most efficient corps'.[16]

Surinam was an unpleasant place to be stationed. Under the terms of the Peace of Amiens in 1802, it was returned to the Dutch. By November the Battalion was in Trinidad, departing for Halifax, Nova Scotia in

Francis, Baron de Rottenburg

Francis, Baron de Rottenburg

Francis de Rottenburg was an Austrian of Polish origin, born in Danzig on 4 November 1757. Like Bouquet and Haldimand before him, he was a soldier of fortune, serving in the French and Polish armies, before, in 1795, entering the service of the British Crown, becoming a major in Baron Carl von Hompesch's Regiment of Hussars. When this regiment was sent to the West Indies in 1796, he remained in Europe to assist in forming Ferdinand von Hompesch's Regiment, which, in early 1798, became a wing of the 5th Battalion of the 60th. His commission in the Regiment as a lieutenant-colonel is dated 30 December 1797.

De Rottenburg was a skilled tactician and author of *Regulations for the Exercise of Riflemen and Light Infantry*, later adopted by Sir John Moore. He was also a very able trainer and popular among the men under his command because of the interest he took in their welfare. Although he could be stern if occasion needed, his system of discipline, like that of Bouquet, was based not on fear and the use of the lash, but on appeal to the moral qualities of self-respect and *esprit de corps.*

De Rottenburg commanded the 5th Battalion until immediately before its departure to Portugal in 1808. He held a number of appointments thereafter, including in command at Quebec from 1810–16, eventually reaching the rank of lieutenant-general. He died at Portsmouth in 1832, aged 75.

Quoting from the *Annals*, Francis de Rottenburg 'was one to whom our Regiment can never adequately express its acknowledgements and whose influence as a trainer of soldiers spread far beyond the limits of his own battalion'. His contribution in imposing values and setting standards for the 60th as a Rifle Regiment, which the Regiment has sought ever since to emulate, was in every respect equal in its importance to that of Bouquet forty years previously.

Reference: Lewis Butler, *The Annals of The King's Royal Rifle Corps, Vol. II.*

October 1803, from where, in 1804, General Bowyer reported:

> *This Battalion is armed with Rifles and swords to fix to them. The present high state and order of this Battalion is due to the solicitude and unremitting attention of Lieutenant-Colonel, Baron de Rottenburg, who has brought it to a principle of discipline suitable to the service for which it was raised and may be required.*[17]

In November 1805 the Battalion departed from Halifax for England, where it was quartered, first, at Hilsea, near Portsmouth, and then at Haslar Barracks, Gosport. In May 1807, expecting to join Lord Cathcart's expedition in Denmark, the Battalion moved to Ramsgate from where, in August, it sailed not to Denmark but to Cork. Here troops were being assembled for possible deployment to South America following the ignominious surrender, in July 1807, of General Whitelocke's forces in Buenos Aires.[18]

The Napoleonic Wars, 1803–15

The Peace of Amiens in 1802 provided little more than a temporary respite. Each side with reason felt it had causes for grievance against the other. On 1 May 1803 Great Britain declared war on France. A titanic struggle ensued involving at different periods every country in Europe.

1803–10: The Regiment in the West Indies

At the outbreak of the War, all six of the Regiment's battalions were in the Caribbean: the 1st, 4th and 6th in Jamaica; the 2nd in St Vincent; the 3rd in Grenada; and the 5th in Trinidad. War, however, had been expected and, on receipt of the news in June, the British immediately captured the French islands of St Lucia and Tobago. News of war with Holland soon followed, resulting in an expedition to capture Surinam, which by September had been partially successful and, by May 1804, wholly successful. The Regiment did not play a major part in these events, with only the rifle company of the 2nd Battalion being used to reinforce the expedition to Surinam.

Meanwhile the mortality rate among the troops began to assume terrible proportions. Two officers and twenty-eight NCOs and men of the 6th Battalion also perished when, on 7 November 1805, the sloop *El Orquixo* foundered off the coast of Jamaica.

In 1806 the 3rd Battalion was sent to Guernsey to recruit. It returned in March 1807, but within eleven months had lost 200 men from fever.

In 1807 the majority of the 2nd Battalion was drafted into the 3rd, with the headquarters staff of the 2nd sent to Jersey to recruit. On completion, in September 1808, the 2nd embarked for Plymouth to join the division of Lieutenant-General Sir David Baird, which was about to reinforce the army of Sir John Moore in Spain. On 4 October the

Battalion sailed for Corunna composed largely of French prisoners of war. Landing on 3 November, it was left to garrison the town. During the battle on 16 January 1809 in which Moore died, the Battalion was held in reserve, embarking shortly thereafter, with the remainder of Moore's army, to return to England. In November of the same year the Battalion departed for Barbados.

In September 1807 Denmark joined the war against Britain. In November an expedition of 2,500 men, including 650 men from the 3rd Battalion, was despatched to the Danish islands, then called The Saints, now known as the Virgin Islands, which surrendered without resistance.

Capture of Martinique, 24 February 1809

On 28 January 1809 a force of nearly 11,000 men in two divisions, one under command of Major-General Sir George Prevost,[19] with the 3rd and 4th Battalion in divisional reserve, set out from Barbados to capture Martinique. On 24 February, after a well-conducted operation during which the actions of Lieutenant-Colonel Mackie and the 3rd Battalion were singled out for praise, the French garrison surrendered. Losses were slight. In September 1817 'Martinique, 1809' was added to the Regiment's growing list of Battle Honours.

Expulsion of the French from The Saints, 17 April 1809

In April 1809 a French naval squadron took refuge in The Saints, resulting in a force of 2,800 men, including the 3rd Battalion and the flank companies of the 4th, being sent to seize the ports in which the French squadron was harboured. A series of sharp encounters followed with a French force of 7–800 men, during which the actions of the 60th were twice singled out for praise. Under threat from the British, the French evacuated their ships and, on 17 April, surrendered. 60th losses amounted to two men killed and sixteen wounded.

In June 1809, 200 men from the 6th Battalion in Jamaica accompanied an expedition to capture San Domingo, where the remnant of the French garrison surrendered without a fight.

Capture of Guadeloupe, January 1810

In January 1810 an expedition of 6,000 men was launched to capture Guadeloupe. On this occasion, and despite the expedition's success, the Regiment disappointed, causing Sir George Beckwith, in overall command in the Windward Islands, to write to the Secretary of State in London: 'I have no confidence in troops recently arrived from England in a motley mixture. The flank companies of the 2nd Battalion of the 60th, and the grenadiers of the 4th Battalion behaved shamefully in the face of the enemy. I repeat my request that certain corps in the army be no longer loaded with men polluted by civil crimes, congregated with French prisoners and deserters.'[20]

Fortunately, with the capture of Guadeloupe, French power in the Windward Islands was extinguished.

1806–19: Service in the Cape Colony

In 1803 Holland had joined the war against Britain. In January 1806 an expedition under command of Lieutenant-General Sir David Baird[21] captured Cape Town from the Dutch. Twice thereafter battalions of the Regiment were redeployed from the West Indies to serve there.

In September 1805 the 4th Battalion moved from Jamaica to the south coast of England and in July 1806 sailed for the Cape of Good Hope where it provided a garrison in the Cape Colony. On arrival a number of Austrian and Hungarian prisoners who had 'behaved without distinction' were, 'in accordance with the bad practice of the time', drafted into the Battalion, which was described by Robert Craufurd on passage to Brazil as 'disaffected'.[22] In May 1808 the Battalion returned to the West Indies.

In 1810 the 1st Battalion followed the same route as the 4th, moving first from Jamaica to England and then, in the second half of 1811, to the Cape Colony where it remained until 1819. Whilst in England its ranks had also been swelled by prisoners of war of all sorts.

The 5th Battalion in the Peninsula, 1808–14

The 5th Battalion arrived in Cork (see page 26) on 16 September 1807 some two months after Russia had concluded peace with France at Tilsit, Austria and Prussia having already done so following Napoleon's victory over the Austrians at Austerlitz (1805) and the Prussians at Jena (1806). Of the Great Powers in Europe, only Great Britain, saved by Nelson at Trafalgar (1805), remained at war with France, and only Portugal remained steadfastly an ally of Britain.

With the Royal Navy supreme at sea and invasion of Great Britain denied, Napoleon decided to subject Britain to commercial ruin by preventing the Country from trading with Europe – a strategy which he termed 'the Continental System'. With the rest of Europe under French control, Napoleon needed to bar Great Britain access to Portuguese ports to make the system effective. He therefore made a compact with Spain, an ally of France, for a joint invasion of Portugal. In November 1807 a combined force under General Junot crossed into Portugal, entering Lisbon on 30 November. By then the Royal Navy had cleared the harbour of its ships which were standing out to sea, and the Portuguese Royal Family had departed for Brazil taking most of the state treasure with them.

Napoleon, however, was not finished. Fearing that Spain was an uncertain ally, he despatched an army of 120,000 to Spain under the pretext of reinforcing General Junot in Portugal. Napoleon then forced

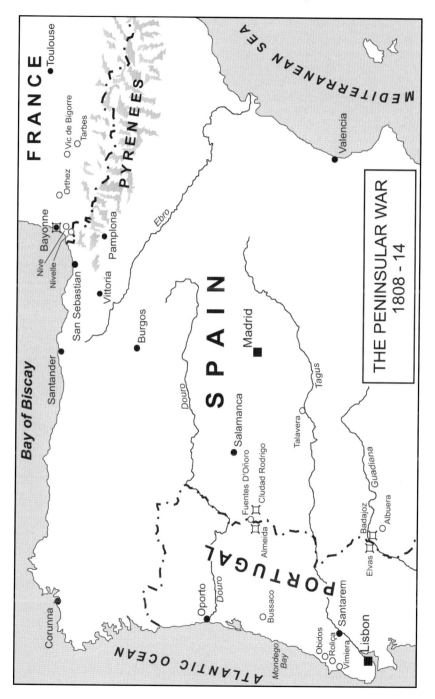

THE PENINSULAR WAR
1808 - 14

the abdication of King Charles IV, proposing that his brother, Joseph Bonaparte, should become King of Spain in his place. Crowned at Bayonne on 7 July 1808, Joseph entered Madrid on the 20th. Most Spaniards were enraged by Napoleon's high-handedness and, as opposition to French occupation grew and the French sought ruthlessly to suppress it, armies formed to fight the French. Forced onto the defensive, the French withdrew north of the River Ebro, leaving Junot with an army of around 25,000 isolated in Portugal.

By now, too, the French were beginning to learn about the inhospitable nature of the climate and terrain in the Peninsula which made campaigning so difficult – poor roads that were often no more than dirt tracks; mountain ranges impassable in winter; rivers and streams that were either dry or flowed in torrents; and countryside that frequently offered little prospect of food or forage.

Operations in 1808

In June 1808 the British Government decided to respond to appeals for help from both the Spanish and Portuguese people. On 14 June Lieutenant-General Sir Arthur Wellesley, recently returned from India and Chief Secretary of Ireland, was appointed commander of an expeditionary force of about 9,000 men already assembled at Cork. Pending Wellesley's arrival, Major-General Rowland Hill, in temporary command, grouped the 5th Battalion, 60th, and four companies of the 2nd Battalion, 95th, into a light brigade, thus initiating a relationship between the two regiments, later The King's Royal Rifle Corps and The Rifle Brigade, which has endured and flourished ever since.

The 5th Battalion, in ten companies, embarked for Portugal on 15 June, but did not sail in convoy with the remainder of the force until mid-July. The Battalion's embarkation strength was 33 officers and 1,007 other ranks, accompanied by 60 women and 50 children. Major William Davy, the senior of the Battalion's two majors,[23] commanded the Battalion in the absence of de Rottenburg, who had been appointed a brigadier-general on the staff at the Curragh. Major William Woodgate was the second major. The Riflemen wore green jackets and blue pantaloons, and were armed with Baker rifles.[24] Officers in command of companies were mounted.

As at the time of the Battalion's formation ten years previously, almost all the Riflemen and many of the officers were Germans, Austrians or Hungarians, with orders in English having to be translated into German.

On 30 July Wellesley's force arrived off the coast of Portugal at Mondego Bay, eighty miles north of Lisbon. On 1 August the companies of the 5th Battalion and the 95th were the first to land to cover the disembarkation of the remainder of the force. On 5 August Wellesley was reinforced by a further 5,000 troops.

Major William Davy

5th Battalion Order – 17 June 1808

The following is an extract of the Battalion Order issued by Major William Davy, embarked on the transport *Malabar* in Cork Harbour, prior to the Battalion's departure to Portugal:

As there is every reason to think that the Battalion will shortly be honoured with an opportunity of distinguishing itself in the field, the Commanding Officer feels it his duty to recall to the attention of the younger part of the Officers to the absolute necessity of making themselves acquainted with the several duties of the outposts, that they may be enabled to lead and instruct the men intrusted to their care. He also expects they will seriously consider that any neglect on their part before the enemy may cause the most fatal consequences not only to themselves, but to the whole Army.

The men are to understand that by the maintenance of order and discipline we can alone look forward to successful opposition to the designs of an enemy: they must on every occasion conform with alacrity to the orders of their Officers; and as great fatigue is often connected with the duties of Light Troops, they must cheerfully submit, and bear like men the hardships attending a soldier's life.

The true 'Rifleman' will never fire without being sure of his man. And he will recollect that a few direct shots that tell will occasion greater confusion than thousands fired at random and without effect.

It is particularly recommended to the men, and will be strictly enforced, to behave with humanity to the people in an enemy's country, and not to plunder or destroy their houses, or attempt their lives without the most urgent necessity or an order to that effect: interest and humanity both require the maintenance of a strict discipline as the only way to conciliate the minds of the people and to make them our friends.

It is the duty of every Officer carefully to provide for the wants of his men. This he may be assured will give him their confidence and esteem.

The Officers should endeavour to learn the capacities and characters of their men that they may employ them to the best advantage; this may be easily done by conversing with them, and hearing their opinion and sentiment on different subjects.

The Commanding Officer will feel sincere pleasure in recommending and rewarding all such non-commissioned Officers and men as may distinguish themselves in the field; but if on the contrary any man should be guilty of cowardice, desertion, or any other such infamous crime as may reflect on the credit of the Corps, he will show no mercy to such an offender, but use every exertion to bring him to the punishment he deserves.

Reference: Lewis Butler, *The Annals of The King's Royal Rifle Corps, Vol. II*, 38–40.

Skirmish at Obidos, 15 August 1808

On 9 August Wellesley ordered Fane's Light Brigade to form an advance guard and move south towards Lisbon. The remainder of his army of 14,500 set off a day later. A further 1,500 Portuguese joined. On 15 August contact with the French was made at Obidos where, in an over-exuberant and injudicious skirmish, the first shots of the Peninsular War were fired and the first losses suffered. Lieutenant Bunbury of the 95th and a Rifleman of the 60th were killed. A number of others wounded.

Battle of Roliça, 17 August 1808

On 17 August Wellesley's force, still advancing, attacked the main body of a smaller French force posted on the hills in front of Roliça. Three companies of the 5th Battalion were detached to a column under Major-General Ferguson's command, while the remaining seven companies plus the four companies of the 95th remained under Fane's command. In the ensuing battle, Wellesley tried to envelop the French, who carried out a well-conducted fighting withdrawal in rugged terrain, eventually managing to break clean to the south. The French lost 600 men and the British nearly 500, with the 5th Battalion losing 56.

At this point Wellesley decided to attach a company from the 5th Battalion to each of his five brigades, with a further two companies to be attached to two further brigades that were about to reinforce his army. Three companies and the Battalion headquarters under Major Davy remained with Fane's Brigade. From now on, and throughout the remainder of the Peninsular War, the 5th ceased to fight as a complete battalion, with companies and detachments operating ahead, in the rear, or on the open flanks of others, with their commanders expected to act on their own initiative when required.

Battle of Vimiera, 21 August 1808

On 18 August Wellesley, hearing that the two reinforcing brigades had arrived, decided to post his army at Vimiera while they disembarked. Three days later, a French force of 13,000 attacked Wellesley's army, which was now close to 20,000 strong. Again the battle was hard fought and again the French were obliged to withdraw, losing 1,800 men. The British lost 720, including 40 members of the 5th Battalion.

During the battle, the Riflemen of the 60th, displaced from their outposts in front of their brigades, had moved to the flanks, where, with well-aimed shots, they continued to inflict their toll on the advancing French. A French officer taken prisoner was later quoted as saying:

> *I was sent out to skirmish against some of them in green, – grasshoppers I call them, you call them Riflemen. They were behind every bush and stone and soon made sad havoc among my men; killing all the officers of my company, and wounding myself without being able to do them any injury.*[25]

Among the two brigades that had reinforced Wellesley's army were the 2nd Battalion, 43rd, and 2nd Battalion, 52nd, thus bringing together at Vimiera, for the first time in battle, battalions of all four regiments which 158 years later, on 1 January 1966, were to merge into a single regiment, The Royal Green Jackets.

Following the defeat at Vimiera, General Junot sued for surrender. Lieutenant-General Sir Hew Dalrymple, now in overall command of the British forces in Portugal, agreed the terms and, on 31 August 1808, signed the infamous Convention of Cintra, permitting Junot's army of 25,000 men with 30 guns to be conveyed back to France in British vessels. A furious controversy ensued in London and Dalrymple was recalled to account for his actions, leaving Lieutenant-General Sir Harry Burrard[26] in command. Meanwhile Wellesley, frustrated in part by the changes in command and seeing no further role for himself, returned to England to resume his post as Chief Secretary of Ireland.

The British Government then decided, on Wellesley's advice, to launch a campaign in the north of Spain. A force of 35,000 was earmarked for the task, under command of Lieutenant-General Sir John Moore. 25,000 of Moore's troops were found from those already in Portugal, while a further 10,000, including the 2nd Battalion (see pages 26-7), were sent from England via Corunna. The 5th Battalion, in two wings, one under Major Davy and the other under Major Woodgate, set off from Portugal with the main body of the army to join Moore in Spain.

It was then that a decision by Major Davy to enlist around 100 deserters from the French Army into the 5th Battalion returned to haunt him. Although endorsed by Burrard, these men behaved so deplorably, with some deserting back to the French with intelligence of British dispositions, that, in November, Woodgate's wing of the Battalion was ordered back to Lisbon. This was followed, on 16 November, with instructions to Davy to do likewise with his wing, although the two wings were not reunited near Lisbon until early March 1809. Once together, Davy set about removing the offenders and restoring the efficiency of the Battalion.

Meanwhile, Napoleon had arrived in Spain with an army of 125,000 to reinforce the 200,000 French soldiers already in the country. He then advanced south of the Ebro routing the Spanish before him. On 4 December the French re-entered Madrid. However, Moore's army was beginning to threaten the French lines of communication to the north. Marshal Soult, with a force of 80,000, was despatched to halt Moore's advance. Vastly outnumbered, Moore, on Christmas Eve 1808, ordered his army back to Corunna. The course of events thereafter will be well known to many. The 5th Battalion, on its way back to Lisbon, was not involved. The 2nd Battalion did play a part as a garrison battalion at Corunna and was in reserve during the battle on 16 January 1809, but it was never on the line of march. Suffice it to state in this Brief History that Moore's audacious advance and epic retreat, executed in atrocious conditions, were of crucial strategic importance in diverting Napoleon from fulfilling his intention of crushing the Spanish and evicting the British from Portugal.

Operations in 1809

The evacuation of Moore's army from Corunna left the British Government undecided as to whether or not to reinforce or abandon Portugal. It decided upon reinforcement and, in April 1809, Wellesley was reappointed to command of an army totalling some 30,000 men.

Major Davy, for his part, was taking every care to encourage good order and military discipline within the Battalion. It seems, too, that Wellesley's confidence in the Battalion was undiminished. On 6 May 1809 he issued a General Order:

> *The Commander of the Forces recommends the Companies of the 5th Battalion of the 60th Regiment to the particular care and attention of the General Officers commanding the Brigades of Infantry to which they are attached. They will find them to be most useful, active and brave troops in the field, and that they will add essentially to the strength of the Brigades.*[27]

Five rifle companies of the 5th Battalion were dispersed to brigades with the remaining five retained as a wing under Major Davy's command. Wellington also directed that the light infantry companies of the regiments in each brigade, still armed with muskets, and the rifle companies of the 5th Battalion attached to brigades should be used in concert. This was followed shortly afterwards by a decision to create divisions, each of two or more brigades, with one or more rifle companies assigned to each division.

Threatened by the French on a number of fronts, Wellesley decided that he must first evict Soult, who, with 20,000 men, had moved into Portugal in late March and was occupying positions astride the River Douro. Preparations complete and with 16,000 men, he began his advance. In a well-conducted campaign of manoeuvre, during which no major battle was fought, Wellesley's army crossed the Douro, threatening the French lines of communication to such an extent that, by 19 May, Soult had withdrawn his army back into Spain.

Having achieved his immediate objective, Wellesley moved his forces south and into Spain to unite with a Spanish army of 35,000, commanded by General Cuesta. His intention then, with a combined force of 55,000, was to move against a smaller French force of some 20,000, commanded by Marshal Victor, which he knew to be in the vicinity of Talavera. In the event, the French army became one of 46,000, while the Spanish proved to be unreliable allies and, in a premature move, were routed by the French on 25 July. This left Wellesley with an effective strength of closer to his original 20,000.

Battle of Talavera, 27/28 July 1809

Expecting battle, the British 3rd Division, to which Major Davy's five companies were attached, was appointed to outpost duty to cover Wellesley's army as it prepared its positions near Talavera. On 27 July the French mounted a surprise attack. In an action in which some regiments started to fall back too hastily, Davy's five companies and the 45th,[28] with Wellesley present, excelled in initially holding their ground and then withdrawing slowly and in good order across six miles of plain to the British main positions. The prospect of a major French breakthrough receded, with a contemporary account stating that: 'a disaster was averted only by the steady conduct of the 60th Rifles and the 45th. There is no doubt that their conduct was magnificent.'[29]

On the next day, 28 July, the French resumed their attack. Fierce fighting followed. Eventually the French withdrew. Losses were high: nearly 7,500 French and around 5,400 British, of whom 47 were from the 5th Battalion, plus a further 31 missing. Indeed, the Battalion's losses since its arrival in Portugal twelve months previously were beginning to concern Major Davy, with the number of fit men in each company reduced to barely 50. Officers were also starting to be attracted by the rewards offered for service in the Portuguese Army, which was being organized and trained by Major-General William Beresford.[30]

Wellesley's success at Talavera was honoured with elevation to the peerage as Viscount Wellington. However, he had little time to celebrate. Stronger French forces threatened, obliging him over the following months to withdraw his army, first, to Badajoz and then, leaving one division forward, to the comparative safety of Portugal. At the same time he initiated the construction of a line of fortifications – the Lines of Torres Vedras – surrounding and protecting Lisbon.

By December all the rifle companies of the 5th Battalion were reunited in winter quarters causing Brigadier-General Cameron of the 7th Brigade to write to Major Davy:

> *My little Company of the 60th marched from hence yesterday morning ... I was sorry to part with it as consisting of the best behaved men I have ever had attached to me in a military situation. There has been no instance of a complaint against any one of them since under my Command. And should a similar distribution take place on any future occasion I hope you will favour me with the same Company back again.*[31]

After his earlier trials, Major Davy was no doubt pleased to receive such a letter, likewise his promotion to lieutenant-colonel. Handing over to Major Woodgate, he travelled to England on leave and, whilst there, was appointed to command a garrison battalion.[32]

Operations in 1810

The year began with Napoleon determined to evict the British from Portugal. More troops were sent to Spain and, in April, Marshal Masséna appointed to command them.

Wellington, for his part, considered that the French would most likely invade Portugal by one of two routes: the northernmost, from Salamanca, and the second, the direct route from Madrid. Two fortresses, Ciudad Rodrigo in Spain and Almeida in Portugal, guarded the route from Salamanca, while Badajoz and Elvas did similar duty on the route from Madrid. He divided his army, which was in the process of being enlarged by the arrival of Beresford's Portuguese, to cover both approaches, with his main effort directed towards the route from Salamanca.[33]

Meanwhile, Lieutenant-Colonel William Williams, who had served as a major with the 81st[34] at Corunna, arrived to take command of the 5th Battalion, the rifle companies of which were again dispersed. Writing to Colonel Davy in May, Captain Andrews of the Battalion wrote:

> *Colonel Williams is a short man; ... his manner is quick, peremptory and at the same time courteous; he speaks with rather a studied tone of voice, something between the agreeable and the commanding; he bows like a Statesman entering into office, and from all I have observed I doubt not that General de Rothenburg has entrusted him with the talisman so essential to command this corps.*[35]

On 10 July Ciudad Rodrigo, held by the Spanish and besieged for two months, fell to the French. On 27 August the Portuguese were no longer able to hold Almeida. The route from Salamanca was open to the French. Wellington had anticipated events. His army had for some while been preparing defensive positions along a rugged range of hills known as the Serra de Bussaco where he resolved to give battle with a force of some 50,000 men, half Portuguese. The French numbered 65,000.

Battle of Bussaco, 27 September 1810

On 27 September, eschewing more subtle approaches, Masséna's army repeatedly attacked Wellington's positions from the front. By noon the French had shot their bolt and retired. They had lost close to 5,000 men while the Anglo-Portuguese army lost about 1,250.

During the battle Lieutenant-Colonel Williams distinguished himself commanding a light battalion made up of three light companies from other regiments and three rifle companies from the 5th Battalion, under Major Woodgate. The battalion, obliged to occupy exposed positions on a forward slope in front of the 3rd Division, fought with great élan, moving to the flanks as the French advanced, from where the rifle companies continued to administer enfilading fire. Williams was twice wounded in a battle which added a further twenty-nine names to the Battalion's casualty lists. Williams, however, never received the recognition that was his due, as Picton, thinking that Wellington had witnessed the action, did not report upon it.[36]

After Bussaco, Wellington declined to turn victory into a pursuit. He withdrew his army behind the Lines of Torres Vedras and to Lisbon where he knew he would be well provisioned by the Royal Navy. The French, meanwhile, finding the Lines impenetrable, withdrew to Santarem to suffer a winter of hardship, ravaged by hunger, disease and guerrillas in the exposed countryside of Portugal, which Wellington's troops had scorched as they withdrew.

Operations in 1811

At the end of February 1811, Masséna, unable to feed his army any longer, withdrew north, with Wellington's troops in pursuit, the rifle companies of the 5th Battalion foremost amongst them. In a series of sharp encounters, Williams, with his light battalion, sought continuously to harass and outflank the withdrawing French. By early April, Masséna had retreated as far as Salamanca, albeit with French troops still holding the key fortresses of Almeida and Ciudad Rodrigo. Wellington needed to capture both if his army was to progress further. He therefore blockaded Almeida. Masséna, in turn, concentrated a force of 47,000 at Ciudad Rodrigo, with which he intended to relieve Almeida. Again anticipating events, Wellington blocked Masséna's approach route by deploying an army of 37,000 on the high ground behind the village of Fuentes D'Oñoro, with Williams's light battalion from the 3rd Division defending the village.

Battle of Fuentes D'Oñoro, 3-5 May 1811
On 3 May the French attacked Fuentes D'Oñoro. In a hard-fought action, during which Williams was again wounded but for which he was praised for his 'spirited conduct', his battalion, including the three rifle companies of the 5th Battalion under Major Woodgate, reinforced by a brigade from the 2nd Division, thwarted a series of French attacks throughout the day.

After regrouping on 4 May, the French resumed the offensive on 5 May, almost succeeding in turning Wellington's flank. But by sunset they were beaten. During the battle the British lost nearly 1,800 men and the French 2,850. The Battalion's losses totalled thirty-six, with Major Woodgate, who had assumed command of the light battalion, wounded on the 5th.

During the night of 10/11 May, the French garrison evacuated Almeida. Marshal Marmont replaced Masséna.

Meanwhile, Wellington could no longer ignore that the fortress of Badajoz had fallen to a French army commanded by Soult on 10 March, and that the approach route from Madrid into Portugal lay open. Having previously sent a force under Marshal Beresford[37] to counter any French advance, he reinforced it with a view to recapturing Badajoz. Soult immediately responded, marching an army of 25,000 towards Badajoz, only to find his way blocked by Beresford.

Battle of Albuera, 16 May 1811

On 16 May battle was joined at Albuera on ground of Beresford's choosing. His positions, though, were poorly selected resulting in a desperate and bloody battle, which his army of 35,000 British, Spanish and Portuguese troops only just won, losing some 7,000 men in the process. Of the 10,000 British present, nearly 4,000 were killed or wounded. Four rifle companies of the 5th Battalion were present, of which only three saw action, suffering twenty-one casualties.

Wellington's route into the heart of Spain, however, remained blocked by French occupation of Badajoz and Ciudad Rodrigo. With his losses at Albuera, he was unable to do much for the moment about Badajoz and therefore turned his attention to Ciudad Rodrigo. A series of British and French moves and counter moves subsequently took place in which Williams, now recovered from his wounds, and his rifle companies again distinguished themselves. In one such action, on 26 September, Captain James Prevost,[38] commanding a rifle company, was killed at Aldea-da-Ponte. In another, Captain Blassière, commanding a rifle company in the south, carried out a daring night patrol into the occupied town of Arroyo dos Molinos, thus gaining intelligence which enabled the British to surround and scatter the French cavalry which was billeted there.

By the end of the year Wellington had succeeded in blockading Ciudad Rodrigo, while further to the south, a corps, now under General Hill's command, remained near Badajoz. Seven companies of the 5th Battalion were with Wellington and three with Hill. During the year the Battalion received 171 men in drafts from England.

Operations in 1812

Capture of Ciudad Rodrigo, 18/19 January 1812

Learning that the French were withdrawing troops from Spain to take part in Napoleon's planned invasion of Russia, Wellington decided to launch a surprise attack in winter on the fortress of Ciudad Rodrigo. On 5 January Colonel Colborne of the 52nd – later Field Marshal Lord Seaton – captured an important outwork. On 15 January a force, including the rifle company of the 1st Division, captured the fortified convent of Santa Cruz. On the night of 18/19 January the main assault took place, during which Craufurd, commander of the Light Division, was mortally wounded. The fortress with its garrison of some 1,800 was taken, for a loss of 500. The 5th Battalion's losses were slight, but included one of the company commanders, Captain Livingstone, who was so severely wounded that he took no further part in the War.

Following the capture of Ciudad Rodrigo, Lieutenant-Colonel John Fitzgerald – another future Field Marshal – replaced Major Woodgate, who returned to England on promotion.[39]

Capture of Badajoz, 6/7 April 1812
Following his success at Ciudad Rodrigo, Wellington swiftly turned his attention to Badajoz, marching his troops south to begin besieging the fortress on 17 March. On the night of 6/7 April the main attack was launched, with Colonel Williams and his light battalion assigned the duty of covering the advance. It was a most bloody occasion, during which Wellington's army sustained 3,700 casualties while storming the walls, to add to the 1,300 lost in the days before. Four companies of the 5th Battalion were involved, with ten killed and thirty-six wounded, including Williams again, and Fitzgerald. To quote from the *Annals*, 'Our troops had not been engaged in so terrible a contest since Ticonderoga [1758]'.[40] But success was achieved and Badajoz captured.[41] Wellington was made an Earl.

With both approach routes into the heart of Spain open, Wellington successfully severed the lines of communication between Marmont's army in the north and Soult's in the south, before deciding to advance on Salamanca and then, with strategic intent, to isolate the French armies in Spain by severing the lines of communication from Bayonne to Madrid. By 27 June Salamanca was safely in Wellington's hands. Wellington's army of 48,000 and Marmont's of 40,000 then sought to outmanoeuvre each other.

Battle of Salamanca, 22 July 1812
On 22 July the armies clashed five miles south of Salamanca. In fierce fighting the French managed to get themselves into a disadvantageous position from which they were only able to extract themselves with great difficulty. By sunset the French had suffered a major defeat. Losses were enormous: over 11,000 French, with 5,000 on the British side. Four French generals were killed and Marmont severely wounded. The British lost General Le Marchant killed and five generals wounded. The 5th Battalion suffered thirty-three casualties. For Colonel Williams, wounded for the sixth time in his career, Salamanca was his last battle with the 5th Battalion before exchanging to the 13th Regiment.[42] Fitzgerald assumed command.

Meanwhile, Wellington followed up his victory at Salamanca by marching upon Madrid, which King Joseph abandoned in haste on 11 August, the day before Wellington's army entered the city. But Wellington did not stay long, moving on to besiege the strategically important fortress of Burgos on the road between Bayonne and Madrid. On 19 September the rifle company of the 1st Division assisted in the capture of an out-work, but the French garrison in the fortress held firm. Losses mounted. In mid-October, with the presence of his army in Burgos and Madrid threatened by the arrival of larger French forces, Wellington lifted the siege. Fearing also that his lines of communications might be severed, he started to withdraw his army back whence it had come. Madrid and Salamanca were abandoned.

After advancing 300 miles since the start of the year, Wellington's army retraced its steps, poorly provisioned and in appalling weather, all the way to the Portuguese border. Losses during the withdrawal were high, with the 5th Battalion reporting 115 missing. Ciudad Rodrigo and Badajoz remained safely in allied hands.

Wellington's army, however, was not the only one retracing its steps. In Russia, Napoleon's army was retreating from Moscow with strategic implications far more severe than the operational and tactical consequences of Wellington's withdrawal.

Operations in 1813

Whilst his army was recuperating, Wellington drew up plans to resume the offensive against the French. Meanwhile, the 5th Battalion's strength was restored to over 800. Eighteen officers were British and twelve foreign. All the NCOs and Riflemen, bar one, were foreigners. In April Fitzgerald departed to assume command of a light battalion in the 2nd Division. Colonel Keane from the 13th Regiment, who had nominally been in command of the 5th Battalion since exchanging with Williams, arrived during the same month, but in August moved to command a brigade in the 3rd Division. Command of the Battalion then passed to Major Galiffe, a Swiss officer of French descent. Galiffe had been a member of the 5th Battalion since its inception, being commissioned into the Regiment on 30 December 1797. He was also amongst those who had embarked for Portugal five years previously.

Wellington initiated his advance in May and by the 26th had re-occupied Salamanca. In a series of rapid and audacious moves, he then bypassed the French as they sought to make a stand at Burgos. Despite their overall superiority in numbers in Spain, the French, with their flanks and rear constantly threatened, were obliged to withdraw north of the Ebro. Here, King Joseph, who had fled Madrid on 2 June, directed his generals to adopt a delaying position on the Bayonne–Madrid road forward of Vittoria, hoping thereby to prevent the lines of retreat of other French forces from being severed.

Battle of Vittoria, 21 June 1813

On 21 June, Wellington, with an allied army of 72,000 men and a further 20,000 Spaniards in support, closed with the French who, on the day, numbered around 65,000. Following a battle in which nearly all the rifle companies of the 5th Battalion were in the thick of the action, the

French were comprehensively routed, losing over 7,000 men and nearly all their 153 guns. British losses amounted to 5,000, including 58 in the 5th Battalion. In the pursuit, the King lost his baggage and his treasure said to amount to £1 million. He quickly abdicated. Wellington was promoted to the rank of Field Marshal.

Such was the crushing defeat imposed on the French that Soult, who was now in overall command, withdrew his armies north of the Pyrenees into France, from where he decided to launch a counter-offensive against Wellington's army. Meanwhile, Wellington concentrated on establishing the port of Santander as his main base of supply in place of Lisbon, and on bringing about the surrender of Pamplona and San Sebastian, which remained in French hands.

The Pyrenees, 25-31 July 1813

Soult's counter-offensive was dependent upon seizing the principal passes through the Pyrenees, after which he intended to march to the relief of Pamplona and San Sebastian. However, he failed in his objectives. During a week's arduous fighting in extraordinarily difficult terrain, Wellington and his generals manoeuvred their forces with great dexterity blocking off and surprising the French time and again in a series of running actions. By the end of July, Soult, realising that his route was barred, withdrew his forces to France, abandoning Pamplona and San Sebastian to their fate. In early September San Sebastian capitulated, to be followed by Pamplona on 31 October.

Losses in the Pyrenees, reflecting the nature of the contest, were heavy: some 13,500 on the French side, of whom 3,200 were taken prisoner, and 7,100 on the British side. The rifle companies of the 5th Battalion were, as usual, in the forefront of the action, with 58 killed or wounded and a further 25 reported missing.[43] An indication of the significance of the role played by the Battalion is reflected in Marshal Soult's report - see next page.

Battle of the Nivelle, 10 November 1813

On 7 October Wellington marched his army into France where Soult's army of 67,000 was deployed in defensive positions along a 16-mile stretch of the Nivelle. Wellington, with an allied army of 90,000, decided to assault the centre, fixing the French with diversionary attacks on the flanks.

On 10 November battle commenced, with Major Galiffe and his three companies with the 3rd Division carrying one of the bridges across the river at the run, for which the Divisional Commander commended him. The remainder of Wellington's army, fighting hard throughout the day, was equally successful, causing the French to use the cover of nightfall to withdraw to a further line of defence behind the Nive.

Casualties, whilst not on the scale of some earlier battles, were still high, with Wellington's army losing 2,700 and the French losing 3,330

41

Marshal Soult's Report to the Minister of War in Paris

St. Jean de Luz, 1st September 1813

The loss in prominent and superior officers, sustained for some time past by the Army, is so disproportionate to that of the rank and file that I have been at pains to discover the reason; and have acquired the following information, which of course explains the cause of so extraordinary a circumstance.

There is in the English army a battalion of the 60th consisting of ten Companies – the regiment is composed of six battalions, the other five being in America or the West Indies. The battalion is never concentrated, but has a Company attached to each Infantry Division. It is armed with a short rifle; the men are selected for their marksmanship; they perform the duties of scouts, and in action are expressly ordered to pick off the officers, especially Field and General Officers. Thus it has been observed that whenever a superior officer goes to the front during an action, either for purposes of observation or to lead and encourage his men, he is usually hit.

This mode of making war and of injuring the enemy is very detrimental to us; our casualties in officers are so great that after a couple of actions the whole number are usually disabled in the ratio of one officer to eight men; I also saw battalions which were reduced to two or three officers, although less than one-sixth of their men had been disabled. You can imagine that if these casualties should recur, it would be very difficult to provide for the replacement of officers even though the nominations were made beforehand.

Reference: Lewis Butler, *The Annals of the King's Royal Rifle Corps, Vol. II*, 200–1.

---

killed and wounded, including 447 officers, with a further 1,230 officers and men taken prisoner. The 5th Battalion lost 73 men, a high percentage of the Battalion's strength and an indication of the part played by the rifle companies in an opposed river crossing against an enemy in prepared positions.

The Passage and Battle of the Nive, 9-13 December 1813
Wellington, having forced the French to abandon their positions along the Nivelle, was determined to force a passage of the Nive in order to threaten the French at Bayonne and to the east. His army attacked on 9 December only to be counter-attacked by Soult. On 12 December Hill's Corps became isolated forward of the rest of Wellington's troops when a bridge was washed away. He was only saved from defeat in the nick of time, after the rebuilding of the bridge, by Wellington's arrival on 13 December with four divisions. With this force Wellington carried the day and drove the French into Bayonne. Losses were again high: 6,000 on the French side and 5,000 on the side of the allies, including 44 members of the 5th Battalion.

Thus closed a memorable year for Wellington and his army, begun in Portugal and ended in France, during which the 5th Battalion did its duty, often at high cost, and with a skill and in a manner which Soult himself recognized to be 'highly detrimental to us'.

Operations in 1814

Wellington resumed the offensive in February 1814, at a time when Napoleon's empire was crumbling. Dividing his army in two, he directed Hope's Corps of 28,000 to invest Bayonne, while the remaining 35,000, under Hill, were directed east towards Toulouse. The 5th Battalion, still commanded by Major Galiffe, started the campaign with around 520 men deployed in nine companies.

The French, fighting in defence of the homeland and no longer molested by Spanish and Portuguese guerrilla bands, resisted all the way as Hill advanced in contact, with the rifle companies in the advance guard suffering frequent losses. On 14 February, Captain Blassière was killed. Meanwhile Hope surrounded Bayonne, during which, on 23 February, a company of the 5th Battalion led the way in a perilous crossing of the Adour estuary below Bayonne. Four days later, the company commander of the same company, Captain Harrison, was severely wounded, losing the sight of both eyes.[44]

Battle of Orthez, 27 February 1814
On 27 February Wellington's army advancing east came up against Soult's army of 37,000 in a strong position near the town of Orthez. In the subsequent battle, and after a hard fight, the French, fearful of being trapped in Orthez, withdrew. Losses were substantial, with the 5th Battalion losing 42.

Vic de Bigorre, 19 March 1814
Continuing to fight all the way, Soult's army fell back on Tarbes. On 19 March three companies of the 5th Battalion under Major Galiffe, no more than 130 strong, attacked a much larger French rearguard at the village of Vic de Bigorre. A fierce engagement lasting three hours then took place among the hedges and enclosures of the village before reinforcements arrived. The French withdrew. In this brave but little-known action, the 5th Battalion lost another 30 men.[45]

By the end of March the French, with 42,000 men, were concentrated in new positions covering Toulouse, an important communications centre with a large military arsenal. Meanwhile the allies had captured Paris and, on 6 April, Napoleon had abdicated. However, neither Wellington nor Soult yet knew this.

Battle of Toulouse, 10 April 1814
On 10 April – Easter Day – Wellington, with an allied army of 53,500, attacked the French positions. Four companies of the 5th Battalion under command of Galiffe, who was promoted a brevet lieutenant-colonel shortly before the battle, were in the vanguard of the 3rd Division. The assault against a strongly-fortified bridge was repulsed with considerable loss but after a day of hard fighting the French eventually withdrew. Two days later Wellington was in possession of Toulouse. The French had lost 3,300 men, the allied army nearly half as many again, of which 64 were from the 5th Battalion.

The War by now was nearly over. On 14 April the French tried unsuccessfully to break out from Bayonne. In a fierce contest to prevent them, the rifle company with the 1st Division, the only one not to take part in the Battle of Toulouse, suffered yet more casualties. Fortunately, news of the events in Paris then reached Wellington and Soult and hostilities ceased.

Operations in 1814 cost the 5th Battalion dear, with 223 officers and soldiers killed, wounded or missing. The company at Bayonne had lost all its officers and was reduced to about 40 rifles. The eight companies with Wellington had only 9 officers and about 250 rifles remaining. Reduced to only 60% of its original strength, it was just as well, from the Battalion's perspective, the War ended when it did.

The 5th Battalion's Contribution

To quote from the *Annals*:[46]

> *The whole duration of the Peninsular War, which had been conducted on both sides with splendid gallantry and chivalrous feeling from start to finish, had been shared with our Riflemen by two regiments only, viz. the 1st Battalion 40th and the 45th.[47]*
>
> *With the exception of the episode in 1809 [1808] when its reputation was tarnished by the conduct of a few individuals who, being prisoners of war, ought never to have been allowed to join it, the career of the 5th Battalion bears comparison with that of any other British unit engaged, and there is not one whose individuality made itself felt in a greater degree. The confidence reposed in the Riflemen by the Duke of Wellington has been abundantly shown; and the practice of detachment into companies, disadvantageous in some respects as a severe test upon their discipline and morale, served only to bring those features to greater prominence. The glorious record of the 95th was almost exclusively confined to the Light Division; our 5th Battalion can claim the honour of furnishing riflemen for a large proportion of the whole army.*

> *In this capacity they attracted the notice of foe no less than friend; and it is remarkable that notwithstanding the exceptionally arduous nature of their duties their regimental system was so good that few regiments had a smaller proportion of absentees on account of sickness.*

In 1808 the Battalion had sailed from Cork with 33 officers and 1,007 NCOs and Riflemen. On 5 July 1814 the Battalion quit France and ten days later landed back at Cork with 18 officers and 232 NCOs and Riflemen. During the war 70 officers were killed, wounded or missing, 784 other ranks killed or wounded and 229 reported missing. These figures, however, are not exact; they overlook, for example, that some men were wounded more than once and will have been double-counted, while others may not have been recorded at all.

In consequence of the 5th Battalion's distinguished conduct in the Peninsula, the Regiment was awarded sixteen Battle Honours,[48] one generic ('Peninsula') and fifteen for particular actions in which the Battalion participated:[49]

Roleia	Vimiera	Talavera	Busaco
Fuentes d'Onor	Albuhera	Ciudad Rodrigo	Badajos
Salamanca	Vittoria	Pyrenees	Nivelle
Nive	Orthes	Toulouse	Peninsula

Quoting again from the *Annals*: 'The Battalion appears to have been well commanded throughout the war; but although Davy, Fitzgerald and Woodgate played their part well, the names of Williams and Galiffe will ever be remembered as those of its most distinguished Commanding Officers.'[50] Williams, Fitzgerald and Galiffe were awarded Gold Crosses. Davy and Woodgate received Gold Medals. Exceptionally, Major Schoedde, who commanded a company at the Nivelle, and Captain Andrews, who commanded a detachment at Talavera, also received Gold Medals.[51]

A number of other officers in the Regiment also distinguished themselves in the Peninsula in other capacities. Among those to receive Gold Crosses were Colonel Keane, commanding a brigade; Colonel James Bathurst, Assistant Quartermaster General on Wellington's staff; and Lieutenant-Colonel Gustavus Brown and Captain Scott Lillie, who commanded Caçadores battalions. Major-General John Hope, who received a Gold Medal, commanded the 7th Division at Salamanca before ill health obliged him to return to England.

Thirty-three years were to pass before the more junior ranks received recognition. In 1847 a Military General Service Medal was instituted and issued in 1848 to fifty-four veterans of the 5th Battalion who had fought in the Peninsular War, were still alive and who claimed their medal. Among them was Rifleman (Private) Daniel Loochstadt who, together with a veteran in the 45th Regiment, received fifteen clasps, the most

5th Battalion in the Peninsula
Battle Honours and Casualty Lists

Action		Date	Battle Honour Awarded	Number of Companies Engaged	Officers			Other Ranks		
					Killed	Wounded	Missing	Killed	Wounded	Missing
1808	Roliça	17 Aug 1808	Sep 1821	10		3		8	39	6
	Vimiera	21 Aug 1808	Sep 1821	10		2		14	23	1
	Others							2	5	9
1809	Talavera	27/28 July 1809	Sep 1821	10		7		10	29	31
	Others						1		4	
1810	Bussaco	27 Sep 1810	Apr 1879	10		5		3	16	5
	Others							1	12	4
1811	Fuentes D'Oñoro	3–5 May 1811	Sep 1821	3		4		3	21	8
	Albuera	16 May 1811	Feb 1825	3		1		2	18	
	Others				2	2		6	31	7
1812	Ciudad Rodrigo	18/19 Jan 1812	Sep 1821	7		1		1	7	
	Badajoz	17 Mar to 7 Apr 1812	Sep 1821	4	1	4		9	32	
	Salamanca	18–24 Jun 1812	Sep 1821	7		3		7	23	3
	Others					1		9	22	118
1813	Vittoria	21 Jun 1813	Sep 1821	10		3		2	53	
	Pyrenees	25–31 Jul 1813	Feb 1825	10	2	5		8	43	25
	Nivelle	10 Nov 1813	Sep 1821	10	1	3		9	58	2
	Nive	9–13 Dec 1813	Feb 1825	10	1	4	1	1	36	1
	Others							13	1	2
1814	Orthez	27 Feb 1814	Sep 1821	9		2		4	35	1
	Toulouse	10 Apr 1814	Sep 1821	9		4		11	48	1
	Others				2	5		46	59	5
Total	Peninsular War		Apr 1815		9	59	2	169	615	229

awarded to an individual in the British Army. Among the officers, Major Schoedde[52] was awarded thirteen clasps for the Peninsula, plus a clasp for service in Egypt earned before he joined the Regiment. No other officer in the British Army was awarded as many clasps. Lieutenant-Colonel Galiffe was awarded eleven clasps.[53]

Wellington was made a Duke and given £400,000.

Peninsular War Medals

During the Peninsular War Gold Medals were awarded to senior officers to the level of commanding officer and staff officers of high grade who performed acts of merit and distinction in battle. The first and subsequent awards were accompanied by receipt of a clasp indicating the action for which the clasp was awarded. On receipt of a fourth clasp, the Gold Medal and earlier clasps were replaced by a Gold Cross, to which subsequent clasps were affixed. The Duke of Wellington received a Gold Cross with nine clasps, indicating his presence at thirteen battles, of which Roliça and Vimiera counted as one. No one else received as many clasps as the Duke.

Peninsular Gold Cross
awarded to Lieutentant-
Colonel William Williams

In 1847 a silver Military General Service Medal was instituted and issued in 1848 to commemorate active service with Britain's land forces between 1793 and 1814. It was awarded to survivors, who had to claim the medal – and over 25,600 did. Twenty-nine clasps were authorised, with two men being in receipt of fifteen. One was Rifleman (Private) Daniel Loochstadt of the 5th Battalion, 60th Rifles.

Military General Service Medal
with nine clasps awarded
to Rifleman (Private) Brandt

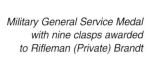

War against the United States, 1812–15

In June 1812, while the 5th Battalion was fighting in the Peninsula, the United States declared war on Britain over matters to do with trade and England's insistence on a right to search American ships for deserters from the Royal Navy.

Although some men from the battalions in the West Indies did act as marine escorts on board British ships sailing in the area, the battalions of the Regiment did not play a great part in the War, and none at all in the south of the United States. However, three members of the Regiment played a major role in the defence of Canada: Lieutenant-General Sir George Prevost, now Governor-General of Canada; Major General de Rottenburg, commanding Montreal District; and Colonel de Salaberry, a Basque and former company commander in the 5th Battalion, who commanded a body of Voltigeurs. Assisted by Colonel Williams, the former commanding officer of the 5th Battalion, who was then serving in Canada, these officers, well versed in the deployment of light troops to best effect, used the few men at their disposal with great skill to defend the Country successfully against a vastly superior number of Americans. They are well remembered in Canada for doing so.

Meanwhile, in 1813, an Act of Parliament was passed authorising the augmentation of the Regiment by another four battalions. On 1 September the 7th Battalion was raised in Guernsey from Dutch, German and other prisoners of war. It was dressed in green and included 640 light infantrymen with muskets and 200 riflemen with rifles. The 8th Battalion was raised in the same year from a provisional battalion composed mainly of prisoners of war being formed in Portugal. It, too, was dressed in green but equipped wholly as a rifle battalion. The authority to create a ninth and tenth battalion was never implemented.

In April 1814 the newly formed 7th Battalion was despatched to Halifax, Nova Scotia, to assist in the defence of Canada. Shortly afterwards, on the cessation of hostilities in the war against France, the 5th Battalion was also warned for service in America but due to its low numbers the order was rescinded and, as already mentioned, it went to Ireland. The 8th Battalion was by then in Gibraltar.

In September 1814 the two rifle companies of the 7th Battalion, including the commanding officer, Lieutenant-Colonel Henry John, took part in an amphibious raid on the State of Maine, entitled the Expedition to the Penobscot, during which a US frigate was destroyed and New Brunswick's border with the United States secured. Although a relatively minor affair, this was the only occasion after the Regiment's departure from America in 1783 that the Royal Americans, as the Regiment was still formally titled, returned to fight on American soil.

In January 1815 the British suffered a major defeat at New Orleans and in the same year the war ended. To quote from the *Annals* written in 1923:

It is much regretted that the war took place at all; a little mutual forbearance should have prevented its outbreak; and that it may be the last ever to sever the relations which should exist between the two countries must be the fervent hope of the Anglo-Saxon race on both sides of the Atlantic.[54]

Postscript

In 1815 Napoleon escaped from Elba and war again erupted with France. However, the battalions of the Regiment, including the 5th Battalion, which remained woefully undermanned, took no part in the *coup de grâce* administered at Waterloo on 18 June. However, two Colonels-Commandant were present: Lieutenant-General Sir Henry Clinton commanding a division and Major-General James Kempt, who was severely wounded, commanding a brigade. A small number of 60th officers were also serving on the staff, including Captain Horace Seymour, ADC to the Earl of Uxbridge, commanding the Cavalry. During the battle Sir John Elley, Colonel of the Blues, and Seymour were reported to have 'performed deeds worthy of the Paladins of the olden time. Horse and man went down before them as they swept onward in their headlong career, and neither helmet nor cuirass could stand against swords wielded by such strong arms.'[55]

Meanwhile, in October 1814, by order of HRH Prince Frederick, Duke of York, Commander-in-Chief of the British Army and Colonel-in-Chief of the 60th, the whole Regiment was directed to wear green uniforms with red facings. Transition from red coats to green jackets was complete.

1815–60: Peace and Imperial Wars

Reduction from Eight Battalions to Two

The end of the Napoleonic Wars was soon followed by calls to cut the size of the British Army. Orders were issued that all line regiments should be reduced to one battalion and the two Rifle regiments, the 60th and 95th, to two battalions apiece. Of the eight battalions in the 60th, the two selected for survival were the 2nd and 3rd Battalion, both then in the West Indies, with the 3rd about to move to Canada. The arrangements to achieve such a substantial reduction were complicated and took four years to complete.

The 8th Battalion in Gibraltar was disbanded first, in 1816, with 334 NCOs and men being transferred to the 5th Battalion, which arrived in Gibraltar from Cork in mid-year.

Next to go, in 1817, was the 7th Battalion, which disbanded at Halifax, Nova Scotia, where it had been since 1814. A draft of 200 men was sent to the 2nd and 3rd Battalion, which were then at Halifax.

In February 1818 the 6th Battalion arrived in England from Jamaica and was immediately disbanded. At the time of its disbandment nine-tenths of the men were foreigners, but almost all the officers were British.

In July 1818 the 5th Battalion, which had returned from Gibraltar during the previous month, was disbanded. Eighteen officers and 400 men from the 5th Battalion were despatched to join the 2nd Battalion in Canada. The remainder were discharged.

In April/May 1819 the 1st Battalion, which had been in the Cape Colony since 1811, returned to England and was disbanded, sending 64 men to the 2nd Battalion and 212 to the 3rd, both battalions still being in Canada. The 2nd Battalion was then renumbered the 1st and the 3rd was renumbered the 2nd.

Finally, in July 1819, the 4th Battalion, on its return from the West Indies, was disbanded for the third time in the Regiment's history.

The measures just described had their purpose for, on 16 July 1818, the Prince Regent signed a memorandum stating: 'That in consequence of the 5th or Rifle Battalion being about to be disbanded, the 2nd Battalion of that Regiment be clothed, equipped, and trained as a Rifle Corps.' It made sense, therefore, that 18 officers and 400 men should be transferred from the 5th to the 2nd (1st) Battalion to assist the latter in their conversion to a rifle battalion. In fact, to most it appeared that far from the 5th being absorbed into the new 1st Battalion, it was the reverse; indeed, for many years members of the 1st Battalion persisted in calling it the 5th! In 1826 Horse Guards, too, referred to it as 'the 1st – late 5th – Battalion'.[1]

On completion of the above reorganisation, both the 1st and 2nd Battalion remained in Canada until 1824.

Change in Title to The King's Royal Rifle Corps

By now the anomaly of the Regiment continuing to be titled 'Royal Americans' was evident to all. By statute the Regiment was still not supposed to serve outside the bounds of North America and the Caribbean, but had done so. Foreigners were also barred from service in Great Britain in peace. While expediency had often resulted in such technicalities being overlooked in war, common sense dictated a need for change. The Regiment, after all, had ceased to be American, other than by heritage and in name, nearly forty years previously. It was also a disincentive to many British, especially officers, to join a regiment that would cause them to spend the greater part of their lives overseas.

It was not, though, until 1824 that a change took place when, in a letter dated 19 June, signed by the Adjutant General, it was written that:

> *His Majesty has been pleased to direct that the 60th Regiment shall cease to bear the appellation of 'The Royal American Regiment' and be termed the '60th Regiment, The Duke of York's Own Rifle Corps and Light Infantry'.*[2]

This was followed by a further letter from the War Office dated 24 July 1824 stating:

> *His Majesty has been pleased to approve of the 2nd Battalion of the 60th Regiment of Foot being equipped and trained as a Rifle Corps, and has also been pleased to direct, as both the battalions of that Corps are to be Rifle Battalions, the Ensigns Rank in future be made Second Lieutenants.*[3]

A process of conversion, initiated by Bouquet and given impetus by de Rottenburg, had run its course and reached its logical conclusion. The 60th was from henceforth, formally and in all respects, a Rifle Regiment, honoured by its Colonel-in-Chief to bear his name and to be designated a Rifle Corps. As a consequence, 'Light Infantry', after an existence of only five weeks, was dropped from the Regiment's title.

In 1827 HRH Prince Frederick, Duke of York, died, to be succeeded as Colonel-in-Chief by his brother, HRH Prince Adolphus, Duke of Cambridge, a gallant old man 'not entirely free from a suspicion of eccentricity'.[4] In 1830 King George IV died, his successor, King William IV, losing little time in bestowing a further mark of Royal favour upon the Regiment. In a letter dated 12 November 1830, the Adjutant General wrote:

I have the honour to acquaint you by the direction of the General Commanding in Chief, that His Majesty has been graciously pleased to approve of the 60th Regiment being in future styled 'The 60th; The King's Royal Rifle Corps' instead of 'The Duke of York's Own Rifle Corps'.[5]

The title by which the Regiment was subsequently, and still is, known – The King's Royal Rifle Corps – was established.

Peacetime Service at Home and Abroad, 1824–47

1st Battalion

In 1824, the 1st Battalion moved to England. Before leaving Canada all foreigners still serving in the Battalion – about 150 – were obliged either to transfer to the 2nd or accept discharge. On arrival in England, Lieutenant-Colonel Thomas Bunbury assumed command. He was of 'the old school', portly in appearance and allegedly quite a character. An inspecting general once asked him whether there was any gambling among the officers in the battalion, to which he replied, 'No, for I have won all their money'.[6]

At the end of 1825 and again in 1826, with social deprivation and unrest prevalent in England, the Battalion was deployed in aid of the Civil Power. On 26 April 1826 a detachment was obliged to open fire on a mob in Manchester, killing six people.

In December 1826 the Battalion formed part of an advance guard sent to Portugal to help the Portuguese defend against the threat of imminent attack from Spain. The attack did not materialise and in March 1828 it left Portugal for Ireland where, in anticipation of Catholic Emancipation, the Country was in a condition of political excitement.

In October 1830 the Battalion embarked for Gibraltar, moving four years later to Malta. In April 1835 Colonel Bunbury, after eleven years in command, exchanged to the 67th Regiment[7] with Lieutenant-Colonel the Hon. Henry Molyneux. Bunbury received £3,500 for the exchange, which it is said he lost at the first subsequent race meeting he attended.

Between 1836 and 1840 the Battalion was stationed on the Ionian Islands,[8] off Greece, where, in 1839, its establishment was augmented to 800 other ranks. There was a considerable Irish element in the Battalion at this time, the best NCOs as a rule being Irishmen. It was whilst in the heat of the Ionian Islands that the officers introduced unbuttoned jackets and waistcoats (mess kit) as a more comfortable form of dress in the Mess, a habit initially frowned upon by higher authority but ultimately approved for the whole Army in 1876.

In 1840 the Battalion returned to England where in January 1841 it was issued with the Brunswick percussion rifle. In May of the same year Colonel Molyneux, who was well regarded as a caring commanding officer, died. The Battalion then moved to Manchester where in 1842, as in 1826, it deployed in aid of the Civil Power. In mid-1843 it was sent to Ireland.

In June 1844 the Battalion was warned for service in India and its strength increased by the induction of 369 volunteers to bring it up to the required Indian establishment of 51 officers, 58 sergeants, 21 buglers and 1,000 Riflemen. Colonel the Hon. Henry Dundas[9] was appointed to command. In June 1845 the Battalion embarked at Cork, arriving in Bombay in October and thence marching to Poona, becoming the first Rifle battalion to be stationed in India.

Arriving after the start of the First Sikh War, the Battalion was soon sent to Karachi in preparation for operations in the Punjab. On reaching Karachi, Colonel Dundas assumed command of all the troops there, while Lieutenant-Colonel Bradshaw assumed command of the Battalion. However, in February 1846, just as it was on the point of engagement, the First Sikh War ended. On return to Karachi, cholera struck, killing eighty members of the Battalion and one-seventh of the European population in the city.

2nd Battalion

In 1824 the 2nd Battalion moved from Canada to British Guiana under command of Lieutenant-Colonel Mackie, who had held the appointment since 1808, serving with distinction at the capture of Martinique in 1809. In 1825, after seventeen years as commanding officer, he handed over to Lieutenant-Colonel Galiffe of Peninsular War fame, but Galiffe did not stay long before retiring to his native country, Switzerland, where he died in 1847. Mackie, meanwhile, was promoted to the rank of major-general.

Life for the Battalion in British Guiana was uneventful, although it did elicit praise:

> *Berbice, 5th July, 1829. The Major General Commanding the District, in his annual inspection yesterday of the Headquarter Division of the 2nd Battalion of the 60th Rifles, was justly gratified with every part of its state and condition. The order of the barracks and the health and appearance of the men were very good. The field exercise deserved especial praise, and well showed how formidable a small body of troops may be rendered if they are well disciplined and judiciously managed.[10]*

The 2nd Battalion left British Guiana for England in early 1830, when Lieutenant-Colonel the Hon. A.F. Ellis, who had been appointed commanding officer over a year earlier, assumed his duties. In early 1832 the Battalion moved to Ireland, then to Gibraltar in 1834, and to the Ionian Islands in 1837, where both battalions of the Regiment served alongside each other until 1840.

In March 1841 the Battalion, about 530 strong, embarked for Jamaica, where it arrived in Kingston in good health but was soon stricken by yellow fever. Within months, 2 officers, 173 other ranks, 10 women and many children were dead, including Colonel Ellis, of whom it was written:

> *During this time the Colonel's exertions had been unremitting to promote the health of the soldiers and to prepare more healthy quarters for them. He was always to be met riding in the sun to visit one or other of his detachments, and hardly a day passed that he did not spend some time in the Hospital endeavouring to raise the spirits of the patients. In fact his only thoughts were for his regiment.*[11]

Soon after, the Battalion moved into the hills where, with the help of a draft from England, it recovered its strength, being deployed from time to time to keep the peace on the island. In April 1843 it received the Brunswick rifle. By May it was fully manned to its establishment of 800 other ranks.

In 1844 the Battalion was ordered to Canada where, in February 1845, Lieutenant-Colonel C.L. Nesbitt assumed command. In 1847 it returned to England and in April 1848 provided aid to the Civil Power during Chartist demonstrations in Macclesfield. In July of the same year the Battalion moved to Ireland where it was constantly required to deploy at short notice in response to the great distress and social unrest caused by failure of the potato crop.

Second Sikh War, 1848–9

The cessation of hostilities with the Sikhs at the end of the First Sikh War in 1846 did not hold. In April 1848 two British emissaries sent to give support to the new Sikh Governor at Mooltan were murdered. Revolt ensued, backed by the Ameer of Afghanistan. After a certain amount of dithering, reinforcement of the region was ordered. The 1st Battalion, under Lieutenant-Colonel Bradshaw, formed part of a reinforcing division commanded by Colonel Dundas.

Siege of Mooltan, 27 December 1848 to 22 January 1849
Mooltan was in rebel hands. On 27 December 1848, Dundas was ordered to capture the enemy's entrenchments on the south side of the city. Five companies of the Battalion took part in the assault, during which Major John Gordon was killed. The city was then besieged with its fortifications gradually being reduced until a final assault on 21 January, after which the rebels surrendered on the following day.

Mooltan was the first battle in which the Regiment had been involved since 1814. The Riflemen quickly showed that they had lost none of the marksmanship or skirmishing skills of their forebears, the

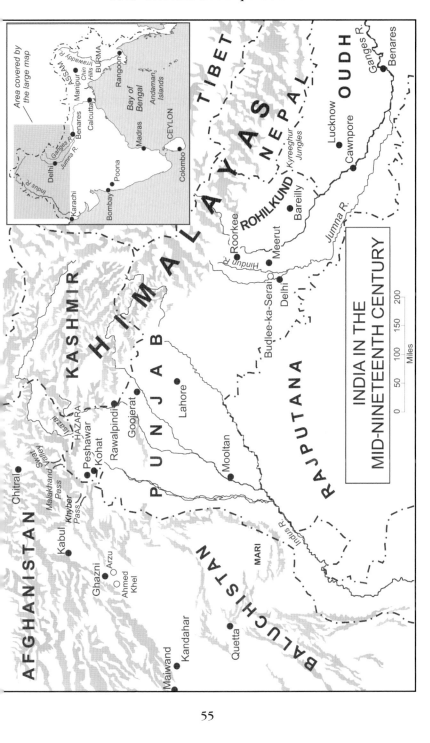

INDIA IN THE
MID-NINETEENTH CENTURY

brigade commander reporting that 'nothing could exceed the gallantry and discipline of the 60th Rifles'.[12] Eleven officers and thirty other ranks were killed or wounded.

Battle of Goojerat, 21 February 1849

Mooltan was followed by a rapid march, with the 1st Battalion in the lead, covering 280 miles to join the forces of the Commander-in-Chief, Lord Gough, in the decisive battle of the War. On 21 February 1849 the British Army of 21,000 confronted 50,000 rebels drawn up on the plain outside the town of Goojerat. Such was the effectiveness of the British artillery that the rebels fled before the infantry could properly close with them. Gough's army suffered 700 casualties with one bugler in the Battalion wounded. In the subsequent pursuit in which the Battalion took part, over 200 miles were covered before the pursuing force was finally halted at the mouth of the Khyber Pass. By the end of March the Battalion had marched nearly 500 miles from Mooltan in under two months. The Second Sikh War was over, for which in 1852 the Battalion was awarded three Battle Honours – 'Punjaub',[13] 'Mooltan' and 'Goojerat'.

Punitive Expeditions, 1849–50

Yussufzai Expedition, December 1849

Following the battle at Goojerat, the Battalion moved to Peshawar from where, in December 1849, Colonel Bradshaw was ordered to lead a punitive expedition against the Sam Barzai tribe who were refusing to pay revenue to the British. Bradshaw's force included two companies of the 60th and a troop of horse artillery (4 guns). Departing from Peshawar on 3 December, two sharp encounters followed on the 11th and 14th before the aim of the expedition was accomplished. A number of villages were destroyed. By 21 December the expedition was back at Peshawar.

Expedition to Kohat, February 1850

In February 1850 another punitive expedition was launched, this time against the Afridi tribes. They claimed that they were not receiving the remuneration due to them for keeping open a pass on the Peshawar–Kohat road and had expressed their displeasure by killing a party of Sappers and Miners. Again, two companies of the 60th took part, with Colonel Bradshaw in command of all European troops in the advance guard. Departing from Peshawar on 9 February, the expedition endured a torrid time forcing its way through the pass under harassing fire from the tribesmen. After the expedition had exacted some punishment upon the tribes by destroying a village, the 60th companies were back at Peshawar by 14 February.

Rifleman Burke and Tullala's Tusk

Rifleman, later Regimental Sergeant Major, Burke

On 14 December 1849, during the Yussufzai Expedition, Rifleman (Private) Michael Burke of the 1st Battalion, 60th, was advancing towards some high ground held by dissident tribesmen, when he and his rear-rank man, Rifleman John Connell, spotted a black flag protruding from behind a rock. Just as the rock was reached, an Afridi fanatic, on horseback and armed to the teeth, dashed out from behind it and shot Connell dead. Without a moment's hesitation Burke sprang upon the man, seized him by the head, hurled him to the ground, and shot him as well as another Afridi who came to his friend's rescue. Burke was slightly wounded and immediately promoted on the field of battle to the rank of Corporal.

Burke's remarkable exploit – he was later the recipient of a Distinguished Conduct Medal – resulted in the commissioning of a large silver centrepiece mounted on a plinth fashioned from the tusk of a huge elephant named Tullala, which on the march to Goojerat carried the pole of the Officers Mess marquee. In 1897 the centrepiece was aboard the Warren Hastings at the time that the ship was wrecked, but by good fortune was the only item of silver to be recovered and is in use to this day.

Rifleman Burke enjoyed a distinguished career in the Regiment becoming Regimental Sergeant Major of the 1st Battalion.

Silver Centrepiece – Tullala's Tusk

The expedition to Kohat was followed by a move to the hill station at Kassowlee where, in October 1850, Colonel Bradshaw died – a man described in the Annals as 'a great soldier, beloved by all ranks', who 'must be accounted as one of our greatest Riflemen'.[14]

War in South Africa, 1850–3

In July 1851 the 2nd Battalion, still under the command of Lieutenant-Colonel Nesbitt, embarked at Cork en route to the Cape of Good Hope where four times previously the native tribes had risen against British rule. By the time the Battalion disembarked at East London in early October large numbers of tribesmen were in the field and, although poorly armed, their knowledge of guerrilla warfare and the difficulties of the country made the task of quelling the revolt a difficult one.

The Governor of the Cape Colony and Commander-in-Chief was Lieutenant-General Sir Harry Smith, famed for his service with the 95th Rifles in the Peninsula where he met his young Spanish bride, Juanita, after whom Ladysmith was named.[15] He knew all about the advantages of using riflemen in broken terrain, where superior marksmanship and fieldcraft were needed, and soon had the 2nd Battalion deployed up country.

On 23 October 1851 an attack, in which the Battalion was involved, was launched against a strongpoint held by local tribesmen and regarded by them as impregnable at the head of the Water Kloof. Here the Rifles were observed hotly engaged with the enemy, 'moving up', to use the words of the Despatch, 'in skirmishing order in fine style along the face of the ridge, receiving the enemy's fire and driving him up the hill'.[16] After an engagement lasting over seven hours the tribesmen withdrew. The debilitating effect upon their morale of being forced to do so was great.

On 15 March 1852, in another significant action, the Battalion was obliged to lead a frontal attack with fixed swords (bayonets) on Iron Mountain, a formidable stronghold held by a large body of tribesmen. The position was carried with the loss of only one Rifleman killed and two wounded. 'The enemy', wrote Sir Harry Smith[17] in his despatch, 'was driven over Krantzes and rocks with great slaughter. Much cattle and many horses were captured, in the defence of which so stout a resistance had been made; and Major Bedford with two companies of the 60th Rifles pursued the fugitives over declivities nearly impassable, many more cattle falling into his hands.'[18]

In May 1852 the Battalion was issued with the Minié rifle in place of the Brunswick. Meanwhile, for the most part, it was hard toil, with the Battalion often operating in small flying columns and patrols. By degrees, however, the tribes were worn down and order restored. By March 1853 the war was over. To quote from the *Annals*:[19]

The news that the long and wearisome campaign had come to an end must have been received with general satisfaction. Hostilities had been forced upon us by the action of the Kaffirs [tribesmen], *for the lives of European settlers and even British dominion had been threatened. But there was little glory to be gained in defeating half-armed savages; and the necessary action of burning their Kraals, destroying their crops, and carrying off their cattle must have been most repugnant to all concerned; the more so, that the conspicuous gallantry of our foe, his commanding presence, and his many good qualities could not fail to excite admiration in the heart of the British soldier. … The almost roadless country, the steep mountains, the unbridged rivers, passable only by drifts which could at one moment be forded dry shod and an hour afterwards be fifteen or twenty feet under water, all combined to make progress extremely difficult and terribly fatiguing; but on the other hand no better school for the training of Riflemen could easily be found.*

On 1 October 1853 Colonel Nesbitt, who had been in command of the 2nd Battalion for nine years, was tragically drowned crossing a river. He was widely considered an able officer. Had he lived, he would no doubt have been pleased that the Battalion's efforts were later rewarded with receipt of the Battle Honour 'South Africa, 1851–53'.

Changes at Home, 1850–8

On 8 July 1850, HRH Prince Adolphus, Duke of Cambridge, died and was succeeded as the Regiment's Colonel-in-Chief by HRH Prince Albert, consort of Queen Victoria. On the Duke of Wellington's death in 1852, the Prince Consort transferred his colonelcy to The Rifle Brigade and was succeeded by General Viscount Beresford, formerly Commander-in-Chief of the Portuguese Army in the Peninsula. On Beresford's death in January 1854, General Viscount Gough became Colonel-in-Chief.

In March 1854 France and England formed an alliance with Turkey and declared war upon Russia. With both 60th battalions already committed overseas, the Regiment took no part in the Crimean War. However, the exigencies of the War led directly to the re-formation of the 3rd Battalion in Dublin in 1855, where it spent the first two years of its existence quartered partly there and partly at the Curragh. The commissioned ranks within the Battalion were filled by promotion within the Regiment. The Battalion was armed with the long Enfield rifle.

In May 1854, in a reversal of the order issued in 1824, the rank of Second Lieutenant borne by the junior officers of Rifle Regiments was abolished and that of Ensign restored.

On news of the outbreak of the Indian Mutiny in May 1857, orders were given for the re-formation of the 4th Battalion. This was done at Winchester. This time the commissioned officers were found largely from other regiments, while the men were principally from the Militia, of which many regiments at this time were embodied for service, together with a number of recruits from London and Lincolnshire.

In 1858 The King's Royal Rifle Corps and The Rifle Brigade jointly established a permanent Depot at Winchester (see Appendix F).

The Indian Mutiny, 1857–9

In 1852 the 1st Battalion moved from Kassowlee to Jullundur where, in 1854, it was commended for pioneering the introduction of 'skirmishing practices' (field firing).

A General Order requiring others to do the same 'as it cannot fail to prove most useful and advantageous', stated: 'in the 60th Rifles a sufficient number of targets are planted out to admit of the extension of a Company. All the usual Light Infantry practice is carried out within a distance of 500 yards, and the men become thereby accustomed to judging distances and consequent range of sight.'[20]

On 1 December 1855 the Battalion marched from Jullundur to Meerut. Its strength was 18 officers and 814 other ranks. In August 1856 cholera accounted for the death of twenty-nine men, seven women and twelve children. On 1 January 1857 the Battalion was armed with the long Enfield rifle and ten rounds per man.

Outbreak of the Mutiny, Meerut, 10 May 1857

The outbreak of the Indian Mutiny, or Sepoy Revolt as it should more accurately be termed, may be attributed to many causes, of which the heavy-handed annexation of Oudh in 1856 was one and the issue of new cartridges greased with animal fat was another. A sense of grievance and signs of unrest prevailed, although few can have anticipated the form, scale and the nature of the horrors that were to take place.

At 6 p.m. on 10 May 1857 members of the 1st Battalion were parading for church in their barracks at Meerut when news arrived that the sepoys in the native regiments in the garrison had revolted.[21] Europeans were being murdered and the town of Meerut was alight. Detachments of the Battalion were immediately despatched to prevent further atrocities and to secure the treasury building, arsenal and magazine. Meanwhile the mutineers set off for Delhi, forty miles to the south-east, where they joined with others in seizing the city.

Despite the prompt response of the Battalion in securing key points and its general state of readiness, no instruction was given for immediate pursuit of the mutineers. Instead, attention was focused on restoring order in Meerut. It was not, therefore, until 27 May that a relief force, under command of Brigadier-General Archdale Wilson, departed for Delhi. The force included a squadron of cavalry, some guns and six companies of the 1st Battalion (16 officers and 450 men) under the command of Lieutenant-Colonel John Jones. Two companies of the Battalion were left at Meerut to guard the garrison and surviving Europeans.

Action at the Hindun, 30/31 May 1857

On 30 May the relief force halted just short of the Hindun River, some nine miles from Delhi. The river, although little more than a rivulet in May, was spanned by a 600-yard causeway at the opposite end of which a strong rebel force of 5,000 was entrenched in a village, supported by five heavy guns taken from the Delhi arsenal. Crossing the causeway under direct artillery fire, the 60th companies stormed the gun positions and routed the rebel infantry from their fortified positions in the village. In this extremely gallant action, during which the Riflemen showed consummate skill in the use of fire and movement, the Battalion lost eleven killed and nine wounded.

After retiring across the causeway to encamp, the relief force was no doubt dismayed to find on the following day that the rebels had reoccupied some of their earlier positions and a further opposed crossing of the causeway was required. During this action, fought in similar fashion to the previous day, the Battalion lost two more killed and six wounded. A further four Riflemen died of sunstroke.

On 1 June the Sirmoor Battalion of Gurkhas joined the relief column, thus initiating a relationship, which, as a consequence of the actions soon to follow, became an Affiliation (see Appendix E). On 7 June the force from Meerut became part of a larger relief column, known as the Delhi Field Force, commanded by Major-General Sir Harry Barnard. A contemporary account states: 'Brigadier Wilson's force marched in this morning and I can't tell you how well they all looked ... Colonel Jones of the Rifles, as fat and rosy as ever ... The Rifles in particular, though they had had a long march, came along stepping out merrily and singing in chorus.'[22]

Action at Budlee-ka-Serai, 8 June 1857

On 8 June a major attack was launched on another strong rebel position at Budlee-ka-Serai, seven miles north of Delhi, during which the 60th companies, crossing canals with water up to their waist, contributed by successfully outflanking the rebels and threatening their rear. The rebels then withdrew into Delhi, while the Delhi Field Force moved to occupy the ridge immediately north of the city, behind which the British encamped.

The Ridge at Delhi, June to September 1857

The Delhi Field Force had too few troops to besiege a city as large as Delhi with a rebel force of uncertain but growing strength congregating behind the protection of its walls.[23] General Barnard, therefore, confined his force to holding its positions on the Delhi ridge overlooking the city from a distance of 1,200 yards and more, in the hope that reinforcements would arrive. Reinforcements, however, were

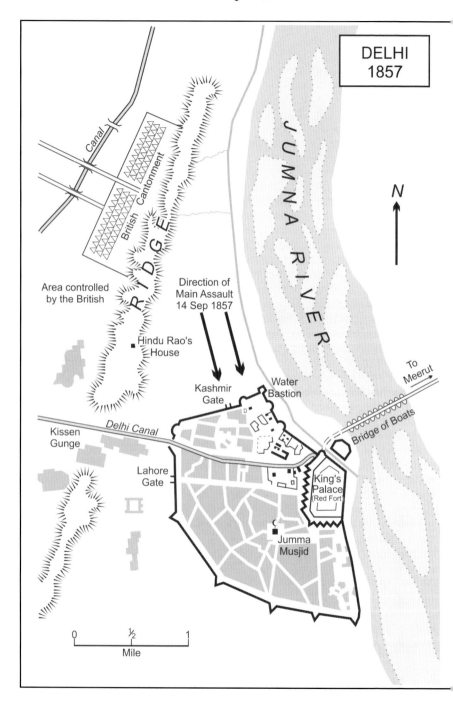

DELHI
1857

J U M N A   R I V E R

N

Canal

British Cantonment

R I D G E

Area controlled
by the British

Hindu Rao's
House

Direction of
Main Assault
14 Sep 1857

To
Meerut

Kashmir
Gate

Water
Bastion

Bridge of Boats

Kissen
Gunge

Delhi Canal

Lahore
Gate

King's
Palace
(Red Fort)

Jumma
Musjid

0   ½   1
Mile

not readily available, as the Mutiny had spread to other cities where the surviving garrisons were in similar need of help. The nearest native troops who might be relied upon were many hundreds of miles away in the Punjab. One small element, however, did arrive – the Guides, a distinguished Frontier corps of cavalry and infantry, after an exceptional march of nearly 600 miles in twenty-two days.[24]

For three months the Delhi Field Force, whose total strength amounted to no more than 4,000 men, hung on to its positions in the face of frequent rebel attacks. Members of the Sirmoor Battalion and the 60th protecting the forward gun batteries ranged on the city, supported by the Guides, repeatedly combined to counter-attack and prevent the rebels from over-running their positions along the ridge. By 30 June the Battalion had lost three officers and forty other ranks killed, and many more wounded. On 1 August Major Reid of the Sirmoor Battalion, commanding a strong detachment of Gurkhas and 60th at Hindu Rao's house, reported that his position had been attacked twenty-four times since he had occupied it in June.

This Brief History does not permit a detailed account of the numerous and often desperate actions involving the Battalion during this period. It is clear, however, from a letter written on 29 June by Ensign Heathcote, who was later awarded a Victoria Cross, that the Battalion was earning a fine reputation for itself when he states: 'Our men are thought a great deal of, and certainly they are beautiful shots; the enemy funk us more than any other regiment, so much so that the King of Delhi has offered a reward for every Rifleman's jacket brought into Delhi.'[25]

Meanwhile, conditions in the encampment were extremely unpleasant. The weather alternated between scorching heat and incessant monsoon rain. Flies abounded spreading disease, with cholera emerging to take its toll, although the Battalion was far less affected than most as the regimental surgeon insisted that the men wore their serge green jackets instead of the linen uniforms worn by others. The Force Commander was among those to die of cholera, being replaced, first, by General Reed and on 16 July by Brigadier-General Wilson. Morale, however, must have remained high with a cricket match and pony race reportedly taking place in the 60th's lines on 4 August.

During these months reinforcements continued to dribble in including, on 14 August, the 52nd Light Infantry. The more, however, that arrived, the greater the pressure on General Wilson to act. A sense of his exasperation is reflected in a letter he wrote on 20 August:

A letter has been received from the Governor-General urging our immediately taking Delhi, and he seems angry that this was not done long ago. I wish to explain to him the true state of affairs – that Delhi is seven miles in circumference, filled with an immense fanatical Mussulman population, garrisoned by fully 40,000

Hindu Rao's House and the Delhi Table

Hindu Rao's house, the deserted home of a Maratha nobleman, was the key position on the ridge overlooking Delhi. It was the headquarters of Major Reid of the Sirmoor Battalion, who commanded the troops protecting the position. From the house it was possible to observe by day each sortie of mutineers leaving the city. It also provided protection to the British camp that lay behind the ridge. It was held against all attack from 8 June to 14 September 1857.

The Delhi table is the best-known artefact to have been recovered by the Regiment from Delhi. During the three months of recurrent fighting on the ridge, all battle casualties among the troops manning the outposts and guarding the gun battery were brought to Hindu Rao's house where the surgeons used the table for operating on the wounded. After the capture of Delhi, the table was divided into its three sections with one section being retained by each of the three regiments which had contributed most to the defence of the house: the Sirmoor Battalion, the Guides and the 60th Rifles. The section retained by the 60th is carved with the badges and mottoes of the three regiments – 'Stout and Steady' for the Sirmoor Battalion, 'Rough and Ready' for the Guides, and *Celer et Audax* for the 60th. It is on permanent display in the Regimental Museum at Winchester.

Hindu Rao's House soon after the Relief of Delhi, 1857

soldiers armed and disciplined by ourselves, with 114 pieces of artillery mounted on the walls; with the largest magazines of shot, shell and ammunition in the Upper Provinces at their disposal, besides some sixty pieces of field artillery, all of our own manufacture, and manned by artillerymen drilled and taught by ourselves; that the fort has been made so strong by perfect flanking defences erected by our own engineers ... and that an attempt to blow in the gates, and escalade the walls was twice contemplated, but it was considered, from the state of preparation against such an attack, ... [that it] would inevitably have failed, and caused the most irreparable disaster to our cause; and that, even if we had succeeded in forcing our way into the place, the small force disposable for the attack would have been most certainly lost in the numerous streets of so large a city, and have been cut to pieces. It was, therefore, considered advisable to confine our efforts to holding the position we occupy - which is naturally strong, and has been daily rendered more so by our Engineers - until the force coming up from below [i.e. reinforcements] could join us.

By early September the culminating point was close at hand, when the long-awaited and extremely slow-moving siege train, with its big guns and howitzers, reached Delhi. On 6/7 September the absent companies from Meerut rejoined the Battalion concurrently with significant numbers of troops from the Punjab. Final preparations for an assault on Delhi began.

Assault and Capture of Delhi, 14–20 September 1857

Within 48 hours of arrival the first siege guns were sited within 700 yards of the city in positions previously reconnoitred and cleared by patrols of the 60th. This had required extreme stealth at night and maximum use of cover in order not to alert the rebels to what was in store. Over the following days additional siege batteries were emplaced and on 12 September all four batteries opened fire simultaneously with devastating effect. On the night of 13 September the walls around the Kashmir Gate and Water Bastion were declared sufficiently damaged for an assault to be considered practicable.

At 3 a.m. on Monday, 14 September 1857, five columns of assault troops awaited the order to storm Delhi (see map on page 62). The first column, commanded by Brigadier John Nicholson - 'a man of overbearing manner and crude notions of generalship, but strong in character, full of energy, and a magnificent fighter'[26] - was directed to carry the walls immediately east of the Kashmir Gate; the second column to storm the Water Bastion; the third column, under Colonel Campbell of the 52nd, including 200 men of his Regiment, to enter the Kashmir Gate; the fourth column, under Major Reid of the Sirmoor Battalion, to take the Kissen Gunge (a village settlement occupied by the rebels) and enter the Lahore Gate from the east; and the fifth column, the strongest of all, to act as a reserve. The 1st Battalion was employed with 200 men covering the advance of the assaulting columns, a company in the column under Major Reid, and a company in the reserve column. The number of assaulting troops including the reserve amounted to about 5,500, while the number of rebels in the city was variously estimated at 40-60,000.

By the time the assault was eventually ordered, it was daylight. Immediately the 200 Riflemen covering the advance of the assault columns skirmished forward in extended line. As Columns 1 and 2 sought to breach the walls, the Riflemen joined in:

> *Carried away entirely with the excitement of the occasion, the Rifles, whose duty it was to cover, and who discharged that duty to the admiration of every beholder, could not withstand the temptation that now met them. Forgetting that being light infantry they were as such essentially skirmishers, they were among the very foremost to mount the walls of the city. Theirs were the first caps waved in token of victory; and theirs among the first human voices proudly raised to proclaim what we had gained and the enemy had lost.*[27]

Meanwhile, Column 3 succeeded with extreme gallantry in blowing in the Kashmir Gate. Column 4, however, was less successful, irrevocably held up by a determined rebel force in the Kissen Gunge and unable to reach the Lahore Gate. Six days of intense and difficult street-fighting then followed, during which the rebels resisted tenaciously, inflicting many casualties on the assaulting troops. Eventually, on 16 September, the magazine was seized and the rebels evacuated the Kissen Gunge. On 20 September the Lahore Gate, the Jumma Musjid (central mosque) and the King's Palace (Red Fort) were occupied. The capture of Delhi was complete. Throughout, the Battalion under Colonel Jones, whose operations had been marked with great skill, had played a leading role.

1st Battalion, 60th Rifles, at the storming of Delhi, September 1857.
Painting by Orlando Norrie.

The price was high. In the assault on 14 September the Battalion lost 27 men killed and 55 wounded, of whom four died later – a greater number of casualties than the Regiment had suffered in its earlier assaults at Badajoz, Ciudad Rodrigo or Mooltan. From the first action at the Hindun River on 30 May to success on 20 September, total casualties in the Battalion amounted to 137 officers and men killed and 252 wounded. The Delhi Field Force's casualties over the same period were 3,854 killed and wounded. The task, though, was crucial. If the position at Hindu Rao's house had fallen to the rebels, occupation of the Delhi ridge – the vital ground – would no longer have been possible. So long as Delhi remained in rebel hands, the upshot of the Mutiny was in doubt. 'It was the fall of Delhi which retained British dominion [over India].'[28]

In one of the finest feats of arms in military history, and certainly in the history of The King's Royal Rifle Corps, Lord Canning, the Governor-General, later commented in his despatch dated 9 November 1857:

All behaved nobly, but I may be permitted to allude somewhat to those Corps most constantly engaged from the beginning: the 60th Rifles, the Sirmoor Battalion, and the Guides. Probably not one day throughout the siege passed without a casualty in one of these Corps; placed in the very front of our opposition, they were ever under fire. Their courage, their high qualifications as skirmishers, their cheerfulness, their steadiness were beyond commendations. Their losses in action show the nature of the service.[29]

The Kashmir Gate after the storming of Delhi, 1857

Jones the Avenger

Lieutenant-Colonel, later Colonel Sir, John Jones,
Commanding Officer of the 1st Battalion at Delhi

Lieutenant-Colonel John Jones commanded the 1st Battalion, 60th Rifles, at the outbreak of the Indian Mutiny and continued to do so until the start of the Rohilkund campaign in April of the following year. Nominally he was the second lieutenant-colonel in the Battalion and had previously been without opportunity to demonstrate his aptitude for command. However, in the space of only a few months, he gained a formidable reputation as a skilled and fearless commanding officer and leader in battle. His determination to suppress the Mutiny and his readiness to deal severely with those mutineers who fell into his hands also earned him the sobriquet 'Jones the Avenger'.

After being given temporary command of a brigade on the Delhi ridge, the Reverend J.E. Rotton, who was present at Delhi, wrote: 'Colonel Jones is without question an able brigadier; his powers of perception in military matters are singularly acute, and his knowledge of strategy has been strikingly displayed on every occasion on which he has had the opportunity of exercising independent command. One of the greatest proofs of his capacity as a soldier is the high state of efficiency and discipline which distinguish his regiment; another is afforded by the universal confidence reposed in him alike by his own officers and men without a single exception. If he does but lead, they are ready to follow wherever he shall direct, not doubting but that in following him implicitly they will assuredly be led to glory and victory. This is a confidence which very few Commanding Officers enjoy.'[1]

Colonel Jones's excellence in command of the 1st Battalion was followed by outstanding success in command of the Roorkee Field Force during the Rohilkund campaign, for which he received a knighthood (KCB) – an unusual occurrence for someone of his rank. That, however, marked the apogee of his career for he was given no opportunity to command a larger force. In later life, it was always said of Colonel Jones that 'he never encountered an enemy whom he did not defeat, never attacked a town that he did not take, [and] never had a gun pointed against him that he did not capture'.[2]

[1] Lewis Butler, *The Annals of The King's Royal Rifle Corps, Vol. III*, 125.
[2] Ibid., 180.

In recognition of his role at Delhi, Lieutenant-Colonel Jones received the brevet rank of Colonel and the CB. Other officers were also rewarded with promotion. Seven men were awarded a Victoria Cross,[30] while another, Ensign Everard Lisle Phillipps, was awarded a posthumous Victoria Cross, but not until 1907 (see page 221). In September 1863 the Battalion received the Battle Honour 'Delhi, 1857', one of the most deserved battle honours in the Regiment's history. However, many actions went unnoticed by authority as the Government of India refused to consider mention of gallant or distinguished conduct unless reports were written in ink. Major Reid at Hindu Rao's house lacked ink. All his reports were of necessity written in pencil.

Delhi, October 1857 to January 1858

Following the relief of Delhi, the 1st Battalion and the Sirmoor Battalion were given time to recuperate by being left to garrison Delhi while others pursued the mutineers. Although the back of the revolt was broken, the province of Bengal was overrun with insurgent bands and the garrison at Lucknow was besieged. Sir Colin Campbell,[31] the new Commander-in-Chief, decided to focus first on the relief of Lucknow in an endeavour in which the 1st Battalion was not involved. On 31 January the Battalion left Delhi and returned to Meerut.

Rohilkund Campaign, 11 April to 24 May 1858

Lucknow was eventually recovered on 20 March 1858, after which Campbell immediately turned his attention to launching a campaign into the province of Rohilkund where many mutineers were taking refuge. Three columns were formed to march into and clear the area, with the columns converging upon Bareilly, the capital of the province. Colonel Jones was given command of one of the columns, entitled the Roorkee Field Force, which included nearly 600 men from the 1st Battalion under command of Major Palmer. The area was a mixture of jungle and more open cultivated land, studded with numerous towns and villages. It was the dry season. The heat was extreme.

Assembling at Roorkee, on 17 April the Force crossed the Ganges at the start of a successful campaign in which superior numbers of rebels were defeated in one battle after another, resulting in the capture of Bareilly on 6 May. Jones excelled in command with his column constantly ahead of the others. Losses inflicted by the enemy were slight. However, more than thirty soldiers died of sunstroke. Jones was knighted for his actions and appointed Quartermaster General in India. Rifleman (Private) Bambrick was awarded a Victoria Cross for his bravery at Bareilly.

Oudh Campaign, 8 October to 31 December 1858

Events in Rohilkund were followed, at the end of the hot weather, by a campaign to complete the subjugation of Oudh. Again, a number of columns were formed, with the 1st Battalion joining the column under command of Brigadier-General Troup. Meanwhile, Colonel Jones had taken up his new appointment and the Battalion passed through the hands of various commanders. Immediately prior to the campaign, the Battalion was re-armed with the short Enfield rifle.

Although the Oudh campaign was neither conducted as swiftly, nor was it, from a Battalion perspective, as remarkable as the Rohilkund campaign, it was similarly successful, with the Battalion forming part of a flying column which cleared the rebels out of the Kyreeghur jungles in the northern part of Oudh.

Arrival of the 2nd Battalion and Conclusion of the Mutiny, 1858–9

At the end of the Kaffir War in 1853 the 2nd Battalion remained quietly in the Cape Colony until the spring of 1858 when the headquarters and four companies totalling 366 all ranks were despatched to India. Arriving in Calcutta in May, the companies were soon deployed in flying columns engaged in expeditions against those mutineers still at large in East Bengal. At the end of the year the remainder of the Battalion arrived from the Cape Colony.

By this time the Mutiny had been almost wholly suppressed, although mopping-up operations continued until mid-1859. Meanwhile, in April 1859, the 1st Battalion moved to Benares where it met with the 2nd for the first time since 1840. In the autumn the 1st moved to Calcutta, where it was fêted before embarking in March 1860 to return to England on a voyage lasting 140 days. On the Battalion's departure after fifteen years in India, the Governor-General published a long valedictory order in which it was written: 'it is not more by the valour of its Officers and men, conspicuous as that has been on every occasion, than by discipline and excellent conduct of all ranks during the whole of their service in India, that this Regiment has distinguished itself.'[32]

Second China War, 1860

At the conclusion of the Indian Mutiny the British Government decided that it was time to resolve its outstanding trade disputes with China. As the Chinese were not amenable to negotiation, the Government despatched an expeditionary force of 11,000 men from India under command of Lieutenant-General Sir Hope Grant. The French sent an expeditionary force of 7,000 men from France to combine with the British.

In February 1860 the 2nd Battalion, the strength of which was increased to ten companies, embarked at Calcutta as part of General Hope Grant's force. Before departure it was re-armed with the short Enfield rifle. Eventually, after a long and tortuous voyage, on 1 August the Battalion, led by its brigade commander,[33] waded ashore close to where the Taku Forts guarded the mouth of the Pei-Ho river, about ninety miles south-east of Peking. Recording the event for posterity, the *Annals* recount that:

The Brigadier (whose command of the Queen's English was so great that he was popularly known as 'Blaspheming Billy') having discarded trousers, boots, and socks, jumped into the water and gallantly led the way. In appearance he was short, somewhat fierce-looking, and bandy-legged. Attired in a big white helmet and a dirty jacket of red serge, beneath which for a very few inches appeared the tail of a slate-coloured flannel shirt, the Brigadier presented a remarkable appearance as he trudged through the mud sometimes up to his knees, carrying his boots and trousers over his shoulder on the end of his scabbard. The host of onlookers was convulsed with laughter; but during the whole mile by unceasing cursing and swearing at the top of his voice, and a wealth of Billingsgate language which all might envy but few attain, he fully maintained his reputation.[34]

After dispersing various Tartar forces in the way, the Taku Forts were assaulted and captured on 21 August in an action in which the British lost 17 killed and 184 wounded. Hope Grant's force then marched via Tien Tsin and Tung Chow towards Peking. After a further attempt at negotiation, marked by treachery on the part of the Chinese, Peking was reached and occupied in October. As punishment for Chinese duplicity, the Summer Palace was burned. Much booty was removed and the Chinese obliged to pay an indemnity of £2.7 million.

In November 1860 the 2nd Battalion, which was the last to leave the Imperial City, moved to Tien Tsin where it spent the winter in fur caps, long boots and sheepskin coats to guard against the freezing weather. In September 1861 the Battalion left Tien Tsin en route for England leaving buried in East Asia just over 100 men who had died at various times from disease and the excessive heat in summer. Two further Battle Honours, 'Taku Forts' and 'Pekin, 1860', were awarded to the Regiment.

1861–98: Peace and More Imperial Wars

Peacetime Service at Home and Abroad, 1861–78

1st Battalion

On returning from India in 1860, the 1st Battalion was stationed at Dover, moving to Aldershot in 1861 and, in early 1863, to the Tower of London. Complimenting the Battalion at the end of their six-month tour of duty at the Tower, the Major-General commanding the Brigade of Guards wrote: 'The smartness in appearance of the Battalion leaves nothing to be desired, and he especially congratulates them upon their behaviour under the peculiar circumstances of garrison life in the Metropolis, so trying to discipline.'[1]

From the Tower the Battalion moved in June 1863 to Ireland, receiving Whitworth rifles of hexagonal bore shortly before departure. The next move, in March 1866, was to Malta, which offered few excitements. On the contrary, 'the atmosphere of the time was still that of the Crimea War, and indeed differed little from that of Wellington's days in Spain and Portugal'.[2] Cricket, racquets and boating were the principal pastimes for officers. In September 1867 the Battalion embarked for Canada where it was quartered at different times over the next few years at Montreal, Quebec, Ottawa and Toronto.

Red River Expedition, May to September 1870

In 1870 French Canadian discontent at the extension of territorial rights, previously claimed by the Hudson Bay Company but purchased from the Company by the Government of the Dominion of Canada, spilled over into rebellion when a group of renegades under Louis Riel seized Fort Garry (now Winnipeg) in a part of Canada known as the Red River Settlement. After a mock trial and the execution of an official surveyor, the Government decided to send an expedition of 1,200 men, commanded by Colonel Garnet Wolseley, to suppress the rebellion.

Fort Garry was 1,240 miles from Toronto, the last 600 miles being through largely uncharted territory, accessible only by small boat and on foot, following the course of extremely fast-flowing rivers. It was a most hazardous expedition requiring completion in the summer season if the soldiers were to avoid the perils of winter. Great care was taken in the selection of troops to join the force, with 400 men from the 1st Battalion being hand picked, including Redvers Buller, a company commander.

After setting out in May on an expedition reminiscent of Forbes and Bouquet's epic journey to Fort Duquesne in 1758, the force reached Fort Garry on 24 August 1870 only to find that Riel and his rebel gang of 200 had fled. The only living creature left in the fort was a fifteen-month old black bear, which was swiftly appropriated and for some years marched in dignified fashion at the head of the Battalion. With no time to lose, the force quickly returned whence it came without a single member of the 1st Battalion being harmed or suffering illness throughout the period it was away.

While the nature of the achievement and the importance of success were fully appreciated in Canada, they attracted little attention in England where observing the course of events during the Franco-Prussian War (1870–71) was of more immediate interest and concern.

Meanwhile, the British Government decided to withdraw all regiments from Canada, leaving it to the Dominion Government[3] to make its own arrangements for home defence. In November 1871 the Battalion moved to Halifax, Nova Scotia. It was the last battalion to leave Canada, representing the Regiment at Quebec as the British flag was lowered just over 112 years after two other battalions of the Regiment had witnessed the flag being raised. In commenting on the occasion in the *Annals*, the author wrote:'The long association of The King's Royal Rifle Corps with the Dominion of Canada is graven on the memory of the regiment and, it is hoped and believed, equally cherished by the people of Canada.'[4]

In December 1876 the Battalion completed its service in Halifax, Nova Scotia, where it had been for the previous five years, and returned to England, from where, in December 1880, it moved to Ireland.

2nd Battalion

In spring 1862 the 2nd Battalion arrived in England from China and was quartered at various stations in the south of England. In 1864 the Battalion was armed with Whitworth rifles, before moving, in early 1866, to Ireland where conditions approaching those of active service prevailed; indeed, the Battalion was constantly under arms in expectation of a Fenian insurrection.

At the end of 1866 the Battalion was issued with Snider breech-loading rifles and in September 1867 moved to India. On this occasion, instead of sailing via the Cape of Good Hope, it became the first battalion to use the new overland route by sea to Alexandria, by train to Suez, and thence by ship to Calcutta.[5] Over the next ten years the Battalion was garrisoned at various stations in India, including Seetapore, Benares, Peshawar, Nowshera, Rawalpindi and Meerut.

Despite the routine of garrison duty, the Battalion continued to excel, as is evident from the Brigade Commander's report following the Battalion's participation in a 'camp of exercise' at Delhi at the end of 1875:

The 2nd Battalion 60th Rifles, commanded by Lieut.Colonel H. P. Montgomery, composed of men in the prime of life, with health, condition, and training to fill up the measure of their efficiency, is, in his [the Brigade Commander's] *opinion, the perfection of a Light Infantry Battalion. Admirably drilled, equipped, and cared for in every respect, the individual intelligence of the soldier developed to the highest extent, with a boundless esprit de corps pervading all ranks, it would be difficult to find its equal as an engine of war.*[6]

3rd Battalion

The 3rd Battalion was re-formed at Dublin in 1855, spending the first two years of its new existence relatively quietly in Ireland. It then moved to India in late 1857 where it was not employed in suppression of the Mutiny but in the unaffected province of Madras. Its strength was over 1,000 and at one point rose to over 1,200. In December 1858 it was issued with short Enfield rifles.

At the end of 1861 the Battalion was sent to Burma with a company detached to the Andaman Islands. At the end of 1865 it returned to Madras with both its transports nearly wrecked during cyclonic storms in the Bay of Bengal. Those on the SS *Devonport* were the worst hit when the main topsail was blown away, followed immediately by the mizzen and foretopsail. The safety of the ship then devolved upon the captain, the 2nd mate, two or three crew and the 350 members of the Battalion on board, the rest of the ship's officers and crew being drunk. For four days the ship drifted helplessly, only being kept afloat thanks, in particular, to the bravery of Ensign Lindesay and the ingenuity of the Riflemen, who, no doubt, had their survival uppermost in their minds.

On eventually reaching port safely, the Battalion remained in southern India until embarking at the end of 1871 for a year in Aden, before arriving back in England at the end of 1872 after fifteen years' continuous service overseas. The next six years were then spent moving around the south of England until embarking for South Africa and the Zulu War in February 1879.

4th Battalion

The 4th Battalion was re-formed at Winchester in 1857, armed with short Enfield rifles, and in the following year moved to Dover, where the legendary Lieutenant-Colonel Robert Hawley assumed command. In September 1860 the Battalion was posted to Ireland. Soon after, the southern Confederate states in America seceded from the northern Federal states in circumstances which led the British Government to decide that it would be prudent to reinforce the regular garrison in Canada. The 4th Battalion was included among the reinforcements, which embarked on the SS *Great Eastern* at Liverpool on 25 June 1861 and arrived at Quebec on 4 July 1861 after the fastest crossing of the Atlantic hitherto achieved. By the end of the year the Battalion was well settled in the performance of garrison duties at Quebec and, from 1863, at Montreal.

The American Civil War ended in the spring of 1865, after which a large number of discharged men of Irish descent established Fenian bands intent on causing trouble on the Canadian border. As a precautionary measure, the Battalion moved to London, Ontario. In June 1866 news arrived that 15,000 Fenians had crossed the Niagara River at Buffalo. Two companies of the Battalion were deployed but by the time they had reached the scene, the Fenians had dispersed. No further problems arose and in May 1868 the Battalion moved to St John's, New Brunswick.

In mid-1869 the Battalion returned to England where, over the next five years, it was stationed variously at Aldershot, Colchester and Winchester. During this period it participated in the Army's autumn manoeuvres of 1871 and 1872, the last for half a century, eliciting the comment that: 'It is probable that no Regiment in the two opposing forces was better known either to the soldiers or the public than the 4th Battalion, which was constantly being quoted as a model of smartness in camp and quickness of movement in the field.'[7] Attributing the Battalion's success to Colonel Hawley, the same author wrote: 'It has probably been given to few Commanding Officers in time of peace to obtain a greater hold of those who served under him than he gained and maintained during the 13 years of his command.'[8] In March 1873 Hawley handed over command of the Battalion on his appointment as Assistant Military Secretary to the Commander-in-Chief.

In 1875 the Battalion was again posted to Ireland and, in November 1876, to India at the start of what was to become an overseas tour lasting sixteen years.

The Period of the Cardwell Reforms

In 1868 Edward Cardwell became Secretary at War at a time when the fear of war with Russia and Prussian successes in 1864, 1866 and, soon after, in 1870, made it clear to all except the most obdurate and conservative that the British Army needed reform. Cardwell initiated a series of changes over the following fifteen years including: abolishing the purchase of commissions and promotion; introducing short service enlistment; pairing single-battalion regiments, giving them territorial instead of numbered designations, and linking them to the reserves; and using the Army at home as a depot for supplying drafts overseas, particularly to India.

During the same period battalions received the Martini-Henry rifle in place of the old Snider. The Martini-Henry was much preferred for shooting; it was lighter with a .45 calibre in place of the .5 calibre of the Snider, but it was apt to jam and bore a heavy kick.

Robert Hawley

Robert Hawley

Robert Hawley transferred from the 89th Regiment (later Royal Irish Fusiliers) to the 4th Battalion, 60th Rifles, in the rank of major on the Battalion's reformation in 1857. He was subsequently the commanding officer for thirteen years from May 1860 to March 1873, during which time the Battalion saw service in Ireland, Canada and England.

Although Hawley is less well known than Bouquet and de Rottenburg, he is often bracketed with them as the third in a trio of innovative and influential commanding officers whose role as trainers was central in setting the tone and standards to which the Regiment thereafter aspired and by which it sought to be judged. He studied Bouquet, de Rottenburg and Moore keenly and modelled his system on theirs. He especially encouraged adventurous training, matched with plenty of leave.

To quote from the *Annals*:

It was said of Sir John Moore, and might equally have been said of Hawley, that his officers were trained for command, and his soldiers acquired such discipline as to become an example to the army, and proud of their profession. Although drill, field manoeuvre, and rifle practice formed an important part of the instruction, it was not by such means only that the character of his men was developed. Every single item connected with the food, comfort, and training, moral or physical, of a Battalion was thought out by Hawley and gradually perfected. His system, also like that of Sir John Moore, was based on the cultivation of morale and of self-reliance on the part of the individual officer or man. Among those who largely owed to their commanding officer the distinction which they subsequently gained [were] Field-Marshal Lord Grenfell, General Sir Redvers Buller, Lieut.-General Sir Edward Hutton ... and many of equal or lesser degree. Colonel Hawley ... was a master of his art, and his influence extended far beyond the limits of his own Battalion.[1]

After command, Hawley became a staff officer and was Deputy Adjutant General when Lord Wolseley was AG. But the two men did not understand each other and in 1883 Hawley retired as a major-general (honorary lieutenant-general). In 1890 he became a Colonel-Commandant of the Regiment. He died much revered in 1898.

[1] Lewis Butler, *The Annals of The King's Royal Rifle Corps, Vol. III*, 254–5

On 1 January 1878, the helmet – described in the *Annals* as 'the most hideous headdress ever conceived by man and the one least suited to our uniform'[9] – replaced the Regiment's busby.

As a result of Cardwell's Reforms, on 1 July 1881 the Regiment was required to drop '60th' from its title and became 'The King's Royal Rifle Corps'. Notwithstanding the change, the titles '60th' and '60th Rifles' remained in informal use, out of sentiment and for convenience.

Prior to the majority of these changes, on 3 March 1869, Field-Marshal HRH Prince George, Duke of Cambridge, succeeded General Viscount Gough as Colonel-in-Chief of the Regiment at the start of an appointment lasting thirty-five years.

Second Afghan War, 1878–80

In 1878 a dispute developed between the British Government and the Ameer of Afghanistan following intrigue with Russia and his rejection of Britain's demand to be diplomatically represented in the capital, Kabul. The British decided to use military force to impose their will upon the Ameer. A number of divisions were assembled for the task.

The 2nd Battalion, quartered at Meerut, was assigned to the Mooltan Division, commanded by Lieutenant-General Donald Stewart. The Battalion was put into khaki for the first time, the officers' swords were bronzed, and Sam Browne belts taken into wear.

At the end of December the Division assembled at Quetta, from where it marched into Afghanistan, occupying Kandahar without resistance on 8 January 1879. A reconnaissance in force was then conducted on the road north towards Kabul. After encountering no opposition, the troops returned to Kandahar. Meanwhile, Afghan defeats at the hands of other columns resulted in the Ameer's abdication and, in May 1879, a peace treaty was signed obliging the new Ameer to accept a British Mission in Kabul. The Mission took up post in July. On 3 September the Residency in Kabul was attacked by a mob of mutinous Afghan soldiers and, after a stout defence, all in it were killed.

So great was the outrage that the immediate occupation of Kabul was ordered. This was achieved in mid-October by forces under the command of Major-General F.S. Roberts VC. The new Ameer resigned, becoming a prisoner of the British. In the absence of further trouble, it was decided in March 1880 that the majority of the Division in Kandahar, where the 2nd Battalion had been for the past year, should return to India.

Actions at Ahmed Khel and Arzu, 19 and 23 April 1880
Marching north towards Kabul, the Division, 7,500 strong, encountered an Afghan force twice its strength blocking the road ahead. Hundreds of Afghan swordsmen then sought to overrun the column before they were checked and routed, leaving at least 1,000 dead in front of the British position. The British lost 17 killed and 124 wounded. The 60th company in the advance guard lost three killed and one wounded.

On 23 April a further action took place at the village of Arzu, near Ghazni, where the Afghans lost another 400 men. Although involved, the 2nd Battalion suffered no casualties. The column then proceeded to Kabul.

The state of affairs in Afghanistan was now such that the return of the troops to India was halted. At the end of July news arrived of the disastrous defeat of the British at Maiwand in southern Afghanistan and of the subsequent siege of Kandahar by the victorious Afghans, under their leader, Ayub Khan. A force of 10,000 men was immediately formed at Kabul to march to the relief of the garrison at Kandahar. The 2nd Battalion was a part of the column, which General Roberts commanded.

March from Kabul to Kandahar, 9–31 August 1880
Roberts's epic march from Kabul to Kandahar was a great physical feat. The distance covered was 326 miles in twenty-three days, of which two were rest days. Although no opposition was encountered, the conditions were extremely demanding, with temperatures varying from 110° in the shade by day to near freezing at night. Dust and sandstorms were a constant irritant, with water often in short supply.

Battle of Kandahar, 1 September 1880
On arrival at Kandahar, General Roberts lost absolutely no time in engaging the Afghans who, having raised their siege of the city on 23 August, were occupying positions about four miles to the north-west. On 1 September, after a battle lasting much of the day, Ayub Khan and his Afghans were routed, for the loss of 30 guns, 35 killed and 213 wounded.

The Second Afghan War was effectively ended. The Battalion then took part in a punitive expedition in the Mari district, south-east of Quetta, entailing much hard marching but no fighting, before returning to Meerut in November. During the expedition, Lieutenant-Colonel Collins, who commanded the Battalion through most of the War, died of dysentery.

In January 1881 the Battalion left India for South Africa in company with other reinforcements destined to take part in the First Boer War, adding 'Afghanistan, 1878–80', 'Ahmad Khel' and 'Kandahar, 1880' to the Regiment's Battle Honours.

Zulu War, 1879

In 1852 Transvaal became an independent Boer Republic, but one whose existence was always threatened by the warlike tendencies of the Zulus. By 1877 the Boer Republic was almost bankrupt and considered by the British to be no longer capable of self-government or self-defence. The British, fearing Zulu intentions and the implications for the security of Britain's possessions in South Africa, annexed Transvaal in April 1877. The Zulus responded by committing several acts of violence on the border with Natal. In December 1878 the British issued an ultimatum demanding, *inter alia*, that the Zulu army should be disbanded. When the ultimatum was ignored, Lord Chelmsford, commanding the British forces in South Africa, immediately launched an offensive against the Zulus. The result was the disastrous defeat of the British at the Battle of Isandhlwana on 22 January 1879. A British column was also blockaded but not attacked at Etshowe.

The British Government immediately despatched two cavalry regiments and six infantry battalions from England, including the 3rd Battalion. On 20 March 1879, six companies of the Battalion, commanded by Lieutenant-Colonel Leigh Pemberton, disembarked at Durban and marched up country to join a relief column of 5,600 men being assembled to march on Etshowe. On arrival, Colonel Pemberton was given brigade command and Lieutenant-Colonel F.V. Northey assumed command of the Battalion. On 29 March, nine days after the Battalion's disembarkation, the advance began. The transport, consisting mostly of wagons drawn by oxen, limited the speed of movement to no more than two miles an hour.

Action at Ginghilovo, 2 April 1879
On 1 April the column reached Ginghilovo and laagered for the night. At 6 a.m. on the following morning, a Zulu force of about 10,000 attacked the laager, working their way through the long grass to within 150 yards of the perimeter. However, after a few determined charges, in some cases getting within 20 yards of the defenders, the Zulus broke off their attack, losing an estimated 1,200 killed. British casualties were light, but included Colonel Northey who was mortally wounded early in the action.

Next day, Etshowe was relieved. Arrangements were then made for an advance on the Zulu capital at Ulundi where, on 4 July, Cetawayo was heavily defeated in a battle in which the Battalion was not involved. It did, however, take part in the subsequent hunt for Cetawayo, resulting in his capture by others at the end of August. This brought the Zulu War of 1879 to a close.

During the war, Lieutenant-Colonel Redvers Buller was awarded a Victoria Cross for an action while in command of the Frontier Light Force. The Battalion was awarded the Battle Honour 'South Africa, 1879'.

First Boer War, 1881

Defeat of the Zulus led to demands from the Boers to recover their independence. By December 1880 the whole nation was in arms and, on the 16th, the independence of the South African Republic was proclaimed. British forces were attacked, garrisons besieged and ultimatums ignored. Major-General Sir George Pomeroy-Colley, Governor and Commander-in-Chief in Natal and High Commissioner in South-East Africa, assembled a force to restore order and relieve the besieged garrisons. Five companies of the 3rd Battalion, under its new commanding officer, Lieutenant-Colonel Cromer Ashburnham, a Delhi veteran, joined the force.

Although highly regarded as an able officer, and under pressure to act quickly to relieve the besieged garrisons before reinforcements were available, Colley proved a poor commander during the events that followed.

Laing's Nek, 28 January 1881

Advancing from Newcastle in mid-January 1881, Colley's entry into Transvaal was blocked by 2,000 Boers in positions at Laing's Nek. Although he had a force not much more than 1,000 strong, he decided upon a plan of attack which went disastrously wrong. The British were repulsed with the loss of nearly 200 killed and wounded, the majority being suffered by the 58th Regiment.[10] The 3rd Battalion lost one killed and five wounded.

Colley had no alternative but to withdraw to a defended encampment in rear and await reinforcements, the first of which, including the 2nd Battalion, arrived at Durban from India on 25 January.

Action on the Ingogo River, 8 February 1881

After Laing's Nek the Boers started to harass Colley's lines of communication, as a result of which, on 8 February, he led a column of no more than 500 men, including the five companies of the 3rd Battalion, to meet and escort some wagons expected from Newcastle. Leaving some guns and one company of the 60th on the home bank, the column crossed the Ingogo River, reaching a plateau on the other side where, at 11.30 a.m., they were attacked and surrounded by 1,000 Boers, who made every use of the cover offered by the higher ground fringing the plateau. A very stiff fire fight ensued, which lasted all day, the Boers constantly threatening to rush the British position, every part of which was under fire at not more than 500 yards' range and in some places less than 100. Soon after 5 p.m. it began to pour with rain. As it became dark, fire ceased. A night withdrawal was ordered which, as the river level was rising rapidly, was only accomplished with great difficulty. The Battalion lost three officers and 55 other ranks killed, two officers and 53 other ranks wounded, and one officer and six other ranks drowned – a total of 120 casualties out of 217 men in the four companies involved. Regimental Sergeant Major Wilkins 'who throughout the day was to be seen wherever the fire was hottest, setting an example to the men by his cool and steady shooting and cheerful gallantry' was later awarded a Distinguished Conduct Medal.

3rd Battalion at Ingogo, 8 February 1881

After Ingogo, Colley wrote:

The comparatively young soldiers of the 60th Rifles behaved with the steadiness and coolness of veterans. At all times perfectly in hand, they held or changed their ground as directed, without hurry or confusion; though under heavy fire themselves, fired steadily, husbanding their ammunition, and at the end of the day, with sadly reduced numbers, formed and moved off the ground with most perfect steadiness and order.[11]

By 21 February the reinforcements from India, including the 2nd Battalion, were at Newcastle, where Colley inspected them. He then decided to have another attempt to dislodge the Boers from Laing's Nek without waiting for the further reinforcements, which would soon have become available to him.

Majuba, 27 February 1881

Departing from the same defended encampment that he had established before Laing's Nek in January, Colley set out at night with a small force of between 4–500 men, including two companies of the 3rd Battalion, to occupy Majuba, a flat-topped mountain, the summit of which, 2,500 feet high, overlooked the Boer positions. Dropping off the two 60th companies on a spur, he proceeded to the summit. Later, a third 60th company was called upon to escort ten pack-mules taking ammunition up the mountain.

At about midday on 27 February, Colley's force on Majuba was attacked by a superior force of Boers and forced to retire. All three 60th companies helped to cover the withdrawing troops, who were being chased off the mountain by the Boers. Colley was killed. Ten other ranks from one of the 60th companies were captured and another wounded.

A stalemate had now been reached between the British and the Boers. Majuba was shortly followed by a truce and, on 23 March 1881, peace was proclaimed with the Transvaal mainly, but not wholly, restored to independent Boer rule.

Despite the speed with which the 2nd Battalion had moved from India to Natal, it did not play a major part in the war and departed for England in December. In February 1882, the 3rd Battalion sailed for Malta, via Zanzibar and the Suez Canal.

Mounted Infantry

There was mention on page 16 of the Regiment's use of mounted infantry at Briar Creek in 1779 during the American War of Independence. It was a tactic with much to commend it to the 3rd Battalion in South Africa where, at the outset of the First Boer War, Captain E.T.H. Hutton commanded a squadron (*sic*) of mounted infantry contributed by the Regiment.

In the Annals the role of a mounted infantryman is described as follows:

> *The mounted Infantryman was an Infantry soldier who fought only on foot and used his horse merely as a means of locomotion. He was trained as an Infantryman, and the extra training required to make him a mounted Infantryman consisted of enough equitation to enable him to get about without damage to himself or his horse and the enlargement of his views by practice in mounted reconnaissance.*[12]

The utility of mounted infantry generated heated debate with the Cavalry, who felt their role was being usurped. However, the Cavalry was not always available and was more expensive to provide and train. Thus, the number of mounted infantry units grew significantly during the period from 1880, with The King's Royal Rifle Corps contributing more officers and men to its ranks than any other corps. It was also the only regiment to turn out a complete battalion of mounted infantry (see page 109).

Captain Hutton, later Lieutenant-General Sir Edward Hutton,[13] became a leading authority on the organization, tactics and training of mounted infantry, founding the Mounted Infantry School at Aldershot in 1888. Prior to that he was instrumental in raising mounted infantry units for service in Egypt and was later to play an even greater part in the expansion and use of mounted infantry in the South African War of 1899-1902.

Unsurprisingly, the role of mounted infantryman appealed greatly to the young officers and Riflemen in the Regiment, who, it must be said, by dint of their background, training and the independence of mind inculcated during their service in the Rifles, were ideally suited to the task. Commanding officers, however, did not always appreciate being deprived of their best men.

Egypt, 1882 *(see map on page 97)*

In the third quarter of the 19th Century, Egypt's external debt became so great that Britain and France took control of the Country's finances. In 1881, the heavily taxed peasantry, led by an Egyptian Army Colonel, Ahmed Arabi, rebelled against the Khedive (Governor) of Egypt, whom they held responsible for their plight. By May 1882, Arabi was effectively master of Egypt, a situation intolerable to the British and French, who were concerned for the safety of their citizens in the Country and for continued free passage through the Suez Canal. A British and French fleet entered Alexandria harbour, prompting a massacre of Christians by Moslems. Plans were immediately initiated to send a British expeditionary force to Egypt, under the overall command of Sir Garnet Wolseley.

On 7 July, the 3rd Battalion, who had only recently arrived in Malta, was warned for service in Egypt, reaching Alexandria on 17 July, six days after the city had been bombarded by the Royal Navy and set alight. Disembarking on 18 July, a body of mounted infantry of two officers and thirty men was formed, under command of Captain Hutton. The men came from both the 3rd Battalion and the 1st South Staffordshire Regiment and were mounted on hardened Arab horses from the Khedive's stables.

Having secured Alexandria, the British, under Major-General Sir Archibald Alison, conducted a reconnaissance in force engaging the Egyptians at Kafr Dowar, near Ramleh, on 5 August, during which Lieutenant Howard-Vyse and a Rifleman with the Mounted Infantry were killed. Rifleman (Private) Corbett was subsequently awarded a Victoria Cross for his gallantry in tending to Lieutenant Howard-Vyse.

Meanwhile the British always intended that their line of advance on Cairo, and the Egyptian Army which stood in their way, should be from the direction of Ismailia and the Suez Canal, and not Alexandria. The 3rd Battalion, therefore, moved by ship from Alexandria to Ismailia, disembarking on 22 August. Wolseley's force then advanced, following the course of the Wadi Tumilef, towards the Egyptian Army's main positions at Tel-el-Kebir, some thirty miles from Ismailia. As the British advanced, so the Egyptians fell back before them in a series of actions in which the 3rd Battalion was not involved.

Battle of Tel-el-Kebir, 13 September 1882
On 9 September, Colonel Redvers Buller VC, the head of Wolseley's intelligence branch, was able to carry out a full reconnaissance of the Egyptian positions at Tel-el-Kebir from a hill overlooking nearly all their entrenchments. No doubt greatly assisted by the information gathered, the British, during the night of 12/13 September, advanced on the Egyptian positions in battle formation. The 3rd Battalion was in the 4th Brigade, commanded by Colonel Ashburnham, in line behind the Highland Brigade. At daybreak (5 a.m.) the attack was launched. The

assault was not easy, with the 3rd Battalion soon engaged with the Highlanders in overcoming stiff resistance. However, as soon as the British cavalry threatened the Egyptian rear, what was a fighting withdrawal became a rout. In not much more than an hour the Egyptians were scattered. Total British losses were 47 killed, 382 wounded and 30 missing, of which the 3rd Battalion suffered 20 wounded.

Two days later Cairo surrendered and the campaign was successfully concluded. The 3rd Battalion became a part of the Army of Occupation, losing twenty men to cholera in the summer of 1883. The Battle Honour 'Tel-el-Kebir' was awarded.

Egypt and the Sudan, 1884–5 *(see map on page 97)*

The British Government, in accepting the task of restoring order in Egypt, unwittingly became involved in trying to find a solution to the problem of Egypt's vast dependency, Sudan, which had been misgoverned for years. In 1881, a certain Mohammed Ahmed took up abode on an island on the White Nile, declaring that he was the Mahdi, foretold by the prophet Mohammed, with a divine mission to reform Islam. He attracted a number of followers and incited rebellion. One of his supporters was Osman Digna, whose forces besieged various Egyptian garrisons in Sudan and then annihilated the relief columns. Although it was the British intention to leave such matters to the Egyptians to resolve, public pressure to act became too strong to resist. A large British expeditionary force was assembled, under command of Major-General Sir Gerald Graham VC. The 3rd Battalion, commanded by Colonel Ashburnham, was assigned to the 1st Brigade, which was commanded by Brigadier-General Redvers Buller VC.

Embarking at Suez on 16 February 1884, the 3rd Battalion, including some mounted infantry, disembarked at Trinkitat on 23 February. The force then encamped two miles inland in the knowledge that an Arab force, approximately 3,000 strong, was entrenched a couple of miles away.

Battle of El Teb, 29 February 1884

On 29 February the British advanced and shortly before noon reached the Arab positions. In the ensuing battle lasting more than two hours, there was much hand-to-hand fighting with charging dervishes wielding fearsome swords. Superior firepower told and eventually resistance ceased, with 825 enemy bodies counted on the ground over which the British had fought. British losses were 30 killed and 160 wounded. Quartermaster Wilkins, who, as Regimental Sergeant Major of the 3rd Battalion, had been awarded the Distinguished Conduct Medal at Ingogo in 1881, was among those killed.

After a few days of retrieving materiel captured by the Arabs from the Egyptians in previous campaigns, the British marched back to Trinkitat to embark for the short voyage to Suakim. Disembarking between 8 and 10 March, the British established a forward base eight miles inland, not far short of Osman Digna's camp at Tamaai.

Battle of Tamaai, 13 March 1884
On 13 March the British, closing in to attack Osman's camp, discovered the enemy in strong positions in a ravine to their front. Disaster nearly followed when the advancing square of the 2nd Brigade was breached by screaming dervishes, the situation only being saved by the steadiness of the British troops and by the flanking actions of Buller's Brigade and the Cavalry. By noon the ravine was crossed and the enemy withdrew, leaving enormous quantities of captured ammunition behind them. Over 1,000 dervishes lay dead on the battlefield out of an estimated force of 10,000. The British lost 115 killed and 110 wounded.

At both El Teb and Tamaai the losses of the 3rd Battalion were slight as, by an act of good fortune rather than intent, on each occasion the squares of which they were a part changed direction, placing the 60th companies in rear. Following the battle at Tamaai, Lieutenant Marling, commanding a detachment of mounted infantry, was awarded a Victoria Cross.

Various follow-up operations took place after Tamaai, during which the troops suffered greatly in the heat. By May the expedition had fulfilled its purpose. The 3rd Battalion returned to Egypt.

Nile Expedition, 1884–5

In 1884, Captain Hutton was pursuing his ideas for enhancing the capability of mounted infantry by contributing to the inception of a Camel Corps with a Mounted Infantry Camel Regiment (MICR).[14] The MICR included a Rifles Company, which was formed in England and took over its camels on arrival in Egypt in September 1884. In total, two out of the four company commanders and six out of the sixteen subalterns in the MICR were from the 60th.

Battle of Abu Klea, 15 January 1885
In late 1884, the Camel Corps played a central role in the unsuccessful expedition to rescue General Gordon at Khartoum.[15] Setting off across the Sudanese desert on 8 January, the main force, 1,500 strong, under command of Brigadier-General Sir Herbert Stewart, encountered and then became involved in a major battle on 15 January with the Mahdi's dervishes at Abu Klea. During the battle, the British suffered nearly 170 casualties, with the enemy leaving 1,100 dead on the battlefield, out of an estimated force of 5,000.

The enemy continued to oppose the advance, with General Stewart mortally wounded on 19 January. Redvers Buller was appointed to command in his place, but by now news had arrived of Gordon's death. After deliberating what to do next, the British Government (Gladstone) decided to withdraw its forces to Egypt, thereby postponing the subjugation of Sudan for a dozen years. The Battalion was awarded the Battle Honour 'Egypt, 1882, 1884'.

4th Battalion in India and Burma, 1876–92

The 4th Battalion arrived in Bombay from Ireland in 1876. The next fourteen years were spent in various stations following the routine of the Army in India - summer in the hills, winter on the plains, interspersed with firing camps and manoeuvres of a sort. The long marches on change of station, often lasting weeks, were one of the more pleasant features of soldiering in India and enjoyed by all ranks. Service in barracks was more tedious and potentially fatal. Peshawar, where the Battalion spent three years from 1885-7, 'was a hotbed of malaria of a most malignant type. A Battalion that had spent the hot weather there looked as if they had been boiled and bleached, and it took the greater part of the magnificent cold weather for them to recover their physical fitness.'[16]

In 1890 Colonel Kinloch arrived to command the Battalion. Recording the event in the *Annals*, the author wrote:

> *Colonel Kinloch was the best-known big-game shikari of his day. In his young days there was no musketry done in India in the hot weather either in the plains or in the hills. The Musketry Staff generally went on leave. Kinloch followed a long spell as Regimental Musketry Instructor by a still longer one as a Musketry Staff Officer. He had six months' leave out of every year for some fifteen years in succession. He had shot nearly every kind of animal in India and Kashmir. After he was married, his wife used to accompany him, and it used to be said that most of his numerous family had been born at over ten thousand feet above sea-level.*[17]

In 1891 the Battalion moved to Burma detaching a party of officers and Riflemen to join the mounted infantry in Upper Burma.

Manipur Expedition, 1891

Manipur was a small protected state in the borderland between Assam and Burma. In 1890 a revolution took place, which, in March 1891, resulted in the murder of a British delegation seeking to negotiate the surrender of the ringleader. A punitive expedition, including the 4th Battalion, was immediately organized. After encountering some initial resistance, the force successfully entered Manipur on 27 April to find the place deserted. With nothing further to be done, the campaign ended and the return journey began. On the way, the Battalion was struck by disease, with twenty-nine dying from cholera and four from other causes.

During the winter of 1891–2, a number of companies took part in operations in the Chin Hills. These involved much marching but no fighting. In November 1892 the Battalion left Burma bound for England.

1st Battalion in Ireland and England, 1880–90

The 1st Battalion arrived in Ireland at the end of 1880 in what were termed 'the Bad Times' and, as in previous years, was frequently called out in aid of the Civil Power. The troops, though, were seldom, if ever, compelled to take action, as the law-breakers always looked upon their arrival as the time to stop. Nevertheless, the Riflemen had to endure many long marches and exposure to all kinds of weather.

In 1886 the Battalion returned to the south of England where, on 9 July 1887, it participated alongside the 2nd Battalion and the 2nd Battalion, The Rifle Brigade, in Queen Victoria's Golden Jubilee Review in the Long Valley at Aldershot. The description in the *Annals* reads:

> *It had been a hot and dry summer and the dust was such as can never ever have been seen in the British Isles before or since. It was a dead still day, and the dust raised by the marching troops went up in a pillar of cloud. Except on the saluting base, where the ground was watered, the troops were enveloped all day in a fog of dust.*[18]

The *Annals* also provide an interesting insight to life in the Army at Aldershot:

> *Aldershot was then a peaceful place compared to what it has been since the South African War; still there was some attempt made there to train troops for the Field, especially after the arrival of Sir Evelyn Wood. There was ground to train on, there were numerous field-days, and what were known as Flying Columns were sent out for a week or so at a time to carry out a sort of Brigade training … but as such things as tactical exercises without troops were unknown outside the Staff College, there were very few company officers who had any idea how even to begin to train their companies, and company training consisted in most cases of a series of cut-and-dried performances taken word for word from the exceedingly formal Drill-book of the day.*[19]

In November 1890 the Battalion departed for India. En route the main crank of the troopship broke in the middle of the Indian Ocean, leaving the ship drifting helplessly for twenty-four hours before another ship helped to tow it to Bombay.

North-West Frontier, 1891–5

On arrival in India, the Battalion travelled by train to Rawalpindi and was almost immediately warned for active service on the Frontier.

Hazara and Miranzai Expeditions, March to May 1891

The Hazara expedition was mounted in early 1881 to quell unrest among the Bunerwals, a large trans-Indus tribe living in the foothills of the Himalayas between Afghanistan and Kashmir. The threat passed, but not before the Battalion had learned the hard way of the importance of acclimatization and physical fitness.

The problem posed by the Bunerwals had no sooner evaporated than a punitive expedition was required to deal with the Orakzais, a tribe of Pathans who had been raiding into British territory from Afghanistan. On reaching the region of the Miranzai border, the Orakzais offered no resistance and accepted terms. Again the Battalion suffered, this time with thirty-three cases of severe frostbite.

Soon afterwards, on 4 April, the young men of the Orakzais, taunted by their mullahs and womenfolk for failing to put up a fight, attacked a military outpost in the border area, killing and wounding a number of soldiers. A more substantial expeditionary force, 7,400 strong, was assembled as other tribes joined the Orakzais. Over the next three weeks a number of sharp exchanges took place during which the British lost 28 killed and 73 wounded. Casualties in the Battalion were light. By 24 April the tribesmen had had enough and terms were again agreed.

After some further forays into tribal territory, the Battalion was back at Rawalpindi by the end of May. Although it had not seen much fighting, it had experienced a lot of hard marching, had received a good training in frontier service conditions, and returned a very different battalion from the one that had set out three months previously.

Isazai Expedition, September/October 1892

In the summer of 1892 it was the turn of the Isazai clan to cause trouble in much the same area as the Hazara expedition had been mounted in the previous year. The Battalion was again involved and again the expedition came to nothing, as the enemy failed to put up a fight and left the country. A few villages were burned and crops destroyed, and the troops withdrew. On the way back to Rawalpindi the Battalion was afflicted by malaria, with half its strength being admitted to hospital.

The Chitral Relief Expedition, 1895

Chitral was a remote, protected, princely state lying at the foot of the Himalayas. In March 1895 one of the claimants to be Mehtar (Prince), besieged the small British garrison in Chitral Fort. A relief expedition,

1st Battalion at Peshawar

and then at the Relief of Chitral, 1895

consisting of three brigades, was assembled. The terrain to be traversed was difficult and mountainous through territory occupied by potentially hostile tribesmen. The 1st Battalion formed a part of the 1st Brigade, commanded by Brigadier-General Kinloch, the former commanding officer of the 4th Battalion.

Action at the Malakhand Pass, 3 April 1895
In order to gain access to the Swat valley, the expedition had to pass through one of three passes. Its commander, Lieutenant-General Sir Robert Low, chose the Malakhand Pass, knowing the other two to be

defended strongly by tribesmen. However, on approaching the Pass it was clear that an estimated 12,000 tribesmen, of whom 3-4,000 had firearms, were defending it and that passage would have to be forced. In the ensuing fight, conducted mostly uphill, the Battalion experienced its first real taste of battle since arriving in the Punjab four years previously. After five hours, involving five infantry battalions, the tribesmen were winkled out of their positions leaving the British in possession of the high ground dominating the pass. The British losses amounted to 11 killed and 51 wounded, the 1st Battalion suffering four killed and four wounded.

With the way open, the expedition moved into the Swat valley, where it was later learned that Chitral had been relieved by a smaller force approaching from a different direction. The troops remained on the Frontier throughout the summer before returning to India in October, adding 'Chitral' to the Regiment's Battle Honours.

The Years Prior to the South African War

1st Battalion

At the end of 1895 the 1st Battalion left India, with half the Battalion bound for South Africa and the other half for Mauritius, via Cape Town. On the last stage of the voyage to Mauritius the RIMS *Warren Hastings* with the headquarters and four companies of the Battalion on board, together with other troops and families, was shipwrecked on the coastline of Réunion, fortunately without loss of life among the troops and families. Continuing to Mauritius, the headquarters and four companies spent two years there before rejoining the remainder of the Battalion in South Africa in March 1899, seven months before the start of the South African War in October.

2nd Battalion

In January 1882 the 2nd Battalion arrived in England from South Africa. It then spent six years in the south of England, furnishing a draft for the mounted infantry in Egypt in 1884 and participating alongside the 1st Battalion in Queen Victoria's Jubilee Review at Aldershot on 9 July 1887. This was followed by a tour in Ireland where it was engaged in a similar pattern of duties and excursions as the 1st a few years previously. At the end of 1891 the Battalion embarked for Gibraltar, moving to Malta in 1895, to South Africa in 1896 and to India in 1899, where, in September 1899, it was warned for service in South Africa.

3rd Battalion

In August 1884 the 3rd Battalion moved from Egypt to Cyprus and in 1886 to Gibraltar. On the night of 17/18 March 1891 Sergeant McQue

Shipwrecks

Crossing oceans in the 18th and 19th Century was a hazardous occupation for soldiers in transit to and from foreign stations. In 1805 thirty men of the 6th Battalion lost their lives when the sloop *El Orquixo* foundered off Jamaica. In October 1845 a sizeable detachment of the 1st Battalion in transit to India nearly died when the troopship *Neptune* was dismasted hundreds of miles south-west of Réunion. In 1861 HM Troopship *Simoon*, with soldiers from the 2nd Battalion returning to England from China, was nearly lost in a hurricane in the South China Sea. At the end of 1865 the transports carrying the 3rd Battalion from Burma to Madras were caught in a cyclone and the SS *Devonport* drifted helplessly for four days before eventually reaching port. But the two best-remembered shipwrecks involving members of the Regiment concern HM Troopship *Birkenhead* and the RIMS (Royal Indian Marine Ship) *Warren Hastings*. Both are well chronicled in the *Annals*.

The Wreck of HM Troopship *Birkenhead*, 26 February 1852
HM Troopship *Birkenhead*, a paddle steamer of 1,400 tons, was en route from England to East London, with 643 people on board, including 500 soldiers bound for regiments fighting in South Africa. Among them was a draft of one sergeant (Andrews) and forty soldiers destined for the 2nd Battalion.

At 2 a.m. on 26 February 1852 the *Birkenhead* struck a submerged rock half a mile off Danger Point at the southernmost tip of South Africa. The night was dark but there was a calm sea and nearly all on board should have been saved but for two fatal errors. The Captain running up on deck ordered the engines to be reversed, which caused the ship to fill with water. He then ordered the lifeboats to be launched, but no drills had been practised and it only proved possible to lower three out of the eight, albeit with all the women and children embarked.

Within minutes of striking the rock, the forepart of the ship broke away. The troops by this time had paraded on deck under command of their officers. When the ship's captain ordered all survivors to jump overboard and make for the lifeboats, the officers had no difficulty in enjoining their men to stand fast for fear of endangering the lives of the women and children. At 2.25 a.m. the ship sank. Some men subsequently made it to the shore, were dragged aboard the lifeboats, or hung to wreckage and were picked up later by a passing schooner. The majority perished, some eaten by sharks. In total, 436 lives were lost and 207 saved. Sergeant Andrews and ten junior ranks from the 60th survived; thirty died.

When the King of Prussia heard what had happened, he was so impressed by the discipline and unflinching self-sacrifice of the troops on board that he ordered that an account of the sinking should be read three times to all the soldiers in the Prussian Army.

The Wreck of RIMS *Warren Hastings*, 14 January 1897
On 6 January 1897 the troopship RIMS *Warren Hastings* left Cape Town bound for Mauritius with 993 passengers, including the headquarters and four companies of the 1st Battalion, four companies of the 1st Battalion, The York & Lancaster Regiment, a detachment from The Middlesex Regiment, and

The wreck of HM Troopship Birkenhead, *28 February 1852*

twenty-seven women and children. Lieutenant-Colonel Forestier-Walker, commanding the 2nd Battalion, was the senior military officer on board.

At 2.20 a.m. on 14 January, the *Warren Hastings*, eight miles off course, steaming at full speed, in pitch darkness and pouring rain, ran straight into the rocks on the coastline of Réunion. The ship stuck fast, allowing time for the troops to fall in below decks without noise and in perfect order. At 4 a.m. the ship's captain ordered disembarkation to begin by rope ladders from the bows, intending not to disembark the women and children until daybreak. However, at 4.20 a.m. the ship began to list badly, so he ordered the men to stand fast while the women, children and sick were helped off the ship. Subsequently, as the position of the ship became even more critical, men clambered ashore as best they could, with many being saved from the sea by their comrades. By 5.30 a.m. all the troops were ashore. Later, some of the baggage was recovered. Miraculously, in an incident reflecting great credit on the discipline and behaviour of the troops, only two Indian members of the crew were lost. After being very well cared for by the French at Réunion, the passengers boarded another ship, maybe a trifle nervously, to complete their passage to Mauritius.

Major H. Gore-Browne and his wife, Lady Muriel Gore-Browne, were among those on board the *Warren Hastings*. He must later have had a hand in recovering the ship's bell because in October 1903, on relinquishing command of the 2nd Battalion, he presented the bell to the Battalion on condition that it should always strike ship's time and that, if no longer required, it should be returned to him. The first condition continues to be met to this day. As to the second, the bell is still required!

particularly distinguished himself, and was later awarded the Albert Medal, for his rescue attempts when an Italian emigrant ship, unfortunately named the *Utopia*, was wrecked in Gibraltar Bay with great loss of life.

Between 1892 and 1898 the Battalion was in England, before moving to Ireland, from where, a year later, in November 1899, it embarked for service in South Africa.

4th Battalion

The 4th Battalion arrived in England from Burma in December 1892, spending the next five years in the south of England, lining the streets in Piccadilly on 22 June 1897 on the occasion of Queen Victoria's Diamond Jubilee and subsequently taking part in a Review before Her Majesty on Laffan's Plain at Aldershot on 1 July. In August 1898 the Battalion proceeded to Ireland, turning out to see the 3rd depart to South Africa in November 1899. It was another two years, however, before it followed suit.

During the 1890s all battalions in the Regiment were issued with Lee-Metford rifles in place of the Martini-Henry. Sealskin busbies replaced the much-reviled helmets.

Mashonaland, 1896

In May 1896, a mounted infantry battalion of four companies was sent to Mashonaland (Rhodesia). This Battalion included a Rifles Company, manned jointly by men from the Regiment and The Rifle Brigade. The aim was to suppress the Mashonas, who had risen in rebellion and had begun to massacre every white man, woman and child in the Country. Arriving off Beira in July, the force, which was extremely small, set off for Salisbury, attacking and destroying the Mashonas' kraals and seizing their cattle as it went. By early November order was restored. The losses in the half company found by the Regiment were one killed and six wounded.

This campaign was the first in which mounted infantry trained at Hutton's Mounted Infantry School at Aldershot had taken part. It was later said that: 'The Mounted Infantry Corps from Aldershot was probably the finest of its kind that had ever taken the field. It was employed entirely in Mashonaland, where its doings in the field drew unqualified praise from Colonials and Dutch alike.'[20]

Chapter 5

1899–1913: The South African War and Subsequent Years

Background

By the middle of 1899 relations between Great Britain and the Boer Republics of Transvaal and the Orange Free State were close to breaking point. British imperialism and access to the mineral wealth of Transvaal were in conflict with Boer nationalism and their intention not to be dictated to or dispossessed by the British. The fiasco of the Jameson Raid in 1896 had served only to confirm the Boers' suspicions. Although governed independently, the Transvaal and Orange Free State pledged to assist one another against any external threat and began to purchase weapons. By October 1899 the Transvaal had imported 80,000 rifles, 80 million rounds of ammunition and a considerable number of guns. The Boers, however, were limited in numbers of men, with 41,000 from the Transvaal and 27,000 from the Orange Free State immediately available to take the field. They also hoped that their kinsmen living in the Cape Colony and Natal would take up arms, and that Germany would provide practical as well as materiel and moral support.

Although Joseph Chamberlain, the British Colonial Secretary, and Sir Arthur Milner, the British High Commissioner in South Africa, were set on war, Lord Salisbury's Government was anxious, for political reasons, that Great Britain should not appear to be the aggressor. It therefore sought to defer sending additional troops to South Africa. Meanwhile, there were no more than 10,000 British troops in the Cape Colony and Natal, insufficient for offence or defence against a determined opposition. As the situation worsened and conflict became increasingly likely, the Government was forced into a decision and, on 8 September 1899, ordered 10,000 reinforcements to be sent to South Africa from the British garrisons in India, Egypt and the Mediterranean. On 22 September, an army corps of 47,000 reinforcements was mobilised in England and Ireland. The Boers, realising that if they were to act they needed to do so quickly whilst they had a numerical advantage, issued an ultimatum to the British Government demanding, *inter alia*, the withdrawal of British troops from their borders and the cessation of reinforcement. Predictably, the ultimatum was rejected and, on 11 October 1899, the South African War began.

By the start of the War, the 1st Battalion, with the return of its headquarters and four companies from Mauritius, had been complete in

Natal for seven months. On 25 September, in expectation of war, it set out from Pietermaritzburg, where it was stationed, to march to Ladysmith, an important junction on the railway system where the lines from the Cape Colony, Transvaal and Orange Free State converged. The Battalion was 17 officers and 767 other ranks strong, with eight rifle companies, and was commanded by Lieutenant-Colonel R.H. Gunning. It was equipped with Lee-Metford rifles and two Maxim machine guns, firing 600 rounds a minute to a maximum range of 2,000 yards. The men wore khaki.

The 2nd Battalion was in the first wave of reinforcements, arriving in Natal from India just before the start of the War. It was 17 officers and 833 other ranks strong, and was commanded by Lieutenant-Colonel G.G. Grimwood. The 3rd Battalion was in the second wave of reinforcements and did not reach Durban from Ireland until 28 November. It was 28 officers and 1,073 other ranks strong, and was commanded by Lieutenant-Colonel R.G. Buchanan-Riddell. Both battalions were similarly equipped to the 1st. The 4th Battalion remained in Ireland, acting as a reinforcement battalion, despatching many of its officers and other ranks to join the staff, the mounted infantry or the 1st, 2nd and 3rd Battalion.

The advantages available to the Boers were exactly those which the British initially lacked. The Boers were hardened to veldt life, acclimatised, familiar with the ground, excellent marksmen,[1] skilled on horseback and adept at exploiting ground and their mobility to outmanoeuvre the more ponderous and less well-adjusted British. The British, on the other hand, were experienced in fighting frontier wars but against far less capable and well-equipped enemies than the Boers. The inadequacies of their doctrine, tactics and training, and the failings of commanders and staff, were soon brutally exposed in an environment where the enemy sought to operate largely unseen and in a manner which at first confounded them. Eventually the strength and resources available to the British from across the Empire prevailed. The experience, however, was to prove painful, costly and ultimately required the deployment of 450,000 men to subdue an enemy that was never stronger than 60,000 at any one time.

The Boer Offensive, October 1899

As soon as the War started, the Boers were intent on exploiting their numerical advantage and decided to take the offensive to isolate or destroy British forces on their borders in the hope of forcing a quick settlement on their terms before the British could muster the resources to overcome them. Striking on a number of fronts, the Boers besieged Mafeking on 13 October and Kimberley two days later. But their main offensive was directed towards that part of Natal (salient), which lay north of the Tugela River and between Transvaal

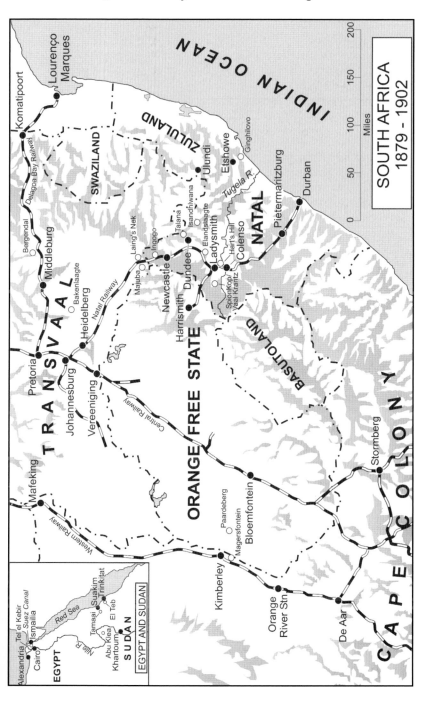

SOUTH AFRICA
1879 - 1902

INDIAN OCEAN

Miles

200

150

100

50

0

Lourenço Marques

Komatipoort

Delagoa Bay Railway

Bergendal

Middleburg

SWAZILAND

ZULULAND

Ulundi

Etshowe

Ginghlovo

Pietermaritzburg

Durban

NATAL

Tugela R.

Laing's Nek

Talana

Isandhlwana

Elandslaagte

Hart's Hill

Ladysmith

Colenso

Majuba

Ingogo

Bakenlaagte

Newcastle

Dundee

Heidelberg

Natal Railway

Harrismith

SpionKop

Vaal Krantz

Pretoria

Johannesburg

Vereeniging

TRANSVAAL

Central Railway

ORANGE FREE STATE

BASUTOLAND

Stormberg

Mafeking

Western Railway

Paardeberg

Magersfontein

Bloemfontein

Kimberley

Orange River Stn

De Aar

CAPE COLONY

EGYPT AND SUDAN

Alexandria

Tel el Kebir

Ismailia

Suez Canal

Cairo

Red Sea

Tamaai

Suakim

Trinkitat

El Teb

Abu Klea

Khartoum

Nile R.

SUDAN

EGYPT

and the Orange Free State. While British occupation of this salient with the limited troops available invited trouble, from a political perspective it was deemed essential; hence, Sir George White, the Commander-in-Chief in Natal, was obliged, against his better judgement, to position a brigade at Dundee. He retained his second brigade with his headquarters at Ladysmith. The 1st Battalion, less one company at Etshowe, was with the brigade at Dundee.

Talana Hill, 20 October 1899
On 13 October the brigade at Dundee received the first reports that the Boers, 8,500 strong, had crossed the Natal border. On 19 October the brigade commander, Major-General Penn Symons, was warned that a Boer attack from east, west and north was imminent. If he were concerned, he neither showed it nor did anything much about it. Meanwhile, during the night of 19/20 October, a Boer force of 1,800 men occupied Talana Hill, a flat-topped feature a mile to the east of, and dominating, Dundee. At 5.30 a.m. the Boers started to shell the British camp to the west of the town. Penn Symons responded by mounting a brigade attack against the Boers, involving four battalions with artillery support assaulting frontally up a steep slope for the most part devoid of cover. It took until after midday to complete and only succeeded thanks to the great determination and courage of the troops involved, especially the 1st Battalion. Colonel Gunning, the commanding officer, was shot dead just below the crest of the hill during the final moments before the Boers withdrew. Penn Symons was mortally wounded. Among the 447 British killed, the 1st Battalion lost 5 officers and 13 other ranks, with 7 officers and 83 other ranks wounded, 10 of whom later died. The Boers lost 150 dead. It was no doubt of considerable consolation that the Battalion subsequently received much praise for the gallantry of its officers and men.

Although the Boers drew back from Talana Hill, they continued to threaten the brigade to the point that the acting brigade commander decided that it would be more sensible to abandon Dundee. After some abortive forays against the enemy (to avoid giving the impression of retreat), and after a difficult march in bad weather, the brigade reached Ladysmith on 26 October.

Meanwhile Sir George White, realising that there was every prospect of his force being besieged at Ladysmith, started to attend to its defences, with the 2nd Battalion arriving to help him. The British also had some success operating forward from Ladysmith, imposing a defeat on the Boers at Elandslaagte on 21 October, in which neither the 1st nor 2nd Battalion were involved. A further encounter, at which the 2nd Battalion was present but did not take part, occurred at Rietfontein on 24 October.

Lombard's Kop, 30 October 1899

On 30 October, both the 1st and 2nd Battalion participated in an ambitious attempt by Sir George White to launch the best part of his force of two brigades, which were now concentrated at Ladysmith, against a Boer position at Lombard's Kop. The outcome is described in the *Annals* as a fiasco with the day being saved by the guns of the horse artillery, which enabled the force to withdraw back into Ladysmith. During the day the British suffered over 1,700 casualties, with the two 60th battalions suffering a total of 12 killed, 61 wounded and 15 missing. In the following days the Boers encircled Ladysmith, with the last train just managing to exit the town on 3 November.

Troops entering Ladysmith after the battle at Lombard's Kop, 30 October 1899

The Defence and Relief of Ladysmith, 30 October 1899 to 28 February 1900

Ladysmith lies in a loop of the Klip River and is surrounded by an outer and inner ring of hills (see map on next page). The outer ring, in places rising to some 700 feet above the level of the town, is some 4-5 miles distant from Ladysmith. The inner ring is slightly lower and less continuous than the outer ring, with its extremities up to 2 miles from the centre of the town. The Boers occupied the outer ring with a force, at its height, totalling 23,000 men. The British perimeter, stretching $12\frac{1}{2}$ miles, embraced the inner ring. As a defensive position it was far from ideal: it was overlooked by the Boer positions; it was within range of their guns; and it lacked depth. From the perspective of the British, the vital ground lay to the south of the town, where loss

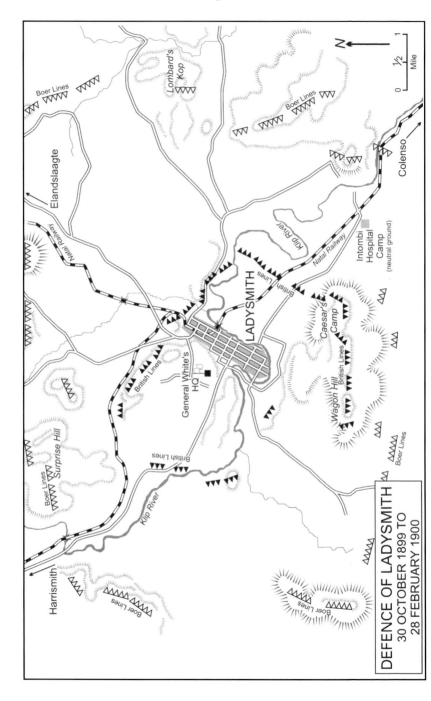

DEFENCE OF LADYSMITH
30 OCTOBER 1899 TO
28 FEBRUARY 1900

of the dominating features within their perimeter, Wagon Hill and Caesar's Camp, would almost certainly have rendered further defence of Ladysmith impracticable.

The besieged garrison numbered just under 13,500 all ranks with 51 guns, of which only eight were long-range weapons.[2] There were also 5,400 civilians, plus a further 2,400 black Africans and Indians. Apart from the 1st and 2nd Battalion, the garrison included the 2nd Battalion, The Rifle Brigade, which had arrived at Ladysmith on 29/30 October. There was a shortage of artillery ammunition. In all other respects, supplies were considered ample for at least a couple of months. Following the loss of Colonel Gunning at Talana Hill, Lieutenant-Colonel H. Gore-Browne assumed command of the 1st Battalion[3].

During November and December the Boers seemed content to invest Ladysmith without attacking it, other than by regular shelling of the town and its perimeter. The British, meanwhile, improved their positions and mounted raids to spike the Boers' guns. The sick, however, began to outnumber the wounded, who were all placed in a hospital, which the Boers chivalrously agreed to treat as neutral ground. As the weeks passed, the concern for relief grew.

Buller's Arrival

At the request of the British Government, Sir Redvers Buller, aged nearly 60, arrived at Cape Town on 31 October to assume the appointment of Commander-in-Chief. His original intention was to use his army corps to advance from the Cape Colony into the Orange Free State and Transvaal, while Sir George White's force contained the Boers in Natal. The situation was now different. Political considerations made it imperative that he should relieve Ladysmith, the loss of which would not only release Boer forces for operations elsewhere but most probably result in their kinsmen in the Cape Colony and Natal joining them. The Boers, meanwhile, were so intent upon bringing about the blow to British prestige that would result from the loss of Ladysmith, that they let slip the opportunity to seize or threaten other parts of Natal, including the key port and British supply base at Durban.

By early December sufficient of the army corps had arrived in South Africa for Buller to initiate action. Sending columns to relieve Kimberley and to check any further invasion of the Cape Colony, he assumed command of a substantial force, including four infantry brigades, each of four infantry battalions, assembling in southern Natal to march to the relief of Ladysmith. The 4th Brigade, commanded by Brigadier-General the Hon N. Lyttelton (Rifle Brigade), included the 3rd Battalion, 60th, and the 1st Battalion, The Rifle Brigade.

Colenso, 15 December 1899

Buller's first problem was to cross the Tugela River, approaches to which were dominated by the Boers, some 6,000 strong, from high ground on the northern side. The river was only fordable in a few places. A road and railway bridge crossed the river at Colenso. After some indecision, Buller, with 21,000 troops at his disposal, elected to force a crossing at Colenso and, on 15 December, attacked. Unfortunately everything went wrong from the start. In particular, the horse artillery advanced too close to the enemy and was decimated. Seeking to cut his losses before disaster ensued, Buller ordered a withdrawal, during which many gallant efforts were made to rescue the guns. Ten out of twelve were recovered, which gave rise to the award of five Victoria Crosses, including to Lieutenant F.H.S. Roberts of the 60th, who died from his wounds two days later.[4] The British suffered around 900 casualties, with a further 220 missing. Boer losses were no more than forty.

The effect on morale of the failure at Colenso was crushing, most of all on Buller, who had already received news in the same week ('Black Week') of British defeats at Magersfontein and Stormberg. He immediately recommended abandoning Ladysmith, but neither the British Government nor Sir George White would hear of it. Instead, the Government appointed Field Marshal Lord Roberts VC to be Commander-in-Chief in South Africa, leaving Buller in command of the Ladysmith Relief Force. Further reinforcements were despatched from England.[5]

Attack on Wagon Hill and Caesar's Camp, 6 January 1900
During the night of 5/6 January, the Boers, after two months of relative inactivity, launched their only major assault on Ladysmith during the period of the siege. Closing in under cover of darkness, 4,000 strong, and attacking Wagon Hill and Caesar's Camp, they almost succeeded in surprising the British. After a desperate defence at close quarters in which both the 1st and 2nd Battalion were involved, the Boers were eventually driven off in a torrential thunderstorm after a battle lasting most of the day. The two battalions suffered over sixty casualties, of whom twenty-one died. Boer casualties were 250, a significant number when the loss of manpower mattered and which, no doubt, determined the Boers to revert to the reduction of Ladysmith by starvation.

As the siege lengthened, the sick list continued to grow and rations started to run out. By the end of January there were 1,900 sick and wounded in the hospital, of whom 848 were typhoid cases and 472 were dysentery. The death rate was eight per day. Horsemeat had long taken the place of beef and, on 9 February, the biscuit ration was halved.

Buller's Offensive, January–February 1900

After Colenso, Buller withdrew his forces to await more reinforcements from England. By mid-January the 5th Division had arrived and he knew he must delay no longer. On 15 January his force set out to ford the Tugela River fifteen miles west of Colenso, after which, to reach Ladysmith, he needed to dislodge the Boers who were occupying the high ground to the north of the river. This high ground, which stretched for nearly twelve miles from west to east, included a peak called Spion Kop near its centre, with two smaller features two miles to the east of it, known as the Twin Peaks. At the eastern extremity of the high ground lay another peak called Vaal Krantz.

As Buller's force, 30,000 strong, advanced, their way was observed by the Boers who were entrenching a line from Spion Kop to Vaal Krantz. On 17 January the Tugela was crossed.

Spion Kop, 24 January 1900

On 20 January the British started to move on to the lower slopes of the high ground from the west. During the night of 23/24 January the Boer picquet on Spion Kop was overrun and the peak occupied, only for the British to endure a torrid time from daylight onwards being raked by Boer artillery and small arms fire. The British held firm, but at considerable cost. Orders from senior British commanders reflected indecision, were slow in coming and lacked clarity.

Twin Peaks, 24 January 1900

Lyttelton, commanding the 4th Brigade, realising that the pressure needed to be taken off the British on Spion Kop, directed the 3rd Battalion to seize the Twin Peaks. This they did, virtually alone and without artillery support, 'crawling, climbing, running, firing from every rock and at every opportunity' over a distance of 1,500 yards until they reached the top. The Boers, 200 strong, hurriedly evacuated the position.

Addressing the Battalion next day, General Lyttelton said: 'I have been a Rifleman for over thirty years, and never, in the course of my experience, have I seen a finer bit of skirmishing and fighting. The men of the 60th, led as I knew they would be led, behaved as Riflemen should.'[6]

The price was high. The commanding officer, Colonel Buchanan-Riddell, a man of sound judgement coupled with an unusual measure of moral as well as physical courage, was killed by sniper fire on the Twin Peaks, with Major R.C.A. Bewicke-Copley taking his place. Two other officers and nineteen other ranks were killed, and four officers and seventy-three other ranks were wounded. Inexplicably Buller then ordered Spion Kop and Twin Peaks to be abandoned, and during the course of the night his forces withdrew back across the Tugela River.

Vaal Krantz, 5-7 February 1900

After reorganizing and regrouping, Buller decided to attack Vaal Krantz. On 5 February his forces crossed the river, with the 4th Brigade attaining the peak only to find itself in a similarly vulnerable spot to that prevailing at Spion Kop twelve days earlier. On 6 February the troops hung on grimly to their positions, during which a half battalion of the 60th launched a spirited counter-attack to overcome a Boer assault. During the night of 6/7 February the brigade was relieved in the line and, at nightfall on the 7th, Buller ordered his forces back across the river. General Lyttelton assumed command of the 2nd Division and Colonel C.H.B. Northcott (Rifle Brigade) of the 4th Brigade.

At this point Buller decided to have another attempt at breaching the Boer positions at Colenso and on the Tugela Heights, north of the river. The second week in February was spent assembling his forces. The Rifle Reserve Battalion, made up of officers and reservists intended to reinforce the 1st and 2nd Battalion, and the 2nd Battalion, The Rifle Brigade, at Ladysmith, joined the 11th Brigade. Meanwhile the garrison at Ladysmith continued to hold out in increasingly difficult conditions. Buller could not afford another failure. No doubt aware of it, his plans for the next phase of his offensive were deliberate and ultimately successful.

The Fight through to Ladysmith, 11–27 February 1900

Buller's offensive took the form of a series of attacks initiated on 11 February, each building on the success of the last, during which the British first dislodged the Boers from positions south of the river and then advanced progressively northwards through the hills leading to Ladysmith.

Hart's Hill, 22/23 February 1900

The fighting was often fierce with the British only managing to cross the Tugela in force on 22 February. The 3rd Battalion was not significantly involved until, crossing the river that evening, it took part in the inconclusive but costly attacks at Hart's Hill, where the four companies involved delivered two bayonet charges and lost over a third of their number in killed and wounded.

After a truce on 25 February to collect the wounded on both sides, the offensive resumed on 27 February with a series of coordinated attacks on a number of Boer positions. By nightfall the Boers were in rapid but orderly retreat, not just from the hills but from around Ladysmith. On 28 February the first troops from Buller's relief column entered the town.

The defence had lasted for 118 days, with 170 of the garrison killed and nearly 400 soldiers and civilians dying of disease, mostly typhoid. Buller's losses over the three months of the campaign from December 1899 to the end of February 1900 amounted to some 5,000, one-sixth of his total force. The Boers had lost around 500. Whilst the British repeatedly blundered at the tactical level, the Boers also erred at the strategic level, failing to exploit their numerical superiority and mobility when they were in a position to do so. By the end of December their offensive had lost its momentum. Although a number of hard-fought battles were still to follow, their failure to capture Ladysmith by storm on 6 January was, in retrospect, the culminating point in their campaign in Natal.

On 3 March the relieving forces marched through Ladysmith. The 3rd Battalion met with their fellow Riflemen of the 1st and 2nd Battalion, no doubt amidst scenes of joy, with the Warrant Officers and Sergeants of all three battalions deciding to remember the occasion by holding an annual Ladysmith Ball. The Rifle Reserve Battalion handed over its officers and reservists and ceased to be a part of the order of battle.

Lord Roberts's Offensive, February to October 1900

On 10 January 1900 Lord Roberts assumed his appointment as Commander-in-Chief in South Africa. Gathering a force of 50,000 reinforcements from England, he decided to adopt Buller's original plan to invade the Orange Free State and Natal from the Cape Colony. Setting off in early February, at the same time as Buller was trying to force his way across the Tugela River, Roberts conducted a successful campaign during which Kimberley was relieved on 15 February and Bloemfontein, capital of the Orange Free State, captured on 13 March. Assembling an even larger force of 100,000, Roberts then set off again in early May, relieving Mafeking on 17 May and reaching Pretoria, capital of the Transvaal, on 5 June. By the end of October both Boer Republics had been annexed. The Boers had fought numerous rearguard actions with skill, but could not match British superiority in numbers. They were determined, however, to continue the War, forming commando groups employing guerrilla tactics to attack the extended lines of communication of the British, especially the railways upon which the British were so dependent for the movement of ammunition and supplies.

Following the relief of Ladysmith, Buller awaited Lord Roberts's order to advance through northern Natal into eastern Transvaal. Setting off in early May, at the same time as Roberts left Bloemfontein, Buller's force advanced slowly, with the 3rd Battalion well forward, while the 1st and 2nd Battalion continued to recover from their ordeal at Ladysmith. Marching via Dundee and Newcastle, by mid-June the British had forced their way around Laing's Nek, which the Boers, denuded of troops sent to oppose Lord Roberts's advance, were no longer able to prevent. Instead, their tactics of attacking the lines of communication, which stretched back 500 miles to Durban, obliged Buller to detach garrisons to protect key points.

At the end of July the 3rd Battalion, after participating in a number of encounters with the enemy, but none on a significant scale, was left for a number of months to look after Heidelberg and the surrounding district. At the same time the 2nd Battalion departed for India, escorting on the way a group of Boer prisoners of war to Ceylon. Meanwhile, the 1st Battalion moved into the vanguard of Buller's advance.

On 15 August Lord Roberts and Buller combined to unite a force of 20,000, opposing a Boer force of 5,000. On 27 August the Boers fought their last stand of the campaign at Bergendal, which lies close to the railway line from Pretoria to Lourenço Marques, and where the 2nd Battalion, The Rifle Brigade, excelled in a successful attack costing it some 80 casualties.

While Lord Roberts's offensive continued for a few months, with the 1st Battalion involved in occasional engagements, the conventional phase of the South African War was over. In October, Buller was ordered to hand over command to General Lyttelton and return to England. In December Roberts also returned to England to become Commander-in-Chief of the Army in succession to Lord Wolseley. Lord Kitchener became the Commander-in-Chief in South Africa.

General Sir Redvers Buller
VC GCB GCMG

Redvers Buller was born in 1839. He attended The Rifle Depot in July 1858 and was posted to the 2nd Battalion in India. He took part with the Battalion in the Second China War and, in 1862, transferred to the 4th Battalion. In 1870 he transferred to the 1st Battalion, taking part in the Red River Expedition in Canada. He left the Battalion in 1871 to attend the Staff College and did not serve at Regimental duty again. In subsequent appointments he took part in the Ashanti Expedition, the Zulu War, and in Egypt and Sudan. During the Zulu War he was awarded a Victoria Cross when in command of the Frontier Light Horse. In 1887 he became Quartermaster General and, in 1890, Adjutant General, an appointment in which he remained until 1899.

Redvers Buller

When Buller assumed command in South Africa, he did so with reluctance. Although his administrative powers shone brightly, he was no longer, at the age of 60, the man he had been. The lack of self-reliance and indecision shown during the Relief of Ladysmith were untypical of his behaviour in earlier years. He did better during the offensive into eastern Transvaal, but by then many lives had been lost. His performance in South Africa elicited much criticism and tarnished an otherwise brilliant career.

Throughout his later life Buller retained his interest in the 60th and was a Colonel-Commandant for thirteen years prior to his death in 1908. He is especially remembered for his support for the Regiment's Veterans Association and was present at its inaugural dinner in 1907. To quote from the *Annals*:

Redvers Henry Buller was a remarkable personality, of independent opinion and habit of thought. Endued with unusual physical strength and clever with his hands, he had in a high degree three qualities – an astonishing capacity for work, whether of mind or body; great love of argument; and a personal magnetism which gained for him the love, confidence and devotion of every N.C.O. and private soldier with whom he came in contact. Buller was the last man to curry favour with them; but that an electric current flowed incessantly between them and him is undeniable. Such a power is given to few English soldiers.[1]

[1] Lewis Butler, *The Annals of The King's Rifle Corps, Vol. III*, 299.

Guerrilla War and the Blockhouse Period

This Brief History does not permit a comprehensive description of the final eighteen months of the War, during which Lord Kitchener endeavoured ruthlessly to wear down the Boers by burning their property, cattle and crops; interning their women and children in (concentration) camps; and restricting the freedom of movement of those Boers who were still prepared to fight. The Boers, for their part, did their best to evade the British and to harass them, including through the conduct of significant offensive operations into the Cape Colony.

The British need to defend their lines of communication meant that the 60th battalions spent most of their time protecting key points, building and guarding blockhouses, usually at a distance of one every mile along the railways, and patrolling between them. Meanwhile, the cavalry and mounted infantry sought to find and destroy the Boer commando groups, who were exploiting their mobility on horseback, and the 150,000 square miles of territory in which they had to operate, to conduct 'hit and run' strikes against the British. Occasionally the battalions would venture forth on operations, which invariably entailed a great deal of marching and very little fighting.

From October 1900 to July 1901 the 1st Battalion was deployed in and around Middelburg and on sweep operations in eastern Transvaal. Thereafter it spent the rest of the War building and occupying blockhouses covering seventy miles of railway line between De Aar and Orange River Station in the Cape Colony. The 3rd Battalion remained in eastern Transvaal on similar duties throughout the period. The 4th Battalion left Ireland in December 1901, just in time for five months on the railway line near Harrismith.

Blockhouse at the railway bridge over the River Tugela at Colenso, December 1900

Mounted Infantry

The nature of the conflict, the vast expanse of countryside and the distances to be covered meant that mounted infantry were much in demand.

1st Battalion

At the beginning of the War, the 1st Battalion had a mounted infantry company, the usual establishment of which was 5 officers and 142 other ranks, organised in four sections. This company fought at Talana Hill and was among the defenders of Ladysmith. It took part in Buller's advance and subsequent sweep operations in eastern Transvaal, becoming a part of the 25th Mounted Infantry Battalion (see next page) in October 1901. During the war the Company lost twenty-five killed and twenty-three wounded.

2nd Battalion

The Mounted Infantry Company of the 2nd Battalion near Ladysmith, 1900

The 2nd Battalion formed a mounted infantry company on its arrival in Natal in October 1899. It was not with the Battalion at the defence of Ladysmith but took part under separate command in the operations to relieve the town. Afterwards it became part of Gough's Mounted Infantry in eastern Transvaal, Zululand and the Orange River Colony.[7] By the end of the War two officers and twenty-nine other ranks of the original company remained, together with 20% of the original horses – a notable record in horse management.

3rd Battalion

The 3rd Battalion, together with the 4th Battalion, and the 3rd and 4th Battalion, The Rifle Brigade, each contributed one section to the Rifles Company of the 1st Mounted Infantry (see next page). A second section from the 3rd Battalion was formed later, which took part with Gough's Mounted Infantry in the relief of Ladysmith. It was subsequently at Blood River Poort, where, on 17 September 1901, the Boers entrapped and attacked the mounted infantry in the flank, taking 6 officers and 235 men prisoner. Lieutenant Price-Davies was awarded a Victoria Cross for his gallantry during this action. This section was united with another, raised in 1901, and together they were increased to company strength on joining the 25th Mounted Infantry Battalion in October 1901.

4th Battalion

From the outset of the War, the 4th Battalion sent many officers and men to join the mounted infantry, including a section to the Rifles Company of 1st Mounted Infantry. In early 1901 it was responsible for creating two mounted infantry companies, which were initially employed in Transvaal before joining the 25th Mounted Infantry Battalion.

1st Mounted Infantry

The Rifles Company formed a part of the celebrated 1st Mounted Infantry, which was organized and trained at Aldershot before the War. On arrival in the Cape Colony in November, it was detached to a force defeated by the Boers at Stormberg on 10 December 1899. The Company then rejoined the 1st Mounted Infantry and took part in Lord Roberts's offensive into the Orange Free State and the Transvaal, seeing action in most of the major battles from Paardeberg on 18 February 1900 through to the final advance on Komatipoort at the end of September. From then onwards until the end of the War, the Rifles Company was in the saddle day and night, marching and fighting Boer commando groups in countless forays and skirmishes. When peace was declared, the Company joined the 25th Mounted Infantry Battalion.

25th (The King's Royal Rifle Corps) Mounted Infantry Battalion

On 18 October 1901, the Regiment formed its own unique battalion of mounted infantry, with one company each from the 1st and 3rd Battalion, and two companies from the 4th Battalion. It joined Benson's column in the eastern Transvaal, of which it was said that no Dutchman dared sleep within thirty miles of its bivouac. Botha, the Boer Commander-in-Chief, became so determined to destroy the column that he collected nearly 2,000 men and attacked it at Bakenlaagte on 30 October 1901. In a rapid charge his forces overwhelmed the rearguard, captured two guns, killed Benson, and surrounded the column, but were eventually kept at bay. The 25th Mounted Infantry upheld the honour of the Regiment in a fierce battle, losing eleven men

His Highness Prince Christian Victor
GCB GCVO

Major HH Prince Christian Victor

Brevet-Major HH Prince Christian Victor of Schleswig-Holstein, a grandson of Queen Victoria, son of HRH Princess Christian, and an officer in the Regiment, died from typhoid at Pretoria on 29 October 1900. He joined the 1st Battalion in 1888, went to India and took part with the Battalion in operations on the North-West Frontier. In March 1896 he was appointed a company commander in the 4th Battalion and shortly afterwards was awarded the rank of brevet-major for service during the Ashanti Expedition of 1895–6. He later served in the Nile Expedition of 1898 and went to South Africa on special service in October 1899. He was attached to the staff of the Commander-in-Chief at the time of his death.

Prince Christian Victor was a keen regimental officer and a good rifle shot. He was also a very fine cricketer. He was universally popular within the Regiment and his loss was keenly felt. There is little doubt that the shock of his death seriously affected the health of Queen Victoria, of whom he was a favourite grandson.

killed, and five officers and forty-five men wounded. Thereafter the Battalion took part in all the major sweeps in eastern Transvaal and Orange River Colony prior to the end of the War.

The End of the War

After prolonged negotiation, the Treaty of Vereeniging, signed on 31 May 1902, brought the War to an end. It had been long and costly for all concerned. The British Imperial forces suffered around 100,000 casualties, including 22,000 dead, 6,000 of whom were killed in action and 16,000 of whom died from disease or from their wounds. The Boers lost at least 7,000, plus a further 28,000 civilians, mostly women and children, who died in the camps. Over 335,000 horses perished. There is no accurate figure for the number of black Africans who died.

For the British, the economic cost of deploying 450,000 troops and associated logistic support to South Africa was enormous. For the Boers, the outcome meant the loss of their independence, although self-government was soon returned to Transvaal in December 1906 and to the Orange Free State in June 1907.[8]

During the service of all four 60th battalions in the South African War, many Riflemen distinguished themselves, including Bandmaster Tyler of the 1st Battalion. Tyler nearly lost his life from drowning when the *Warren Hastings* was wrecked in 1897. His conduct was subsequently singled out for mention during the battles at Talana Hill, Lombard's Kop and Wagon Hill, for which in April 1901 he received the Distinguished Conduct Medal – an award unusual for bandmasters.

During the war 29 officers and 516 non-commissioned officers and Riflemen of The King's Royal Rifle Corps were killed in action or died. The Regiment was granted three more Battle Honours, 'Defence of Ladysmith', 'Relief of Ladysmith' and 'South Africa, 1899–1902'.

Service between the South African and First World Wars

1st Battalion

The 1st Battalion left South Africa for the Mediterranean in September 1902, basing the headquarters and four companies at Alexandria, three companies in Crete and one in Cyprus. Crete at that time was being garrisoned by troops from Great Britain, France, Russia and Italy, whose duty it was to see fair play between the majority Christian and minority Moslem populations. Every now and again trouble flared. In one incident a Rifleman was seriously wounded.[9]

In March 1906 the Battalion was reunited in Egypt and in October departed to Khartoum for a year, before returning to Egypt for nine months and thence to England in early 1909. At the outbreak of the First World War, the Battalion was at Aldershot.

2nd Battalion

The 2nd Battalion arrived in India from South Africa, via Ceylon, in January 1901, spending the next nine years in various places in the Country. On 1 January 1903 it took part in the Delhi Coronation Durbar. In January 1910 it left India for England (Shorncliffe) in time to line the streets for the Funeral Procession of King Edward VII in May and the Coronation Procession for King George V in June 1911. It then spent a week in August 1911 at Hull during a strike by dockworkers, coalminers and railwaymen. At the outbreak of the First World War, the Battalion was at Blackdown in Surrey.

3rd Battalion

The 3rd Battalion remained in South Africa until early 1903 before moving to Ireland and, in March 1904, to Bermuda, where it spent eighteen months creating the best water polo team in the British Army. It returned to England (Aldershot) in 1905 for three years before moving in early 1908 to Malta and Crete. Following the end of allied occupation of Crete in 1909, the Battalion was concentrated at Malta before, in November 1910, embarking for India where it took part, together with the 4th Battalion, in the 1911 Delhi Coronation Durbar.

4th Battalion

The 4th Battalion remained in South Africa until June 1904 before returning to occupy barracks over the next five years at various stations in the south of England. In 1909 it preceded the 3rd Battalion to India. At the outbreak of the First World War, both battalions were still in India.

25th (KRRC) Mounted Infantry Battalion
Somaliland, 1903–4

Towards the end of 1900 Mahommed-bin-Abdullah Hassan, more usually known as the Mad Mullah, started to cause trouble in the British Protectorate of Somaliland. Expeditions in 1901 and 1902 failed to resolve matters, leading to a larger expedition in 1903. This included a company from the 25th (KRRC) Mounted Infantry Battalion, which was despatched from South Africa. This expedition, after long and trying operations in waterless country and after receiving reinforcements from India, succeeded in defeating the Mullah's army of around 7,000 at Jidbali on 10 January 1904. The British force of 4,000 suffered just over 60 casualties, including some in the Regiment's mounted infantry company. The Mullah, although still alive and free, became a fugitive without a following, and nothing more was heard of him for some years.

Other Events, 1902–13

From 1906 onwards the 60th battalions started to receive .303 short magazine-fed Lee Enfield rifles, which the Regiment used to good effect in achieving numerous successes in Army Rifle Association competitions. Sport also played a major role in the life of battalions, with the 4th Battalion winning the Army Football Cup in 1908.

Members of the Regiment were less happy with the changes ordered to mess kit which prompted the author of the *Annals* to write that: 'By War Office letter 61002, Inf. 812, A.G. 7, Dress, December 1, 1902, the old braided mess dress was abolished, being succeeded by the present abomination.'[10]

The same author also observed that: '[In India] in January 1904 the old pattern of helmet was replaced by the Wolseley, or Egyptian pattern, a much more serviceable form of headdress. It was impossible to see to shoot, lying down, with the old helmet, without turning it back to front.'[11]

On 1 May 1904, HRH The Prince of Wales, later King George V, succeeded HRH Prince George, Duke of Cambridge, as Colonel-in-Chief of the Regiment. One of the first acts of the new Colonel-in-Chief was to sanction that 'The Duke of York's March' should become the Regimental slow march during inspections. This prompted the author of the *Annals* to write:

> *At one time the Band of the 1st Battalion, if not others, used to play it* ['The Duke of York's March'] *before 'The Huntsman's Chorus' at the end of every programme. This practice of playing a succession of tunes before 'God Save the King' can be very wearisome. Under one C.O. the 1st Battalion Band played no less than three times – 'The Duke of York's March', 'The Huntsman's Chorus' (at that time our Regimental March), and then a melancholy, wailing thing called 'The Queen-Empress', which I really think the C.O. and the Bandmaster must have composed between them, as I can thankfully say that I have never heard it since.*[12]

Memorials and Institutions

The South African War gave rise to a number of initiatives during the first decade of the 20th Century, including, in 1901, publication of the first *King's Royal Rifle Corps Chronicle*. This was followed immediately after the War, with the establishment of a Memorial Fund to which all in the Regiment were invited to subscribe. The money from the Fund was used, first, to erect obelisks and crosses over the graves in South Africa of those in the Regiment who died during the War. Secondly, four cottage homes, costing £6,000, were built at Winchester for the use of old Riflemen, with a further four built and paid for by The Rifle Brigade. On 15 July 1904 HRH Princess Christian, mother of the late HH Prince Christian Victor, opened the homes, which were administered by the Riflemen's Aid Association, established jointly with The Rifle Brigade in 1883/4. The third and last portion of the Fund was used to place a stained glass window in

*KRRC Memorial Cottages opened in 1904 in memory of
the Riflemen who died in the South African War*

Winchester Cathedral, which was unveiled during a grand Service of Dedication on 6 April 1910. The brass tablets beneath the window, on which the names of all those who died in the War were inscribed, and which were later considered unsightly by the Dean and Chapter, were removed in 1948 and a Memorial Book substituted in their place.

On the seventh anniversary of the Relief of Ladysmith, 28 February 1907, the Veterans Association (now The King's Royal Rifle Corps Association) held its inaugural dinner at 56 Davies Street, London. General Sir Redvers Buller, the senior Colonel-Commandant, presided, with 44 officers and 365 veterans present. In the same year the Regimental Needlework and Clothing Guild (later the Ladies Guild) was instituted for the purpose of making and collecting garments, particularly of underclothing, for the benefit of the wives and children of married Riflemen.

On General Buller's death in 1908, Field Marshal Lord Grenfell[13] succeeded as senior Colonel-Commandant, extending, with the support of Lieutenant-General Sir Edward Hutton, the role of the *Celer et Audax* Club from being just an officers' dinner club instituted in 1859, to one embracing other interests and activities.[14]

These developments indicated not only the Regiment's concern for the welfare of all those associated with it, but its desire that service in the Regiment should be enjoyable and rewarding, on and off duty. The new institutions, and what they stood for, served to provide the glue that bonded the Regiment and the elements that enabled it to prosper and to cope in adversity. It was as well, too, that they were in place before the First World War, which was to have such a shocking effect on the lives of so many.

Chapter 6

1914–18: The First World War

Background

The genesis of the First World War may be attributed to many factors, of which the impact of Germany's imperialist ambitions and its prolonged efforts to become the dominant power in Europe are the most usual. The more immediate cause was the murder at Sarajevo on 28 June 1914 of the Archduke Franz Ferdinand, heir to the Austrian Empire. His death sparked a chain reaction that led to German forces crossing the Belgian frontier and initiating the outbreak of war on 4 August. The principal Allies were Great Britain, France and Russia, while Germany and the countries of the Austro-Hungarian Empire constituted the Central Powers.[1]

The scale and nature of the First World War, and the extent of the Regiment's participation, preclude detailed coverage in this Brief History of all the actions and activities in which each battalion and individuals in the Regiment were involved. Only the more significant engagements are included, without always listing the numbers of casualties, not because they were unimportant – on the contrary, they were often horrific – but to avoid the narrative becoming a litany of statistics.

The British Army in 1914

At the outbreak of the War, the British Army, including the Territorial Force and reservists, totalled 733,000. Unlike France and Germany with conscription, the British Government decided to rely on voluntary enlistment to increase the size of its Army and recalled Lord Kitchener from Egypt to become Secretary of State for War. He called for 500,000 volunteers to form the New Army.

The principal offensive component of the British Army, the British Expeditionary Force (BEF), consisted of six Regular divisions of infantry, each of three brigades with four battalions, and one cavalry division: in all, 120,000 men.[2] A second line of fourteen Territorial divisions and fourteen cavalry brigades existed, but was only attested for home service.

The BEF, commanded by General Sir John French, was well organized and highly trained, with infantry battalions having recently changed to an establishment of four large, instead of eight small, companies, plus a headquarter company. The most obvious weaknesses were a lack of automatic weapons (each battalion having only two Maxim guns) and a shortage of heavy artillery and artillery ammunition.

The Regiment, 1914–18

At the outbreak of the War, the Regiment consisted of four Regular battalions and two Special Reserve battalions.

The 1st and 2nd Battalion were quickly deployed to France in August as a part of the BEF. The 1st was in the 6th Infantry Brigade, 2nd Division, and the 2nd in the 2nd Infantry Brigade, 1st Division. Both Divisions were in I Corps, commanded by Lieutenant-General Sir Douglas Haig. During the War a Rhodesian contingent, No 8 (Rhodesia) Platoon, served with the 2nd Battalion.

The 3rd and 4th Battalion sailed from Bombay to England in October. Both were in the 80th Brigade, 27th (Lahore) Division, which included the 4th Battalion, The Rifle Brigade. After a month of training and acclimatization, the Division moved to France just before Christmas. During the War a contingent of over 250 Fijians served with the 4th Battalion.

The 5th and 6th Special Reserve Battalion were made up of reservists. In August 1914 the strength of each was immediately raised to 2,500, but they were soon unable to cope with the call for battle casualty replacements. However, they still managed during the War to despatch drafts totalling 1,575 officers and 35,626 other ranks to the battalions overseas.

In the New Army, the Regiment raised nineteen Service battalions between 1914–18.[3] Thirteen of these, including two pioneer battalions, served on the Western Front. The other six were reserve battalions preparing drafts for service overseas. The six reserve battalions ceased to be a part of the Regiment on transfer to the General Training Reserve on 1 September 1916.

Of the thirteen Service battalions that fought on the Western Front, eight were raised in 1914 and were officered largely by ex-Rifle officers, with many ex-Regular warrant and non-commissioned officers re-enlisting. Two or three Regular officers, plus a number of warrant and non-commissioned officers, were also posted to each Service battalion. These arrangements became more difficult to sustain as the War progressed. None of the Regiment's Service battalions went to France before 1915.

The 7th and 8th Battalion were grouped with the 7th and 8th Battalion, The Rifle Brigade, in the 41st Brigade, 14th (Light) Division. The 10th and 11th Battalion were grouped with the 10th and 11th Battalion, The Rifle Brigade, in the 59th Brigade, 20th (Light) Division. The 16th (Church Lads) Battalion was raised on the initiative of Field Marshal Lord Grenfell, senior Colonel-Commandant of the Regiment and Commandant of the Church Lads Brigade.

KRRC Battalions During the First World War

Regular Battalions

1 KRRC	Western Front 1914–18	2nd Division
2 KRRC	Western Front 1914–18	1st Division
3 KRRC	Western Front 1914–15	27th (Lahore) Division
	Salonika 1918–18	
4 KRRC	Western Front 1914–15	27th (Lahore) Division
	Salonika 1915–18	
	Western Front 1918	50th Division

Special Reserve

5 (Huntingdon Militia) KRRC	Reserve/Drafting 1914–18
6 (Royal 2nd Middlesex Militia) KRRC	Reserve/Drafting 1914–18

Service Battalions

7 KRRC	Western Front 1915–18	14th (Light) Division
8 KRRC	Western Front 1915–18	14th (Light) Division
9 KRRC	Western Front 1915–18	14th (Light) Division
10 KRRC	Western Front 1915–18	20th (Light) Division
11 KRRC	Western Front 1915–18	20th (Light) Division
12 KRRC	Western Front 1915–18	20th (Light) Division
13 KRRC	Western Front 1915–18	37th Division
14 KRRC	Reserve/Drafting 1914–16	
15 KRRC	Reserve/Drafting 1914–16	
16 KRRC (Church Lads)	Western Front 1915–18	33rd Division
17 KRRC (British Empire League)	Western Front 1916–18	39th Division
18 KRRC (Arts and Crafts)	Western Front 1915–17	41st Division
	Italy 1917–18	
	Western Front 1918	
19 KRRC	Reserve/Drafting 1915–16	
20 KRRC (British Empire League Pioneers)	Western Front 1916–17	3rd Division
	Italy 1917–18	
	Western Front 1918	
21 KRRC (Yeoman Rifles)	Western Front 1916–18	41st Division
22 KRRC	Reserve/Drafting 1915–16	
23 KRRC	Reserve/Drafting 1915–16	
24 KRRC	Reserve/Drafting 1916	
25 KRRC (Pioneer)	Western Front 1918	Corps Troops
51 KRRC	Young Soldiers 1917–18	
52 KRRC	Young Soldiers 1917–18	
53 KRRC	Young Soldiers 1917–18	

In addition to those already listed, three other battalions became a part of the Regiment's organization in 1917: the 51st, 52nd and 53rd Battalion. These were created as a result of the National Service Act, 1916, when a large number of boys became liable for service on attaining their eighteenth birthday. The 53rd Battalion carried out the boys' initial training as Young Soldiers. They then graduated to either the 51st or 52nd Battalion for five months' continuation training before joining the field army.

In 1914 The Rifle Depot played a crucial role on mobilization. It had the task of clothing, equipping, arming, feeding and posting over 5,000 reservists in five days in early August. Subsequently, before the Service drafting battalions were properly established,[4] the Depot handled the main influx of volunteers for the New Army. Some 30,000 destined for The King's Royal Rifle Corps and Rifle Brigade were handled by the end of September 1914. They arrived without notice and in varying numbers: over 6,000 in one 24-hour period. All, however, were comfortably fed and billeted, the necessary staff being created as the situation demanded, with the local authorities and citizens of Winchester doing everything they possibly could to help.

Territorial Battalions

On 1 April 1908 The London Regiment was formed as a part of Haldane's new Territorial Force. The King's Royal Rifle Corps had historic links with a number of battalions of The London Regiment but, between 1908 and 1916, they were not a part of The King's Royal Rifle Corps. In July 1916 the majority of the pre-1908 affiliations were restored, but the battalions continued to serve and fight as battalions of The London Regiment. The distinguished record of these battalions during the First World War is not covered in this Brief History but may be found in the many well-documented histories of The London Regiment (see also Appendix D).

The Western Front, 1914

Retreat from Mons, 24 August to 5 September 1914

The 1st and 2nd Battalion arrived in France on 13 August, marching into Belgium and occupying positions near Mons on 23 August. However, the unexpected withdrawal of the French on the BEF's right flank, and the possibility of being outflanked by the Germans on the left, necessitated a British retreat to the line of the River Marne. The 1st and 2nd Battalion saw little action, with most of the fighting carried out by II Corps, in particular, in a successful delaying action at Le Cateau on 26 August. During this period the 2nd Battalion marched 180 miles in 13 days.

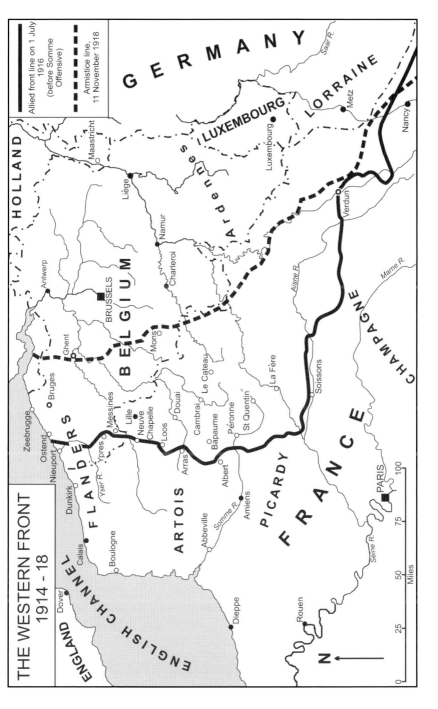

THE WESTERN FRONT 1914 – 18

Allied front line on 1 July 1916 (before Somme Offensive)

Armistice line, 11 November 1918

GERMANY

HOLLAND

LUXEMBOURG

LORRAINE

Ardennes

BELGIUM

BRUSSELS

FLANDERS

ARTOIS

PICARDY

CHAMPAGNE

FRANCE

ENGLAND

ENGLISH CHANNEL

Maastricht
Liège
Namur
Antwerp
Ghent
Bruges
Zeebrugge
Ostend
Nieuport
Dunkirk
Calais
Boulogne
Dover
Messines
Ypres
Neuve Chapelle
Lille
Loos
Arras
Albert
Abbeville
Amiens
Somme R.
Dieppe
Rouen
Seine R.
PARIS
Soissons
Aisne R.
Marne R.
La Fère
St Quentin
Péronne
Bapaume
Cambrai
Douai
Le Cateau
Mons
Charleroi
Verdun
Luxembourg
Metz
Nancy
Saar R.
Yser R.

N

Miles
0   25   50   75   100

Advance from the Marne to the Aisne, 6 September to 13 September 1914

The Allied retreat was stopped on the Marne. The right flank of the advancing German Army was counter-attacked by the French Sixth Army. The BEF advanced towards the River Aisne.

Hautevesnes, 10 September 1914

On 10 September the 1st Battalion, 1,150 strong, in the advance guard of the 2nd Division, came upon the rearguard, 1,200 strong, of the withdrawing Germans in the Regiment's first major engagement of the War. A battalion attack was ordered, supported by others, which resulted in the Germans surrendering. The Germans later explained their surrender by stating that the Battalion's skirmishing and marksmanship were so good that they could neither move nor return fire. Just over seventy members of the Battalion were killed or wounded.

Battle of the Aisne, 13 September to 27 September 1914

The Germans halted their retreat on high ground east of the River Aisne. On 13 September the British crossed the river and, on 14 September, attacked in strength. Fierce fighting followed as the British sought to expand their bridgeheads across the river and to seize the high ground occupied by the Germans. On the 14th and subsequent days casualties mounted alarmingly as each side engaged in a tactical battle of attack, counter-attack and counter-counter-attack, with the superior musketry of the British preventing the Germans from pushing them back across the Aisne. The outcome was a stalemate with both sides forced into trench warfare, for which the Germans, in terms of materiel, were very much better equipped. The 1st and 2nd Battalion between them lost over 450 men killed and wounded.

First Battle of Ypres, 19 October to 22 November 1914

At the beginning of October the BEF moved to the left flank of the Allied armies to cover a 35-mile frontage immediately to the north, east and south of the Belgian town of Ypres in Flanders. With the arrival of I Corps on 19 October the move was complete. Meanwhile, the BEF's strength was growing as new formations arrived from England and overseas.

By now the Western front was close to extending to the sea. With the Germans and the Allies unable to outflank each other, it became a matter of whether one side was strong enough to break through and overwhelm the other.

The First Battle of Ypres was hard fought over a number of weeks. The 1st and 2nd Battalion were constantly involved in the many attacks and counter-attacks, which held the salient against a much larger

German force with greater and heavier artillery. On 23 October the 2nd Battalion was involved in a successful counter-attack to recover lost trenches near Langemarck, but, on 31 October, was reduced to 150 all ranks after losing over 400 men in the recovery of the captured village of Gheluvelt. Its numbers were made up and, on 11 November, the Battalion played an important part in the repulse of a German attack at Nonne Boschen.[5] On the following day, at Klein Zillebeke, Lieutenant Dimmer performed the act of gallantry for which he was later awarded a Victoria Cross.[6]

Meanwhile, on 2 November, disaster struck the 1st Battalion when B, C and D Company were surrounded and forced to surrender near Hooge. When the remnants of the Battalion were withdrawn from the battle on 18 November, its losses in the previous six weeks exceeded 1,000, of which half were missing, presumed prisoners of war. HH Lieutenant Prince Maurice of Battenburg was among those killed.[7]

By 22 November the First Battle of Ypres was over with neither side having achieved the breakthrough that it sought. Winter set in and, with it, snow. The Germans switched their attention to the Russians, transferring four cavalry and eight infantry divisions to the Eastern Front. These early battles, however, had taken a very heavy toll of the Regiment's Regular officers, warrant officers and NCOs, with the BEF losing nearly 90,000 officers and men between August and December 1914.

The Western Front, 1915

The year began with all four of the Regiment's Regular battalions in France. The first of the Service battalions did not arrive until May.

Winter with the BEF in Flanders was not pleasant. The trenches filled with water, mud was everywhere, and the men were never dry and never warm. The trenches occupied by the 3rd and 4th Battalion in January were particularly susceptible to flooding, with many men suffering from trench foot. Attacks continued to be mounted by both sides, but not with the vigour of earlier months, as each side awaited better weather. On 1 March 1915, the 4th Battalion lost over 100 men out of 300 at St Eloi.

Battle of Neuve Chapelle, 10–12 March 1915

The Allies, realising that the Germans were competing on two fronts, and fearing the loss of troops to the Dardanelles, decided that they must launch an offensive while there was hope of success and they had the means to achieve it.

The British attack was made at Neuve Chapelle, providing a further 'foretaste of what was to happen again and again during the next three years: a rapid success where the bombardment had been effective; a

'Coal-Box'

'Coal-Box' was a German pony, which strayed into the lines of the 2nd Battalion in Belgium in 1914. He served with the Battalion throughout the First World War, being looked after by Lance-Corporal Geary of the Band. He accompanied the Band and Bugles on parade and always marched at the head of the Battalion, except on long marches when the Quartermaster provided a special box on the back of a lorry. When he arrived at Portsmouth after the War, he was practically blind in one eye. The other deteriorated while the Battalion was in Ireland. Eventually, as a kindness, he was shot in 1921. It was said that 'Coal-Box' would lie down and die for his Country or go anywhere – with a little persuasion!

'Coal-Box'

costly failure where it had not; a little ground gained; a failure to get any farther as soon as the enemy's reserves came up; and heavy losses, about equal on both sides.'[8]

None of the Regiment's battalions took part in the main attack at Neuve Chapelle, although the 1st Battalion was involved in a diversion near Givenchy, where small groups, with great gallantry, reached the

German positions but were subsequently obliged to abandon them, suffering nearly 250 casualties. The main attack achieved some success, but not on the scale desired.

The Second Battle of Ypres, 22 April to 25 May 1915

On 22 April the Germans attacked the northern flank of the Ypres salient, using poison gas for the first time, invoking panic amongst the French and Algerian troops most affected, and exposing the left flank of a Canadian division to direct attack. This was the start of a month as testing as the First Battle of Ypres had been six months previously, with the Germans using poison gas on a number of further occasions.

St Eloi, 8-10 May 1915

On 8 May the Germans launched a major attack against the 80th Brigade, 27th (Lahore) Division, which included the 3rd and 4th Battalion and the 4th Battalion, The Rifle Brigade. The line held but the losses were enormous. Further attacks were repulsed on 9 and 10 May, during which the front trenches of the 4th Battalion were destroyed and the support trenches became the line of defence. Over the three days the Battalion suffered over 500 casualties, reducing its strength to 3 officers and 100 men. Between 22 April and 14 May the 3rd Battalion suffered a similar number of casualties.

Bellewaarde Ridge, 24/25 May 1915

With barely time to reorganize, the 3rd and 4th Battalion were rushed up into the line for a night attack at Bellewaarde Ridge. Initially successful, the attack was aborted at dawn with the battalions suffering another 200 casualties. The German Army then issued orders to cease further offensive operations and the Second Battle of Ypres ended.

Allied Offensive in Artois, 9–27 May 1915

While the Second Battle of Ypres was in progress, the Allies launched an offensive to the south, in Artois, towards the plain of Douai and Aubers Ridge. On 9 May the 2nd Battalion supported the initial attack on Aubers Ridge, which lasted all day, was unsuccessful, and cost the Battalion 250 casualties.

Festubert, 15 May 1915

In the light of French successes elsewhere, General French was prevailed upon to continue the offensive, with the 2nd Division, on 15 May, launching the first night attack made by British troops on the Western Front. The 1st Battalion was in the first wave of assaulting troops, which by daybreak had very successfully reached the third line of German trenches, which were held until the Battalion was relieved on 17 May. The attack, however, once again proved costly with the Battalion losing its commanding officer, Lieutenant-Colonel G.C. Shakerley, killed in action, and a further 300 men killed or wounded.

The offensive ended on 27 May, the BEF having achieved small territorial gains at a cost of 16,000 casualties. On 23 May, Rifleman (Private) Mariner, a member of the 2nd Battalion in the front line near Cambrin, performed the act of gallantry for which he was later awarded a Victoria Cross.

Hooge, 30/31 July 1915

The 7th, 8th and 9th Service Battalion arrived in France with the 14th (Light) Division in the middle of May, assuming responsibility for a part of the trench line in the Ypres salient, which in places was no more than fifteen feet from the German line. On 30 July the 7th Battalion and the 8th Battalion, The Rifle Brigade, were in the line when the Germans attacked using flamethrowers for the first time against British troops in what was literally a baptism of fire for these New Army battalions – 'a trial in which they showed that in courage and devotion they were the equals of any of their predecessors in the Regiment'.[9] All but a few of the front-line trenches occupied by the 7th Battalion were overrun. A counter-attack was ordered.

> *Nothing in First or Second Ypres was more resolute than the counter-attack made by* [these] *battalions. ... The ground over which they attacked had not a vestige of cover, the three-quarters of an hour's preliminary bombardment had been devoid of effect, no one, from the Divisional Commander downwards, could have had any hope of success ... but the new battalions went forward as if they were determined to show that when called upon they could give their lives as freely as those whose blood had already soaked the ground for which they were fighting.*[10]

Predictably, the attack failed. The 7th Battalion lost just over 300 men, the 8th close to 200, and the 9th nearly 350, including its commanding officer, Lieutenant-Colonel C.S. Chaplin, killed in action. The 8th Battalion, The Rifle Brigade, suffered almost 500 casualties.

In July the 10th, 11th, 12th and 13th Service Battalion arrived in France, to be followed in September by the 16th Battalion. None of these battalions experienced battle on the scale of the 7th, 8th and 9th Battalion at Hooge until the following year.

Battle of Loos, 25 September to 15 October 1915

Following the offensive in May, the French pressed for a further offensive against the Germans in Artois and Champagne. General French was opposed to the plan because he had insufficient forces and the ground over which the BEF was expected to attack was unsuitable. Lord Kitchener, for wider political and strategic reasons, directed him to accept it 'even though by so doing we may suffer very heavy losses'.

On 25 September the British attacked with six divisions on a 6-mile frontage in Artois, with the French Tenth Army of seventeen divisions on a 12-mile frontage to their right. The 1st and 2nd Battalion were involved in the main attack. To compensate for a lack of artillery, the British used gas for the first time. With the wind varying in direction, the gas proved to be a double-edged weapon with 200 men in the 2nd Battalion, who were about to leave the jump-off trenches, being incapacitated. Indeed, whenever the gas went the right way, the enemy's resistance crumbled. When it went the wrong way, the attack failed.

Meanwhile, in a subsidiary attack on Bellewaarde, the 9th Battalion went to the support of the 9th Battalion, The Rifle Brigade, who had reached the second line of German trenches. Subsequently, between 26 and 29 September, the 1st Battalion was engaged in occupying and holding an extremely vulnerable position known as the Quarries, halfway between the German first and second lines.

Although the Battle of Loos dragged on until the middle of October, the Regiment ceased to play a major part much beyond the end of September. Once again its casualties were considerable – about 400 in the 1st, over 500 in the 2nd, and over 250 in the 9th Battalion. In total the BEF lost 50,000 men for no strategic gain. Although the 7th and 8th Battalion were held in readiness, they were not used. On 25 September, the opening day of the battle, Rifleman (Private) Peachment, aged 18, a member of the 2nd Battalion, performed the act of gallantry for which he was later awarded a posthumous Victoria Cross.[11]

The campaign of 1915 had gone badly for the Allies. Germany's successes on the Eastern Front meant that she would soon be able to turn her attention fully to the Western Front, while the efforts of the Allies to take advantage of her temporary weakness had failed, and failed at far greater losses than they had inflicted. France had almost reached her limit in the provision of manpower. The attempt to relieve the pressure on Russia by opening the Dardanelles had foundered. The only glimmer of light was that a large reserve of British manpower was still untapped and munitions in large quantities should soon be available.

In November the 27th (Lahore) Division, with the 3rd and 4th Battalion, left France for Salonika. On 19 December General Sir Douglas Haig succeeded General Sir John French as Commander-in-Chief, British Forces in France.

The Western Front, 1916

The Allied grand-strategic plan for 1916 was to mount major offensives simultaneously on the Eastern and Western Fronts, with the British taking something of an equal share to the French on the Western Front. At the operational level, the objective was to wear down the enemy's resistance through attrition of his forces. For a variety of reasons the Allied offensive was set to begin in July. The Germans, however, pre-empted the Allies by launching a grand offensive against the French at Verdun in February, which lasted nine months, cost each side over 350,000 casualties, and resulted in the Germans finishing up where they started.

During the first six months of 1916 there were no grand offensives on the British Front, although both sides engaged in constant activity to gain some tactical advantage and to discourage the other from thinning out their line so as to send reinforcements to Verdun. There was little peace for those in the trenches as the battalions spent one-third of their time in the front line, one-third behind the line in brigade or divisional reserve (where they were never quite free from shell fire), and one-third in rest billets.

Meanwhile, the 17th and 20th (Pioneer) Battalion arrived in France in March and the 18th and 21st Battalion in May. The 21st Battalion (The Yeoman Rifles) was commanded by Lieutenant-Colonel the Earl of Feversham, who was personally responsible for raising the battalion from among the farming class in the north of England. By early 1916, however, the number of volunteers to join the British Army had declined to such an extent that conscription for single men was introduced in January and for married men in May. By June 1916 the BEF was over one million strong.

Battle of the Somme, 1 July to 25 November 1916

The desperate battles being fought by the French to contain the Germans at Verdun meant that British and Dominion forces assumed the greater role in mounting the planned Allied offensive in July. The objects were to prevent the transfer of German troops from the Western to the Russian front; to wear down the strength of the opposing forces; and to lighten the pressure on the French at Verdun.

Responsibility for mounting the offensive fell to General Sir Henry Rawlinson, commanding Fourth Army.[12] The area chosen lay north of the River Somme, with a centre line running north-east from Albert to Bapaume. On 1 July the British attacked on a 15-mile frontage with 19 divisions (247 infantry battalions) in the front line or in immediate reserve. The French attacked on the right flank with five divisions on an 8-mile frontage.

Two days before the battle the 2nd Battalion took part in a diversionary attack, which resulted in over 200 casualties. None, however, of the Regiment's battalions were directly involved in the main battle until 14 July. Thereafter all fourteen battalions took part at some point or other in the grim and gruelling conflict, which continued for four and a half months until eventually, as the weather worsened, the battle petered out in the second half of November.

The number of actions involving the Regiment are too numerous to list, with bitter fighting taking place to secure features such as High Wood, Bazentin-le-Petit, Pozières, Delville Wood, Guillemont, Flers-Courcelette, the Schwaben Redoubt and Ancre Heights.[13] Throughout, the officers and Riflemen repeatedly performed acts of great courage, with eleven Military Medals awarded to members of the 16th Battalion for their bravery during a single attack on 15 July – their first major action of the war. On 27 July Sergeant Gill of the 1st Battalion performed the act of gallantry at Delville Wood for which he was later awarded a posthumous Victoria Cross. On 27 September Number 8 (Rhodesia) Platoon excelled in a bombing attack that resulted in the capture of a 130-yard stretch of German trench line.

By the middle of October the weather had completely broken and the battle became a struggle against mud. Battalions were often in the line for long periods of great strain. Trenches were frequently obliterated and whole sections of men buried. The state of the German trenches was as bad or worse. When staff work was good, limited success was attained. However, effort was habitually dissipated in small and costly attacks, which were easily countered by enemy machine-gun fire. Not enough time was given over to preparation and reconnaissance. Fire plans were too rigid and the use of ground was unimaginative. Accurate maps were not always available.

By the end of the Battle of the Somme the BEF had achieved territorial gains measuring about twenty miles wide and six miles deep, and suffered nearly 420,000 casualties. The Regiment lost some 200 officers and 4,000 men, killed, wounded or missing, with the Service battalions, which distinguished themselves greatly on the field of battle, sustaining the majority. Four commanding officers were killed, including the Earl of Feversham. Command of battalions sometimes devolved upon captains, while junior officers and NCOs frequently found themselves in command of companies. German losses, however, were also considerable[14] and, in the wider context, the actions of the BEF on the Somme probably saved the French from defeat at Verdun and Russia from invasion.

The Western Front, 1917

The year 1917 opened full of promise. The effects of the fighting on the Somme, at Verdun and against the Russians were forcing the Germans on to the defensive, while changes in the French High Command led to optimism that a decisive breakthrough of the German positions in Champagne was possible. The British, who had spent much of the winter seeking to learn the lessons of the Somme and to improve the handling of their infantry and artillery on the battlefield, were initially assigned a supporting role. This required the BEF to take over more of the front line and to conduct subsidiary

Resting in the trenches, August 1916

KRRC transport delivering officers' kit during the Battle of Arras, 1917

operations to prevent the Germans from redeploying to oppose the French. The strength of the BEF now exceeded 1.5 million and was continuing to grow, while heavy artillery, tanks and ammunition were more readily available.

128

Operations in the Ancre Valley, January to April 1917

Early in January the British began limited operations in the valley of the River Ancre, north of the Albert to Bapaume road. On 17 February the 1st Battalion was involved in a costly assault in bad ground conditions at Miraumont, ultimately achieving the objective but suffering nearly 200 casualties. On 4 April the 10th and 11th Battalion succeeded in 'a brilliant attack' at Metz-en-Couture, with the battalions between them losing 300 men. Resistance, however, was sometimes lacking as the Germans retired to heavily fortified positions on the newly constructed Hindenburg Line, reducing their frontage between Arras and Soissons by twenty-five miles and freeing fourteen divisions for operations elsewhere.

Battle of Arras, 9 April to 17 May 1917

The Battle of Arras, fought on ground immediately to the east of the town, was aimed at achieving limited territorial gains, while tying down as many German forces as possible prior to the French offensive in Champagne (16 April). Thanks to careful planning and preparation, considerable ground was taken in the early stages. The 1st, 7th, 8th, 9th and 13th Battalion were involved in the opening days of the battle between 9 and 13 April, with the 16th Battalion joining in on 23 April. Successful actions took place near Tilloy-lez-Mofflaines, Wancourt, Monchy-le-Preu, Oppy and Gavrelle, but often with losses of 200 or more in a battalion. As the battle proceeded, the successes became fewer with reverses at Croisilles and Chérisy, and with the battalions of the Regiment ceasing to play a major role after 4 May. Haig, meanwhile, had to prolong the battle longer than he wished in order to keep the pressure off the French whose offensive was failing.

Plans for an Offensive in Flanders

By the middle of May it was clear that the French had temporarily exhausted themselves and that the morale of their army was close to collapse. With the burden of maintaining the momentum of operations on the Western Front now falling to the BEF, Haig decided that this was the moment to launch a long-planned offensive in Flanders to capture the high ground near Passchendaele, seven miles north-east of Ypres. From there his aim was to achieve a breakthrough to the Belgian coast, ejecting the Germans from the ports from which they were mounting submarine operations against Allied shipping. But first it was necessary to seize and hold the Messines Ridge on the southern flank of the planned offensive.

Messines Ridge, 7 to 14 June 1917

On 7 June the attack on the Messines Ridge was launched to the sound of 19 mines containing 470 tons of explosives being detonated beneath the German positions. The 18th and 21st Battalion both took part in the

The scene at Passchendaele, November 1917.

battle, which, by 14 June, had secured all the ground that was wanted. However, another six weeks were to pass before the BEF was ready to initiate its offensive east of Ypres.

Nieuport Bains, 10 July 1917

Meanwhile, as a preliminary to an advance along the Belgian coast, the British relieved the French on the frontline on the River Yser, occupying, in particular, a small bridgehead in the sand dunes on the north side of the Yser estuary opposite Nieuport Bains.

On 10 July the 2nd Battalion was one of two battalions holding the bridgehead[15] when the Germans launched a major and prolonged bombardment of the area, including machine-gunning the Battalion's positions from the air. During the course of the bombardment, trenches and breastworks collapsed, men were choked and buried in the sand, and, as the day wore on, devoid of heavy artillery support, the position became untenable. Despite a heroic stand resulting in a number of gallantry awards, the Battalion was overwhelmed. In the final stages, the commanding officer, Lieutenant-Colonel R.N. Abadie, defiant to the last, killed five Germans with his revolver before himself being shot dead. Out of a battalion 520 strong, only 40 escaped. Just over 400 were taken prisoner, including 100 wounded, among them the 19-year old Battalion Intelligence Officer, Lieutenant, later General, W.H.E. 'Strafer' Gott. Miraculously, by the end of July the Battalion was reformed and, in September, gave a demonstration of 'the battalion in attack' before a distinguished gathering of American officers, the United States having declared war on Germany on 6 April 1917.

Photo no CO2265 courtesy Imperial War Museum, London.

The Third Battle of Ypres (Passchendaele), 31 July to 10 November 1917

The Flanders offensive (Third Battle of Ypres) began on 31 July, after twelve days of heavy preliminary bombardment, which damaged the agricultural drainage and, as rain set in, turned the ground into bog. The well-constructed concrete pillbox and wire defences of the German positions presented a formidable obstacle to the assaulting troops. Everywhere the enemy resisted strongly, mounting frequent counter-attacks. Inevitably attacks faltered and, as the battle turned into one of attrition and endurance, so the number of casualties grew.

Eight of the Regiment's Service battalions were major participants in the battle – the 8th, 10th, 11th, 12th, 16th, 17th, 18th and 21st Battalion. The 17th and 18th Battalion were in the assaulting waves of infantry attacking Picklem Ridge on the first day, with the 21st Battalion subsequently holding the line against German counter-attacks. On 16 August the 12th Battalion succeeded in capturing all objectives in a major attack near Langemarck, during which Sergeant Cooper performed the acts of gallantry for which he was later awarded a Victoria Cross. On 23 August the 8th Battalion participated in fierce fighting near Inverness Copse. On 20 September a major attack was launched on a 4-mile sector of the front with the 10th, 11th and 12th Battalion involved in further battles near Langemarck, and the 17th, 18th and 21st Battalion engaged in assaults in the vicinity of the Menin Road. During the following days the 16th Battalion, in reserve, deployed companies forward to reinforce battalions in need.

Although the Third Battle of Ypres dragged on in seas of mud until 10 November, the battalions of the Regiment ceased to play a major part after the end of September. By the end, some but not all of Passchendaele Ridge was captured. Casualties were severe, with both the BEF and the Germans losing around 250,000 men. The commanding officers of the 10th Battalion, Lieutenant-Colonel T.M. Rixon, and 13th Battalion, Lieutenant-Colonel R.C. Chester-Master, were both killed in action during this period.

Battle of Cambrai, 20 November to 6 December 1917

As the offensive east of Ypres ground to a halt, it was decided to mount a major attack on the German positions on the Hindenburg Line, south-west of Cambrai, where the ground was much more suitable for tanks, even in wet weather, and to capture Cambrai.

Dispensing with the usual lengthy preliminary bombardment, over 470 tanks supported by infantry were massed and the attack launched on a 6-mile front on 20 November. The 10th, 11th and 12th Battalion were all involved in the initial phase during which the BEF penetrated the German line up to a distance of four miles, with Rifleman (Private) Shepherd of the 12th Battalion displaying great leadership and gallantry on the first day, for which he was later awarded a Victoria Cross. Subsequently the 1st Battalion entered the line near Bourlon Wood, capturing 300 yards of German trenches on 29 November.

On 30 November the Germans mounted a fierce counter-attack using gas and aircraft. The onslaught was so great that they very rapidly broke through the British lines, attacking the 10th and 11th Battalion, who were in the front line, in their flanks and rear. The Riflemen fought well but there was little opportunity for escape. The 12th Battalion in reserve was ordered into positions behind the 10th and 11th, which it just managed to hold with every man lining the trenches. The 1st Battalion distinguished itself in similar fashion but at less close quarters, inflicting considerable losses on the Germans with accurate shooting from a flank near Bourlon Wood.

By now both sides were exhausted and, although fighting continued over the next few days, the BEF withdrew to less exposed positions, giving up most of the ground that had been gained. Each side suffered losses of around 40,000, with the 10th, 11th and 12th Battalion between them losing over 1,000 men, the majority being captured when the 10th and 11th Battalion were overwhelmed on 30 November.

The year 1917, which had opened with such promise, ended in disappointment. The British and French offensives had failed. The Russians were virtually out of the War. The Italians had been defeated at Caporetto (24 October), leading to the redeployment of a number of Allied divisions from France to Italy, including the 41st Division with the 18th and 21st

Battalion. Salvation, however, was potentially at hand; by December 1917 the Americans had 130,000 troops in France with more on the way.

The Western Front, 1918

For the Germans the situation at the beginning of 1918 was obvious; the Allies had to be defeated before the Americans brought a sufficiently large and well-trained army to bear upon them in France to ensure an Allied victory. The British and French, on the other hand, had every reason to favour a defensive posture while waiting for the Americans to conclude the assembly and preparation of their forces. The outcome was predictable and anticipated – a German offensive.

Meanwhile, the BEF reorganized. Each infantry division was reduced in strength from twelve to nine infantry battalions, with the 10th Battalion disbanded in February 1918 and the 21st Battalion in March, on its return from Italy with the 18th Battalion. The manpower from both battalions was redistributed to other battalions. Subsequently, in April 1918, the Regiment raised another Service battalion, the 25th (Pioneer) Battalion, which carried out much valuable work in France during the remainder of the War. The BEF also reorganized its defences in similar fashion to the Germans with a forward zone, a battle zone and a reserve or rear zone. However, preparation of the new positions was not complete by the time the Germans launched their grand offensive.

First German Offensive, 21 March to 5 April 1918

The Germans chose to mount their offensive against the BEF between Arras and La Fère, with the main effort on a 20-mile front west of St Quentin. They did so with a numerical superiority of three to one, having recovered more than thirty divisions from the Eastern Front. They also reorganized their forces with specially equipped and trained storm troopers in the assault formations, leaving their less well trained and equipped troops to defend the trench line.

Early on 21 March the enemy unleashed a terrific bombardment, with a large percentage of gas shells, prior to launching their offensive in thick fog a few hours later. The impact was immediate not least upon the 7th, 8th and 9th Battalion in the front line of the 14th (Light) Division a few miles south-west of St Quentin. The 8th and 9th Battalion in the forward zone and the 7th Battalion in the battle zone were soon overwhelmed by sheer weight of numbers. Many small parties fought gallantly to a finish, while those who were able, conducted a fighting withdrawal. By 26 March the total strength of the three battalions, which numbered close to 2,000 on 20 March, was less than 250. After receiving some reinforcements, the exhausted remnants were relieved in the line during the night of 4/5 April. The 14th (Light) Division went in to reserve and was later disbanded; so, too, were its battalions, with the 7th Battalion providing the nucleus of a new battalion of The London Regiment, and the 8th and 9th Battalion being absorbed into the 12th and 16th Battalion respectively. To quote from the *Annals*: 'It was a sad ending to a grand Division, which had gloriously upheld the best traditions of the old Rifle and Light Infantry Regiments.'[16]

The 11th and 12th Battalion were in Corps reserve and were quickly deployed into the front line east of the River Somme. Having covered the withdrawal of the forward divisions, they continued to hold their positions until being ordered to retire on 24 March. Withdrawal continued until the end of the month, but cohesion was never lost, with the battalions taking part in many hard-fought and often successful actions. During this period the two battalions between them lost over 900 men, including the commanding officer of the 11th Battalion, Lieutenant-Colonel G.K. Priaulx, killed in action. Although the two battalions were subsequently in and out of the trenches, they did not take part in any further major engagements during the remainder of the War.

On 21 March, the 17th Battalion, in reserve, was deployed into the front line north-west of St Quentin. Retirement soon became necessary and was continued in good order until 30 March. During this period of constant battling the Battalion lost nearly 400 men.

Meanwhile, the 1st Battalion was south of Arras, having lost 320 men in the trenches earlier in the month from mustard gas attacks. Ordered into the line on 22 March, it was obliged to retire in extremely difficult and confused circumstances, and by 26 March was six miles north of Albert. After sustaining nearly 500 casualties, the Battalion was taken out of the line on 1 April to reconstitute.

The 18th Battalion, recently returned from Italy, was the eighth of the Regiment's battalions to be swept up in countering the German grand offensive. Initially in Corps reserve, it deployed forward into positions east of Bapaume, where, on 24 March, it became so involved in the fighting that it could not be extracted. Out of a battalion of 900, only 80 escaped either being killed or captured.

On 4/5 April the German advance was halted ten miles east of Amiens, a key centre on the BEF's lines of communications. The Germans had penetrated forty miles and captured Péronne, Bapaume and Albert, but during the 16-day offensive they had lost 250,000 men. The BEF lost nearly 180,000, including close to 80,000 taken prisoner, while the French, who had been rushed in to stem the tide of the German advance, lost around 80,000. On 5 April Ludendorff, the German Commander-in-Chief, ceased the offensive in Picardy and turned his attention to Flanders.

Second German Offensive, 9 to 29 April 1918

On 9 April the Germans attacked between Ypres and Neuve Chapelle on a smaller scale than on 21 March but with a numerical superiority that was just as great. The Germans quickly penetrated the line, obliging the British to abandon the Messines and Passchendaele ridges. By 11 April the situation was so desperate that Field Marshal Haig instructed the BEF 'to fight it out. Every position must be held to the last man: there must be no retirement.'

The 16th Battalion was the only battalion of the Regiment to be significantly involved in countering the German offensive in Flanders, moving into the line five miles south of Ypres on the evening of 11 April. On the following day their flank was turned and the Battalion was attacked in the rear, with isolated elements continuing to fight on gallantly for a further 72 hours. Nearly 570 members of the Battalion were either killed or captured, with the remainder temporarily formed into a composite battalion with the 9th Battalion, Highland Light Infantry.

Eventually the German advance was halted and after a further unsuccessful attempt to break through in Picardy, Ludendorff called off the offensive against the BEF on 29 April. Both sides were exhausted. Time, however, was running out for the Germans, if they were to achieve a favourable outcome to the War before the Americans engaged in strength. On 27 May Ludendorff ordered the first of three more offensives initiated over the next two months, all of which were primarily directed against the French. At one point the Germans came within 60 miles of Paris. The tide, however, was turning. American divisions took to the battlefield. As the Allies hit back and the situation improved, so that of the Germans worsened.

Allied Offensive, 18 July to 11 November 1918

On 18 July the French and Americans launched a major counter-offensive against the Germans between the River Marne and River Aisne. On 8 August the BEF started to recover some of the ground lost in March and April. These actions very soon developed into an advance along the whole Allied line against a German army that was becoming increasingly dispirited.

The 1st, 2nd, 4th, 13th and 16th Battalion were the most prominently involved in the Allied offensive, taking part in a series of successful attacks, beginning with the 13th Battalion at Bucquoy, north-west of Bapaume, on 21 August and continuing through until the end of the War. Casualties during this period, while still significant, were much lighter than in previous offensives as German resistance in some areas collapsed. Significant numbers of prisoners were taken. Between 22 and 24 August, the 1st Battalion, attacking in the same area as the 13th Battalion, captured one and a half times its own strength of prisoners, losing less than 70 men in the process.

In September the momentum of the Allied advance increased as the Germans withdrew to the Hindenburg Line. On 11 September, the 13th

Battalion captured Trescault, west of Cambrai. On 18 September the 2nd Battalion captured Berthaucourt, north of St Quentin. On 23 September the 16th Battalion met stiff resistance in an extremely hard-fought and successful action at Villers Guislain, south of Cambrai, which resulted in the award of one Distinguished Service Order, four Military Crosses and fourteen Military Medals to members of the Battalion. By the end of September the Hindenburg Line had been breached and the Germans were in retreat.

In early October the 4th Battalion, which returned from Macedonia in July, entered into the attack, successfully seizing Le Catelet and Marliches, south of Cambrai. On 8 October, the 1st Battalion, advancing in the same area, took part in its last significant engagement of the War at Niergnies. On 17 October the 2nd Battalion encountered the same German battalion south-east of Cambrai that had overwhelmed it at Nieuport Bains in July 1917. This time the boot was on the other foot as the Battalion captured 14 field guns, 12 trench mortars, 100 prisoners and numerous machine guns.

By now the pattern of advance was well established with only occasional reverses. By early November it was apparent that the German withdrawal was rapidly becoming a rout, with the 2nd, 4th, 13th and 16th Battalion in the vanguard of the BEF's advance. The last of the German prepared defensive positions west of the River Rhine was breached. On 4 November over 19,000 prisoners and 450 German field guns were taken. The Germans, having used the last of their reserves, sued for peace. On 11 November the Armistice was signed.[17]

Operations on Other Fronts, 1915–19

Salonika and Macedonia, 1915–18

In September 1915, Germany, Austria and Bulgaria determined to crush Serbia, an ally of Britain and France. Reinforcements were immediately sent to Serbia's aid, including the 27th (Lahore) Division from the Western Front, with the 3rd and 4th Battalion. By the time reinforcement was complete, it was too late to prevent the Austrians and Bulgarians succeeding in their invasion of Serbia; instead, the Division occupied defensive positions in Salonika, a part of neutral Greece, which had reluctantly consented to an Allied presence on its soil.

The winter of 1915-16 and the spring and early summer of 1916 passed off quietly, albeit with the troops decimated by a particularly virulent form of malaria. In September the French mounted a successful offensive against the Bulgarians, with the British on the right flank holding positions on the line of the River Struma. For nearly two years there was no serious fighting on this part of the front, although the 3rd and 4th Battalion were frequently engaged in minor operations and patrol encounters in the two and a half miles of No Man's Land between the British and Bulgarian positions.

In July 1917 Greece entered the war on the side of the Allies. In the spring of 1918 the great German offensive on the Western Front led to the recall of the 4th Battalion to France. In September 1918 the Allies in Salonika launched a major offensive against the Bulgarians in Macedonia. After an initial stiff resistance the Bulgarian army was routed and, on 29 September, Bulgaria sued for peace. The 3rd Battalion was in reserve during the offensive and saw no action.

Italy, 1917–18

Following the defeat of the Italians by the Germans and Austrians at Caporetto on 24 October 1917, the Allies despatched reinforcements to Italy, including the 41st Division from the Western Front, with the 18th and 21st Battalion. Arriving in November, and after holding the line on the River Piave for three and a half months without serious fighting, both battalions returned to France in March 1918.

North Russia, 1918–19

In early 1918 the Allies sent a small expedition to Murmansk in North Russia in the hope of rallying sufficient anti-Bolshevik elements to the Allied cause to remain a thorn in Germany's side, and to prevent the Germans from gaining access to an ice-free port from which to mount submarine operations against Allied shipping. However, by the time of the Armistice, the Allies were engaged not against the Germans but the Bolsheviks, who objected to the Allied presence on Russian soil.

In April 1919 a composite rifle company of three platoons from the Regiment and one from The Rifle Brigade was formed at The Rifle Depot and despatched to Murmansk to join the forces already there. In harsh conditions in a sparsely populated area, it took part in many minor operations and engagements against the Bolsheviks with invariable success and with few losses. When the expedition was withdrawn in October, the Company was amongst the last to leave, having provided the rearguard to cover the evacuation of the main force from Murmansk.

The Regiment's Contribution

Seventeen battalions from the Regiment – four Regular and thirteen Service battalions (including two pioneer battalions) – fought on the Western Front, in Italy and in Salonika between 1914 and 1918. They did so with great distinction, being awarded a total of seventy Battle Honours.

Losses were appalling. 12,824 officers and men of the Regiment were killed or died during the War.[18] Their names are recorded in the Roll of Honour in Winchester Cathedral and on countless war memorials and headstones in France and the United Kingdom. John Tweed's imposing statue of a First World War Rifleman, which has stood outside the West Door of Winchester Cathedral since 1922, provides an evocative and constant reminder of their sacrifice and a particular focus for the Regiment's annual Act of Remembrance (see picture on page ii). About 130,000 members of the Regiment were wounded.[19]

Seven members of the Regular and Service battalions of the Regiment were awarded a Victoria Cross, including Lieutenant J.F.P. Butler (not previously mentioned), who performed his act of gallantry while serving with the Gold Coast Regiment in the Cameroons in November 1914. Victoria Crosses were also awarded to members of two of the Regiment's affiliated Territorial battalions, Second Lieutenant G.H. Woolley of Queen Victoria's Rifles and Lance Corporal J.A. Christie of the Finsbury Rifles. Additionally, Captain H.S. Ranken, Royal Army Medical Corps, serving with the 1st Battalion, was awarded a posthumous Victoria Cross for his acts of gallantry at Hautevesnes on 9/10 September 1914.[20]

Other gallantry awards included:[21]

Officers:

Distinguished Service Order	101
Bars to Distinguished Service Order	11
Military Cross	321
Bars to Military Cross	27
Distinguished Flying Cross	2
Mentioned in Despatches	432

Other Ranks:

Distinguished Conduct Medal	240
Bars to Distinguished Conduct Medal	21
Military Medal	1260
Bars to Military Medal	139
Military Cross[22]	15
Mentioned in Despatches	304

During the War, forty-two officers with previous service in the Regiment held command or staff appointments in the rank of Brigadier-General or above. General Sir Henry Rawlinson, Commander of the Fourth Army, was the most senior. Lieutenant-General Sir Thomas Morland,[23] Commander X and later XIII Corps, and Lieutenant-General Sir William Pitcairn Campbell,[24] were the next most senior, both later becoming a Colonel-Commandant of the Regiment.

For the most part the Regiment was not used as Bouquet or de Rottenburg advocated but, in the way of all other infantry regiments, committed to a war of attrition, of frontal assaults and life in the trenches. A readiness and ability to skirmish and to shoot straight were marked assets, but rarely were these skills employed imaginatively ahead of and on the flanks of others in the manner that had earned the Regiment its reputation for effectiveness in North America, in the Peninsula and during the frontier wars of the 19th Century. Fortunately, the corporate memory of the Regiment outlived the horrors and circumstances of the War, thanks, in part, to the previous generation who took such care to ensure that the history of the Regiment and its *raison d'être* were properly recorded for the benefit of, and to guide, subsequent generations. The sense of purpose, role and characteristics that distinguished Rifle regiments from other regiments would soon be restored.

Chapter 7
1919–38: Between the Two World Wars

Occupation and Demobilization, 1919

As soon as the First World War ended, the Allies moved into Germany, with the British Army of Occupation, under Lieutenant-General Sir Thomas Morland (60th), billeted in the Rhineland towns and villages in the flat countryside between Cologne and Düsseldorf. The 1st, 2nd, 13th, 18th and 20th[1] Battalion all formed a part of the occupying force, with the three Service battalions being grouped in the 1st (Light) Brigade under command of Brigadier-General G.V. Hordern (60th).

The 3rd Battalion finished the War in Salonika, from where it moved by train to Constantinople in February 1919 to occupy a part of Anatolia in defeated Turkey.

The 4th, 11th, 12th, 17th and 25th Battalion all remained in Northern France on salvage duties. The 16th Battalion ran a demobilization camp on the coast.

In June 1919 the four Regular battalions returned to England, the 3rd and 4th to prepare for service in India, and the 1st and 2nd to become Home battalions. All but three of the Service battalions overseas also returned to England during the year and were demobilized. The 13th, 18th and 20th were not demobilized until February 1920.

In England, the 1st Battalion moved into barracks at Aldershot and the 2nd Battalion into barracks at Portsmouth, where both embarked upon a period of reorganization and training, as well as preparation for the despatch of drafts to the 3rd and 4th Battalion, which sailed for India in October.

In 1919 HRH Prince Henry, the future Duke of Gloucester, was gazetted to the Regiment, transferring to the 10th Hussars in 1921. He became Colonel-in-Chief of The Rifle Brigade in 1942.

Ireland, 1920–1

With the War over, the situation in Ireland deteriorated as demands for Home Rule resurfaced. On 31 August 1920 the 1st Battalion was ordered at short notice to deploy to Belfast, where it arrived on 3 September with 22 officers and 575 men. Commenting on the period, the commanding officer, Lieutenant-Colonel R.G. Jelf, wrote:

[It may be of interest to give] *some idea of the situation in Ireland, as seen through the eyes of those who, like ourselves, had had practically no experience of the country, and who were suddenly launched upon the difficult and complex task of attempting to restore order in that distressed country. ...*

The Sinn Fein system of intelligence is well organised, and, of course, one has to remember that the greater part of Ireland is on their side, either voluntarily or by systematic intimidation.

In almost every instance we have found that employees in the Post and Telephone Offices are not only undependable, but even actually hostile, the direct result being that most military correspondence of a secret nature has to be transmitted either by cipher code, or by a system of couriers, travelling by train.

It has been established beyond doubt that a great number of the raids, carried out by the Sinn Feiners, have been planned and executed by men who have gained considerable experience in the same line, in France and Flanders, and the detail with which everything is carried out has been remarkably well thought out. ...

The real difficulty in Ireland at the present time is to differentiate between friend and enemy, with the direct result that we have all come to the conclusion that the best policy to pursue is to trust nobody, and to keep one's own counsel with regard to any impending operations. ...

[The principles guiding officers in selecting whom to arrest are:] *First and foremost, anyone in possession of arms, or even a single round of revolver or S.A. ammunition, is liable to arrest, and on conviction by Court Martial would certainly be awarded three years' penal servitude or even five years. It is an undoubted fact that the Sinn Feiners have made a most careful study of the art of hiding arms and ammunition, and a search of a moderate sized house may easily take six men a couple of hours to do, quite apart from the outhouses, coal and peat stacks, potato patches, and stooks of standing corn, all of which are favourite hiding-places.*

The next sure guide for arrest is the possession by anyone of the official organ of the Irish Republican Army, a paper published fortnightly, and officially recognised as their mouthpiece. The paper is known as Antoglac *(The Volunteer) and contains excellent articles on the methods to be adopted for carrying out raids, ambushes, etc., and evidently written by men who were fighting on our side in the World War of 1914-18. The paper is only sold to members of the Irish Republican Army, and the fact that any single individual is in possession of a copy of it is a tacit acknowledgement that the owner is a member of the force, and can be arrested accordingly.*

To sum up the whole situation, it is most difficult to foresee any end to the present deadlock, and I must honestly confess that, during my month's leave in England, the one thing that at once

*struck me was the appalling ignorance and apathy of everyone
with regard to the real situation in this country*[2]

During the initial months of deployment the Battalion was extremely
busy conducting cordon and search operations, pre-empting ambushes
and initiating surprise raids on suspect individuals. In one 3-week
period in September/October 1920, 140 houses plus two complete
villages were searched in the vicinity of Omagh. Soon after, the Battalion
moved into a hutted barracks at Ballykinler, County Down, where it built
an internment camp 'for the reception of those who were known to be
imbued with Sinn Fein tendencies'. This subsequently kept the guards
busy countering sophisticated attempts by the detainees to escape by
tunnelling under the wire.

Meanwhile, in December 1920, the 2nd Battalion was ordered to
Ireland at short notice, conducting operations in the rural areas of
Monaghan and Cavan, where patrols, and those moving on the roads,
were occasionally shot at by flying columns of Republicans. The
tension, however, eased a little when, on 12 July 1921, the British
Government agreed a truce, which, on 6 December 1921, extended to
an Anglo-Irish Treaty agreeing to the establishment in the following year
of an Irish Free State. On 7 December all internees were released.

Throughout their time in Ireland both battalions continued to send
substantial drafts to the 3rd and 4th Battalion in India, where many of
the men were still on short engagements of two, three or four years. This
resulted in each of the battalions being reduced to about 300 men by
the time they returned to England in early 1922.

Service Abroad, 1922

After arrival in India at the end of 1919, the 3rd Battalion went to Mhow
in central India and the 4th to Quetta. Apart from improving their
standards of training, each sought to capitalize on the opportunities to
compete for rifle shooting and sporting prizes, with members of the
Regiment excelling on the range and in the boxing ring. In 1921
Sergeant-Bugler Gilmore of the 3rd Battalion won the Army Rifle
Association Gold Jewel for the best rifle shot in India, while Colonel
Saunders-Knox-Gore won the King's Medal at Bisley, the first time that
the Championships at home and abroad had been won by
representatives from the same regiment in the same year.

There were also opportunities for big game shooting (shikar). On one
expedition Captain H.O. Curtis of the 3rd Battalion killed 'Alphonse', a
notorious cattle-killing tiger, whose skin subsequently graced the walls of
the Officers Mess. Big game hunting, however, was not just the preserve of
the officers. The *Annals* record that on another expedition: 'CSM Buchanan
shot a fine 9 foot 10½ inch tiger, Cpl Curtis another, and [Sergeant-Bugler]
Gilmore the varied bag of a wild goat, a crocodile and a chital stag.'[3]

Meanwhile, the 2nd Battalion, on returning to England from Ireland, was soon required to join the British Army of Occupation in Germany, being sent in April 1922 to Lublinitz in Upper Silesia, the future of which – whether it should form a part of Poland or Germany – was being disputed by the Poles. The Battalion's duties included the manning of frontier posts and armoured trains. However, soon after arrival the frontier was fixed and Lublinitz transferred to Poland. In July the Battalion moved to join the rest of the Army of Occupation in the Rhineland.

Reduction to Two Battalions, 1922–3

In 1922 the economic state of Great Britain and the conviction that there would not be another war for at least ten years ('The Ten-Year Rule'⁴), and certainly not on the scale of the last, led to inevitable reductions in the size of the Regular Army ('The Geddes Axe'), with the 3rd and 4th Battalion of The King's Royal Rifle Corps and The Rifle Brigade required to disband. Sadly, the ruling as to which battalions should be disbanded took no account of their quality.

Within the Regiment it was decided that the 1st Battalion should relieve the 4th Battalion in India, and that the 2nd Battalion should be the Home battalion. In October 1922, elements from the 1st, 3rd and 4th Battalion united at Quetta to form the new 1st Battalion, with the rump of the 3rd and 4th Battalion returning to England to be struck off the Army's order of battle in early 1923, thus ending for all time the service of two very fine battalions.

By way of compensation, although not intended as such, the War Office in June 1923 at last agreed, after years of struggle, that the rank of a private soldier in Rifle Regiments should be Rifleman, the rank used unofficially since the days of the 5th Battalion and the Peninsular War.

The Route to Mechanization, 1923–38

2nd Battalion

The 2nd Battalion remained a part of the Army of Occupation in the Rhineland until moving to Aldershot in January 1925, where it was chosen, from 1 April 1926, to carry out trials as the first mechanized infantry battalion in the British Army. This did not remove the requirement for rifle companies to march from one point to another, but replaced horse-drawn transport with motor transport in the form of a variety of trucks. On 1 March 1928 the new infantry battalion organization was adopted, replacing one of the four rifle companies with a machine gun company, which, at war establishment, consisted of four sections of four guns each. Soon after this change, the Battalion formed the first experimental machine gun company equipped with Carden-Loyd carriers driven by personnel from the Royal Tank Corps. Members of the Battalion drove the remainder of the transport.

On moving to Tidworth in 1929, the machine gun company received its own Carden-Loyds. In the same year a mechanized anti-tank platoon was formed in Headquarter Wing. The platoon consisted of two sections, each with two 0.5-inch Vickers anti-tank machine guns carried in Carden-Loyds with trailers for the gun crew. In 1931 a mechanized mortar platoon of two sections carried in Carden-Loyds, each with two 3-inch Stokes mortars, was added.

The Battalion's first experience of mechanization ended in June 1932 when it moved to Belfast. In accordance with War Office policy that no infantry unit should remain mechanized for longer than two changes of station (Aldershot and Tidworth), it reverted to horse-drawn transport. During the trial it received twenty-six satisfactory inspection reports and took part in many exercises and demonstrations, including one for the Colonel-in-Chief, King George V, and was well prepared to reassume the mechanized role when the opportunity arose five years later. It had also not neglected other important aspects of a Rifleman's life. It won the Britannia Trophy for rifle shooting in 1928 and 1932, and the non-central Queen Victoria Trophy in 1926, 1932 and 1933. RSM W. Jagger won the King's Medal for best individual rifle shot in 1925 and 1927. In 1933 the Battalion won the Army Inter Unit Team Boxing Championship, with Rifleman Thorne becoming the Army heavyweight champion.

Palestine, 1936-7
The Battalion enjoyed a very different and altogether much quieter time in Ireland between 1932 and 1935 than it had experienced in 1921. In November 1935 it moved to Aldershot, winning the Britannia Trophy again in the following July. In September 1936 it was warned for an emergency tour in Palestine, sailing two weeks later by troopship to Haifa with 27 officers and 683 men, of whom about half were reservists. On arrival, the Battalion was immediately employed on internal security duties to contain an Arab revolt aimed against the rapid economic

Carden-Loyd carrier and trailer of the Machine Gun Platoon,
2nd Battalion, Tidworth 1930

Regimental Sergeant Major W. Jagger,
Winner, King's Medal, Bisley, 1925 and 1927

domination of Palestine by the Jews. The rifle companies patrolled by vehicle and on foot, guarding key points including Jewish settlements, enforcing curfews, and cordoning villages while the police searched for arms. Within a fortnight of their arrival, the revolt was over, the reservists returned to England, and the Battalion, now only 300 strong, moved into billets at Tel Aviv.

For the next year Palestine was relatively quiet until violence broke out again in October 1937, requiring a reversion to the same sort of internal security duties as a year previously. At the end of November the Battalion embarked at Haifa to return to Aldershot.

On arrival in England on 17 December 1937, the 2nd Battalion was placed under command of the 1st Cavalry Brigade as a mechanized infantry (motor) battalion – a role defined in 1938 as 'a battalion of infantry equipped with transport down to a truck for each individual section and providing all its own drivers'. The other motor battalion in the Brigade, 1st Battalion, The Rifle Brigade, was more advanced in its training having assumed the role some months earlier.

The Brigade was an experimental one, intended to trial new arms and equipment, and to develop tactics, practices and procedures to facilitate infantry/tank co-operation. The organization of the Battalion was designed to enable the companies to act independently and to be self-supporting. It was, therefore, equipped with rifles, light machine guns, mortars and anti-tank and anti-aircraft weapons, with a high proportion of the men trained as drivers.

Much effort was expended and progress made in acquiring the individual skills and studying the tactics required to make a success of

2nd Battalion on Salisbury Plain, 1930s

being a motor battalion. In October 1938 the Battalion moved to Tidworth where, during the winter of 1938-9, the increasing likelihood of war provided added incentive to train and prepare well.

1st Battalion

The assumption of the 3rd Battalion's role at Quetta in 1922 marked the start of an unbroken spell of overseas service for the 1st Battalion, lasting until 1947. A note, therefore, of what service in the East was like for the Rifleman of the 1920s may not be out of place. To quote from the *Annals*:

> *After recruit training at the Rifle Depot, drafts for India would be made up in the trooping season during the winter months; this allowed men to settle in before the hot weather. A newly enlisted Rifleman would be single and probably on an initial engagement committing him to seven years active service and five on reserve. On embarkation in a troopship he would be starting an overseas tour of six years with no home leave and therefore no opportunity of getting married during the tour. Since marriage under the age of twenty-five in the case of soldiers and thirty in the case of officers was not recognised by grant of quarters or allowances, a battalion in which the vast majority were bachelors was inevitable. The result was a team whose members knew each other exceedingly well; and, if the officers applied themselves with imagination and skill, the basic infantry requirements of marksmanship and fitness could easily be built up. Furthermore, the free time available after the few types of weapon had been mastered made the effective organisation of sport and entertainment essential.*[5]

During the 1st Battalion's time in India there was not much to disrupt the normal pattern of life. A year spent in 1927 in an extremely rugged and mountainous district on the North-West Frontier at Razmak was the closest to active service. The Battalion by then had moved from Quetta to Rawalpindi and marched 262 miles to reach Razmak, where its role was to prevent the notoriously blood-thirsty Mahsuds and Wazirs from fighting. This was successfully achieved. Commenting at the end of the Battalion's tour, the Battalion's brigade commander wrote:

> *The training and tactical efficiency of the Battalion is of a very high standard, due to the excellent supervision and instruction of an able commanding officer* [Lieutenant-Colonel F.G. Willan], *backed by a keen and capable team of officers. The N.C.O.'s are well trained and know their jobs, with the result that the training of smaller formations is good. The men are fit and keen and move extremely well on the hillside. The efficiency of the Battalion in mountain warfare is excellent.*[6]

Rifle shooting, sport and big game hunting all played a major part in the Battalion's programme of activities. In 1926 the Orderly Room Sergeant, Sergeant F.E. Dracott, won the Gold Jewel for the best rifle shot in India, demonstrating his versatility and combining his success with membership of the Battalion hockey team that won the Army and All-India tournaments in the same year. In 1928 Rifleman Lewis won the Gold Jewel.

On leaving Razmak in November 1927, the Battalion went to Lucknow where it adopted the new infantry battalion organization of three rifle companies and a machine gun company, consisting of two platoons, each of three sections, with two gun detachments per section. The company was supported by an Indian platoon of Ahirs to look after the pack mules and to drive the animal carts carrying the machine guns and ammunition.

At the end of 1931 the Battalion moved from Lucknow to Calcutta, where ceremonial took precedence over all other military activity and where even rifle ranges were virtually inaccessible. Calcutta, as well as being an unhealthy and venal city, was very expensive for a Rifleman, whose rate of pay on first joining was two shillings a day, on which, in 1931, the Government imposed a 10% cut because of the financial crisis and general depression affecting Great Britain at the time. Nevertheless, some managed to get away to the mountains, to Sikkim, Kashmir and elsewhere, including Second Lieutenant H.C.J. (John, later Lord) Hunt, who led the 1953 expedition that conquered Everest.

In November 1934 the Battalion left India for Burma, with the District Commander in Calcutta reporting upon 'an exceptionally fine Battalion imbued as it is with a rare and genuine esprit-de-corps throughout all ranks. Everything is done well and thoroughly'.[7]

Burma, 1934–8

The Battalion spent four years in Burma, with one company detached during the first year to the Andaman Islands. Burma at this time was still a part of India, although those serving there most probably felt far removed from the hierarchy and bureaucracy of India, a feeling no doubt reinforced when Burma was formally separated from India on 1 April 1937.

Meanwhile, Hitler's rise to power became ever more threatening. Although the Munich Settlement, signed on 30 September 1938, temporarily averted war, the fear was sufficiently great for the War Office to bring forward the 1st Battalion's intended move to a mechanized role in Egypt. In November 1938 the Battalion arrived in Cairo where it was met by its new commanding officer, Lieutenant-Colonel W.H.E. 'Strafer' Gott. A hectic period of preparation and training as a motor battalion began. The 2nd Battalion, The Rifle Brigade, formed the other motor battalion in what was soon to become the 7th Armoured Division, the Desert Rats.

New Colonel-in-Chief

In January 1936 HM King George V, the Regiment's Colonel-in-Chief, died after holding the appointment for nearly thirty-two years. It was not until the Coronation in May 1937 that the Regiment learned that HM King George VI had graciously consented to succeed his father as Colonel-in-Chief.

Chapter 8

1939–45: The Second World War

Background

The events that led to the start of the Second World War are well known: Hitler's appointment as Chancellor of Germany on 29 January 1933; the reoccupation of the Rhineland in March 1936; the annexation of Austria in March 1938; and the invasion of Czechoslovakia in March 1939. Hitler's intentions that the territories lost in 1918 should be recovered, that Germany's power and prestige should be restored, and that Germany and its people should dominate a European continent cleansed of alien races, were well advertised. For six years his militant oratory, the course of events and the pace of German rearmament signalled what the British and her allies tried so hard to avoid – war. On 1 September 1939 Germany invaded Poland, a country with which Great Britain and France had a mutual assistance pact. After issuing Germany with an ultimatum to desist, which was ignored, Great Britain and France declared war on Germany on 3 September 1939.

Immediately a British Expeditionary Force (BEF) of 140,000 troops was despatched to France, under the command of General Viscount Gort. A period of relative inactivity followed (the 'phoney war') lasting until May 1940.

The Regiment, 1939–45

In April 1939, following the German invasion of Czechoslovakia and the Italian invasion of Albania, the British Government passed the Militia Act initiating conscription. In a belated effort to increase Britain's preparedness for war, the Territorial Army (TA) was authorized to recruit up to war establishment and to expand existing regiments to two battalions. This was quickly achieved, resulting in the Regiment entering the War with two Regular battalions, the 1st and 2nd, both motor battalions, and six TA battalions, which, in 1940, began to be equipped and trained as motor battalions and which, in 1941, became numbered battalions of The King's Royal Rifle Corps:

7th and 8th Battalion (Queen Victoria's Rifles), The King's Royal Rifle Corps

9th and 10th Battalion, The King's Royal Rifle Corps (The Rangers)

11th and 12th Battalion (The Queen's Westminsters), The King's Royal Rifle Corps

KRRC Battalions During the Second World War

Regular Battalions

1 KRRC	Motor Battalion	North Africa 1940–3 Italy 1944–5
2 KRRC	Motor Battalion	Calais 1940 North Africa 1941–3 Italy 1943–4 North-West Europe 1944–5

Special Reserve Battalions

5 (Huntingdon Militia) KRRC	Emergency Reserve	
6 (Royal 2nd Middlesex Militia) KRRC	Emergency Reserve	

Territorial Battalions

7 (Queen Victoria's Rifles) KRRC	Motor Cycle/Motor Battalion (Disbanded 1943)	Calais 1940
8 (Queen Victoria's Rifles) KRRC	Motor Battalion to 1944 Holding Battalion 1944–5	
9 KRRC (The Rangers)	Motor Battalion (Disbanded 1942)	Greece and Crete 1941 North Africa 1941–2
10 KRRC (The Rangers)	Motor Battalion replacing 1 MTB (1943)	
11 (The Queen's Westminsters) KRRC	Motor Battalion	North Africa 1942–3 Italy 1943–4 Greece 1944–5 North-West Europe 1944–5
12 (The Queen's Westminsters) KRRC	Motor Battalion	
30 KRRC	Old Soldiers Battalion (Disbanded 1943)	
70 KRRC	Young Soldiers Battalion (Disbanded 1943)	
1 Motor Training Battalion	Replaced by 10 KRRC (1943)	

In November 1939 the Regiment acquired a further TA battalion manned by soldiers over the age of forty-five in the displaced Home Defence companies of the three TA regiments. This was initially numbered the 7th (Home Defence) Battalion, which changed in December 1941 to the 30th Battalion, The King's Royal Rifle Corps. The soldiers carried out static guard duties on vulnerable points in and around London. The Battalion was disbanded in April 1943.

With the outbreak of War, there was insufficient space at The Rifle Depot to accommodate all the recruits in training. The 60th element moved two miles out of Winchester to a hutted camp at Bushfield, where an attack by a German aeroplane in 1940 caused some casualties. In the autumn of 1942, the arrival of the US Army in the south of England and the need to vacate Bushfield to provide accommodation for the Americans[1], led to the move of the Regiment's recruit training organisation from Bushfield to Fulford Barracks, York, where it assumed the unexciting title of 27 Primary Training Centre.

In September 1940 a Young Soldiers Battalion was formed – 70th (YS) Battalion, The King's Royal Rifle Corps – which disbanded in 1943.

Since members of motor battalions required specialist training, the Regiment formed a motor training battalion – 1st Motor Training Battalion (1 MTB) – which was initially based at Chiseldon, near Swindon in Wiltshire. A blend of reservists, unfit Regulars and emergency-commissioned or enlisted individuals provided the staff. In autumn 1942 the Battalion moved to Strensall, near York, where, in 1943, the 10th Battalion assumed the role, allowing 1 MTB to disband.

The Regiment went to great lengths to recruit and train its officers properly. While Officer Cadet Training Units (OCTU) and selection boards continued to handle officer entrants centrally, the Regiment established its own system to meet the special requirements of motor battalions. In May 1941 a Motor Wing, staffed by Green Jackets for the potential officers of both the Regiment and The Rifle Brigade, was established in 103 OCTU run by the Royal Armoured Corps at Perham Down in Wiltshire. Potential officers were also encouraged to volunteer for service before call-up, which enabled them to enlist in the regiment of their choice. In 1942 the Motor Wing was replaced by a self-standing Green Jacket OCTU at York, thus achieving a high level of synergy and efficiency adjacent to the Regiment's Motor Training Battalion and recruit training depot. The excellent material that resulted from the Green Jacket OCTU ended up right across the Army, for whenever a tedious lull in fighting occurred, Green Jacket officers often volunteered for special duties, for example, as parachutists, with the Special Air Service or with the Special Operations Executive.

During 1939 a short khaki serge blouse and trousers (battle dress), worn with web anklets, replaced the long-established service dress and long puttees, and a two-piece suit of denims supplanted the brown boiler suit for dirty work. A khaki-coloured 'fore and aft' replaced the peaked forage cap. This was swiftly supplemented by the private purchase of a Rifle green version for 'walking out'. Similarly, Rifle green berets later replaced the issue khaki model. The Regiment and its role were emblazoned distinctively on this new dress with metal shoulder titles and a narrow flash of Rifle green exclusive to Green Jackets, differentiating the motor from the marching infantry battalions whose flash was scarlet. Badges of rank remained black on scarlet. Despite the earnest striving of War Office egalitarians, black buttons were retained.

Defence of Calais, 22–26 May 1940

When the BEF departed to France in September 1939, none of the battalions of the Regiment was included, the two motor battalions of the Support Group of 1st Armoured Division (the 2nd Battalion and 1st Battalion, The Rifle Brigade) being held in reserve in England.

On 9 April 1940 Hitler invaded Denmark and Norway. Denmark capitulated on the same day; the Norwegians resisted. On 20 April, anticipating a need for British reinforcements, a new brigade, 30 Infantry Brigade, was formed at Tidworth for service in Norway. The 2nd Battalion (Lieutenant-Colonel E.A.B. Miller[2]) together with the 1st Battalion, Queen Victoria's Rifles (1 QVR) (Lieutenant-Colonel J.A.M. Ellison-Macartney) and 1st Battalion, The Rifle Brigade, were the principal units in the Brigade, which was commanded by Brigadier Claude Nicholson.

On 10 May 1940 Hitler invaded France and the Low Countries. Ten days later it was clear that the French High Command, under whose orders the BEF operated, had lost control of the battle. On 20 May Guderian's XIX Panzer Corps reached the French coast near Abbeville. Evacuation of the BEF became a possibility, requiring the Channel ports to be secured. 20 Guards Brigade was ordered to Boulogne and 30 Infantry Brigade to Calais, where a small number of British troops from the BEF and a French garrison of Territorials were already in place.

The battalions of 30 Infantry Brigade received the order to move during the evening of 21 May. The 2nd Battalion, 750 strong, was at the time in East Anglia guarding against possible German invasion. 1 QVR, a motor-cycle reconnaissance battalion, 550 strong, was on similar duty in Kent. It was instructed to deploy on light scales without vehicles. The Brigade was joined by 3rd Royal Tank Regiment, with cruiser and light tanks, and 229 Anti-Tank Battery, Royal Artillery. No field artillery or engineer support was included.

22 May 1940

On 22 May Guderian's XIX Panzer Corps began advancing north towards Boulogne, Calais and Dunkirk, with 10th Panzer Division directed to capture Calais. 1 QVR and the 3rd Royal Tank Regiment arrived in the afternoon. 1 QVR was ordered to move on foot into the surrounding countryside and block the main approach roads to Calais (see map).

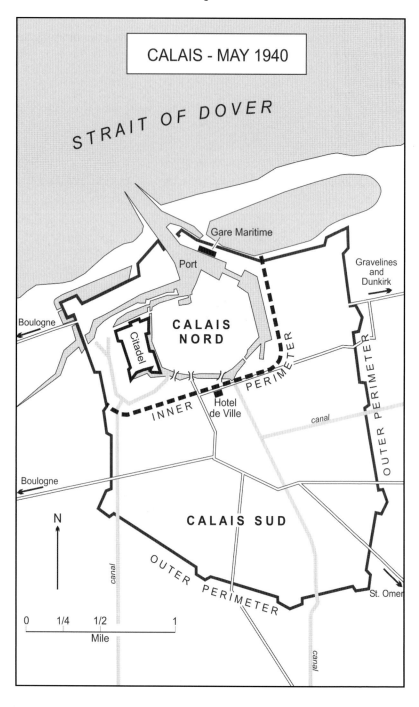

CALAIS - MAY 1940

STRAIT OF DOVER

Gare Maritime

Port

Boulogne

Gravelines
and
Dunkirk

CALAIS
NORD

Citadel

PERIMETER

INNER

Hotel
de Ville

canal

OUTER PERIMETER

Boulogne

N

CALAIS SUD

OUTER PERIMETER

canal

St. Omer

0   1/4   1/2   1

Mile

canal

23 May 1940
3rd Royal Tank Regiment engaged the Germans during the morning. In the afternoon, the 2nd Battalion and 1st Battalion, The Rifle Brigade, arrived in pouring rain and as shelling of the port began. Realising that Calais was likely to be surrounded, the brigade commander concentrated his few forces on defence of the town, with the 2nd Battalion manning an outer perimeter in the south and west, and The Rifle Brigade in the east. 1 QVR was ordered to provide elements to both battalions on withdrawal from its outposts in the countryside.

24 May 1940
At dawn the leading regiments of 10th Panzer Division attacked the outer perimeter positions held by the 2nd Battalion and elements of 1 QVR. During the day, and despite support from the Royal Tank Regiment, the RAF and Royal Navy destroyers offshore, the attacks intensified. As dusk fell, and in preparation for evacuation at short notice, the order was given to close in under cover of darkness and defend a shorter inner perimeter in the northern part of Calais (the old town). Meanwhile, 20 Guards Brigade was evacuated from Boulogne.

25 May 1940
By morning the Germans had moved into the southern part of Calais and were attacking the inner perimeter and, in particular, three key canal bridges, which the Germans were able to overlook from the top of the town hall (Hotel de Ville). These bridges were held by companies of the 2nd Battalion, supported by 1 QVR, and became the scene of intense street fighting. Soon after 11 a.m. the brigade commander rejected an offer to surrender. This prompted a major bombardment and attack upon the British positions. Around 4 p.m. a further offer to surrender was rejected and the battle resumed. By now it was clear that there would be no evacuation.

Much of the northern part of the town was in flames. The heat and smoke were intense. Houses were in ruins and the streets strewn with rubble. German snipers were everywhere. Movement immediately attracted fire. Casualties were mounting. Water and ammunition were in short supply. Virtually all the Brigade's tanks and anti-tank guns were out of action.

Undeterred, small groups of exhausted Riflemen, commanded by equally exhausted junior officers and NCOs, continued to hold doggedly to their positions in the face of overwhelming odds. Realising that the British were not going to give in, the Germans halted their attacks at nightfall in readiness for an all-out assault in the morning.

26 May 1940
At dawn the German assault recommenced with an intense artillery bombardment followed by air attack from wave upon wave of Stuka dive-bombers. Gradually the defenders, under relentless pressure, were forced

*The barricade at Pont Faidherbe, scene of bitter fighting
at Calais on 25/26 May 1940*

Calais after the battle, May 1940

Officers of the 2nd Battalion captured at Calais photographed at Oflag VII C, September 1941. Lieutenant-Colonel E.A.B. Miller seated, centre.

157

from their positions, with the remnants of the 2nd Battalion and elements of 1 QVR conducting a last stand in the north-east part of the old town, and 1st Battalion, The Rifle Brigade, with other elements of 1 QVR, holding out to the north of the nearby railway station (Gare Maritime). By 4.30 p.m. the Citadel had fallen. Soon afterwards, the last positions were overrun. There was no sensible alternative but to surrender.

The Defence of Calais in Context

The Defence of Calais was, by any standards, heroic. Against a backdrop of chaos, confusion and uncertainty, outnumbered, outgunned and with their backs against the sea, the British, with three Green Jacket battalions at their centre, plus 800 valiant Frenchmen, held a German panzer division at bay for the best part of three days. Hurriedly despatched, lacking all arms support and without hope of evacuation, officers and soldiers alike fought with a tenacity, courage and gallantry, which, ever since, have provided an example to others. That it was possible is a reflection upon the high morale and determination of individuals not to fail their comrades or their Regiment.

The strategic importance of the Defence of Calais has often been argued. Churchill was in no doubt that it contributed to buying vital additional time for the subsequent successful evacuation of 360,000 Allied troops from Dunkirk. Sir Anthony Eden, Secretary of State for War and a former 60th officer, also identified its significance when he signalled to Brigadier Nicholson on 25 May: 'Defence of Calais to utmost is of vital importance to our Country and BEF and as showing our continued cooperation with France. The eyes of the whole Empire are upon the defence of Calais and we are confident you and your gallant regiments will perform an exploit worthy of any in the annals of British history.'

The human cost, borne by so few for the benefit of so many, was high. 300 British troops were killed and 700 wounded. 130 members of the Regiment's two battalions died, including 11 officers.[3] Only a handful escaped. The majority faced five years in prisoner of war camps, which some, including Brigadier Nicholson, did not survive. Furthermore, the British had lost the manpower and expertise of two motor battalions. Calais, though, will always be remembered as one of the finest hours in Regimental and Green Jacket history.

The battalions lost at Calais were reconstituted at Tidworth in the autumn of 1940. They very soon reached a high state of training and were operational by the end of the year.

North Africa, 1940–1

In June 1940 Italy declared war on Britain, threatening British domination of the Mediterranean, its important bases in Egypt, and its lines of communication to India and the Persian Gulf. Immediately, and

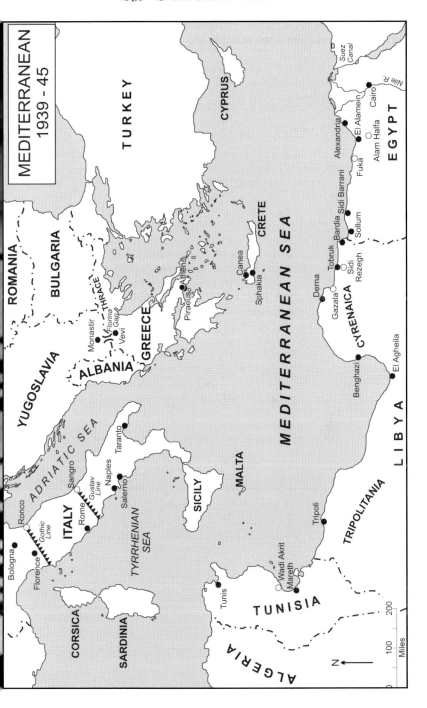

MEDITERRANEAN
1939 - 45

ROMANIA

BULGARIA

YUGOSLAVIA

ALBANIA

GREECE

Monastir

Florina Gap

Vevi

THRACE

TURKEY

CYPRUS

Suez Canal

Nile R.

Cairo

El Alamein

Alam Halfa

Fuka

Alexandria

EGYPT

Sidi Barrani

Bardia

Sollum

Tobruk

Sidi Rezegh

CRETE

Canea

Sphakia

Piraeus Athens

Derna

Gazala

CYRENAICA

Benghazi

El Agheila

MEDITERRANEAN SEA

LIBYA

ADRIATIC SEA

ITALY

Ronco

Bologna

Florence

Gothic Line

Rome

Gustav Line

Sangro

Naples

Salerno

Taranto

TYRRHENIAN SEA

SARDINIA

CORSICA

SICILY

MALTA

TRIPOLITANIA

Tripoli

Wadi Akrit

Mareth

Tunis

TUNISIA

ALGERIA

N

100 200 Miles

until May 1943, all convoys were routed round the Cape of Good Hope on a journey of 13,000 miles to the Middle East, instead of 3,000.

Libya was an Italian colony with 250,000 troops based there, greatly outnumbering the 36,000 British and Dominion soldiers under Lieutenant-General O'Connor, commander of the Western Desert Force (renamed 13 Corps on 1 January 1941). 7th Armoured Division, with the 1st Battalion in its Support Group, was one of two divisions in the Western Desert Force. Lieutenant-Colonel S.C.F. De Salis commanded the 1st Battalion, while his predecessor, now Brigadier Gott, commanded the Support Group. The Battalion had been a motor battalion for eighteen months and was familiar with the desert, although not yet with desert warfare. In April 1940 detachments of Rhodesians joined it and by the end of the month a Rhodesian platoon had been formed. This later expanded to a Rhodesian company, one of the finest companies in the Regiment.

An extensive barbed-wire fence marked the frontier between Egypt and Libya. As soon as war was declared, the Western Desert Force took the offensive, patrolling aggressively across the border, establishing moral ascendancy over the Italians. On 13 June, D Company of the 1st Battalion played a leading part in an attack on an Italian patrol base, Fort Capuzzo, which resulted in the capture of its garrison of 246 men. Mussolini then directed a reluctant Marshal Graziani, commander of the Italian forces, to advance into Egypt, which he did in September, but only as far as Sidi Barrani, some 60 miles from the frontier, where the Italians leisurely set about establishing themselves before making a further move.

1st Battalion at Fort Capuzzo, Libya, June 1940.
Photo no. E1434 courtesy Imperial War Museum, London

The British responded by establishing desert mobile columns. These generally comprised one motor company with a troop or battery of guns. Their role was to harass, delay and observe the enemy, a task ideally suited to Riflemen used to acting imaginatively and on their own initiative. They operated very successfully against the Italian defended localities and logistic dumps, providing company commanders with valuable experience in this type of warfare. They also identified the weaknesses in the Italian front, which General Wavell, Commander-in-Chief, Middle East Command, and O'Connor's Western Desert Force were shortly to exploit.

Wavell's Offensive, December 1940 to February 1941

'The Wavell Offensive' was launched in December 1940 and, although it initially had limited objectives, it quickly developed into a series of outflanking movements, which constantly threatened to envelop the Italians. In a 10-week period the Italians were hustled out of Egypt and Cyrenaica, yielding 130,000 prisoners and a mass of tanks, guns, ammunition, equipment and vehicles. Commonwealth losses amounted to 500 killed and just under 1,400 wounded.

The 1st Battalion played a full part in these astonishing successes, cutting off the Italians' line of retreat from, first, Bardia and, then, Tobruk. When the offensive was halted in mid-February 1941, the Battalion had covered 764 miles in 7 days of actual motoring, ending up astride the Benghazi to Tripoli road west of El Agheila. Despite ten continuous months in very rough desert conditions, very few vehicles broke down. The Battalion, together with 7th Armoured Division, was then sent back to Cairo for a welcome rest and refit, but not before it had been subject to frequent German air attack in the forward area as Rommel's Afrika Corps began to arrive in Libya.

Greece, 1941

On 7 April 1939 Italy invaded Albania as a step towards achieving Mussolini's ambition to turn the Balkans into a sphere of Italian influence. In October 1940 the Germans entered Romania to secure the oilfields upon which they were so dependent. Mussolini, fearing German encroachment into his intended sphere of Italian influence, impetuously ordered the invasion of Greece. The invasion, launched on 28 October 1940, quickly foundered. The Greek Army, supported by the RAF, advanced thirty miles into Albania. Meanwhile, Churchill saw opportunity to open up a Balkan front and, in February 1941, persuaded the Greeks to accept Allied troops on their soil. Hitler did not want this, not least because he feared the threat that this would pose to the southern flank of the forthcoming German attack on the Soviet Union.[4] On 2 March Bulgaria admitted German troops on her soil. On 6 April Germany invaded Yugoslavia and Greece.

In early March the first of 50,000 Commonwealth troops under the command of Lieutenant-General Sir Henry 'Jumbo' Maitland Wilson (Rifle Brigade)[5] arrived in Greece. The force, known as W Force, included two Australian divisions, a New Zealand division and 1st (British) Armoured Brigade,[6] of which the 9th Battalion (The Rangers) was a part. The Battalion, under command of Lieutenant-Colonel G.C. Ashburner, had become a motor battalion in 1940 and arrived in Egypt on 31 December. It spent the next two months training in the desert. It came as something of a surprise, therefore, to be redeployed to Greece, where the Battalion disembarked at Piraeus on 15 March 1941.

In the days that followed, the Battalion travelled 300 miles over difficult mountain roads, very different from the desert to which it was just becoming accustomed, to prepare defensive positions on the line of the River Vardar, in order to delay any German advance westwards through Thrace from Bulgaria. However, the German invasion of Yugoslavia on 6 April prompted a rapid redeployment to the Greek frontier with Yugoslavia in order to block the road south from Monastir where it passes through the Florina Gap, near Vevi.

Florina Gap, 9 to 13 April 1941
Arriving on 9 April, the Battalion had little time to prepare good defensive positions on ground that was exposed and on a frontage of 4,000 yards, which allowed no reserve. First contact with an Adolf Hitler SS mechanized division occurred during the night of 10/11 April, followed by heavy bombardment and some ineffectual enemy probing attacks on the following day, during which it snowed hard. On 12 April the Germans attacked in force. By mid-afternoon, after six hours of battling, the Battalion was no longer able to hold its positions and was forced to withdraw, requiring the flanking Australian units to evacuate their positions in haste. Fortunately, good discipline and fighting spirit prevented the withdrawal turning into a rout, and by nightfall C Company had occupied an intermediate position, four miles to the rear, affording excellent fields of fire to repel any attack which might be made in the morning.

On 13 April (Easter Day), in bitterly cold weather, the Germans mounted a series of dismounted attacks against C Company's position, during which the company commander[7] counted up to 500 dead in front of his position. However, some German penetration took place, resulting in an orderly withdrawal to new positions further south. On 14 April these were abandoned as the Germans on other axes threatened to outflank W Force.

During the next two weeks a difficult fighting withdrawal was conducted along muddy roads clogged with traffic and under constant air attack. Meanwhile the Greeks decided that further resistance was pointless and on 21 April the evacuation of W Force was ordered.

162

Lieutenant-Colonel Ashburner was medically evacuated, leaving Major D.R.C. Boileau in command of the Battalion. After covering the east flank of the evacuation area, the Battalion abandoned its heavy equipment and vehicles and, during the nights of 27 and 28 April, moved across the beaches east of Athens to be taken, in the nick of time, on board the waiting Royal Navy destroyers.

During the campaign in Greece, W Force lost around 13,000 men, mostly prisoners. The 9th Battalion lost around 150. The commander of 1st Armoured Brigade later reported to one of the Regiment's Colonels-Commandant:

> *I am so glad to get the chance of telling anyone about the Rangers, for although I only had them under me for a few weeks in Greece, I have never been fonder or prouder of any unit I have had fighting with me. … The line was terribly thin, but was held for four days in bitter, snowy weather against frequent attempts at penetration by a Hitler S.S. division, including several night attacks – a pretty trying experience even for seasoned troops, and this was their first experience of war.*[8]

Crete, 1941

When the 9th Battalion was evacuated from Greece, it fully expected to return to Egypt. The 165 all ranks evacuated on 27 April did so. The remaining 400, who were evacuated on 28 April, finished up on Crete, an island of strategic importance to the Royal Navy as a fuelling base between Alexandria and Malta. It was also of value to the Germans as its possession would protect the sea route for Romania's oil to Italy and offer airfields from which to attack the North African coast and Malta. Hitler, therefore, decided to capture Crete. On 20 May German glider-borne and parachute troops landed on the island.

Lieutenant-General Bernard Freyberg VC, the New Zealand commander of the garrison of 35,000 Allied troops, had an extremely difficult task on his hands to defend Crete. The island was large and in easy reach of the German-occupied airfields in Greece, while the priority for Allied air support lay elsewhere in North Africa. His troops, too, were poorly equipped, with those just arrived from Greece, such as the 9th Battalion, having only small arms for their protection.

The Battalion was deployed in defensive positions around Canea on the north coast of Crete and, although the Allies put up an extremely stout resistance, the weight of the German landings, together with their air superiority, was too great to counter. On 23 May an unsuccessful attack by B Company on a sizeable group of German parachutists resulted in the company suffering 25% casualties. By 26 May the position was hopeless. Orders to withdraw across the mountains to Sphakia on the south coast were slow in reaching the Battalion, which became involved during the night of 26/27 May in fruitless attempts to stem the German attack. Thereafter, late on 27 May, the Battalion was instructed to make its way south in small groups avoiding German patrols and air attack. However, insufficient shipping, the short hours of darkness and the presence of the Germans did not permit a full evacuation.

During the campaign on Crete the Allies lost 16,000 men. Nearly 70 out of the original 400 members of the Battalion who arrived on the island escaped. The rest were either killed or, in the case of the majority, were taken prisoner, among them, the commanding officer, Lieutenant-Colonel Boileau. Some managed to evade the Germans and join the Cretans who continued their resistance until the end of the War. Those who did make it back to Egypt, including those evacuated directly from Greece, provided the cadre around which the Battalion was later re-formed.

North Africa, 1941–3
Rommel's First Desert Offensive, March 1941 to October 1941

On 5 February 1941, Hitler, fearing that an Italian collapse in Libya might unseat Mussolini, advised the Italians that he was sending Rommel and the 5th Light Division to North Africa forthwith, to be followed by 15th Panzer Division in May. General Wavell, however, applying conventional criteria, did not expect an immediate German attack and, with his extended lines of communication stretching back over 1,000 miles to the Nile Delta, reduced his forces on the front line at El Agheila in western Cyrenaica. Rommel saw an opportunity and, although his forces were untrained in desert warfare, he seized the initiative. On 24 March the British were driven out of El Agheila. On 29 March, the 1st Battalion, together with the 7th Armoured Division, which was resting in Egypt, was ordered forward to Cyrenaica to counter the increased level of German activity. On 31 March Rommel's offensive began.

Rommel's forces moved swiftly and aggressively, forcing the Allies, in a replay of Wavell's earlier offensive but in reverse, to withdraw 700 miles in two weeks to where they had started in December 1940. The 1st Battalion was involved in numerous close encounters along the way, including a sharp engagement with a German battlegroup at Derna aerodrome on 7 April. Only the garrison in Tobruk held firm. During the night of 11/12 April the Battalion crossed through a gap in the wire into Egypt.

The Western Desert Force was reconstituted with Brigadier Gott responsible for a mobile force, including the 1st Battalion, which sought constantly to harass the Germans whose lines of communication and forces were now stretched to the point that further advance was not possible. On 15/16 May an attempt by Gott to advance west of Sollum (Operation Brevity) was aborted after heavy tank losses. Between 15 and 17 June a more ambitious plan (Operation Battleaxe), hastily launched by Wavell under pressure from Churchill, using tanks that had recently run the gauntlet of a Mediterranean convoy to Alexandria, also failed. The Allies were now finding out that mere quantity of tanks mattered little unless they were mechanically sound, reasonably fast and armed with an adequate gun. They also had no tanks with armour thick enough to prevent penetration by German 88 mm guns.

During the next four months a relative lull occurred as each side sought to build up its strength for future operations. The 1st Battalion took turn and turn about with the 2nd Battalion, The Rifle Brigade, observing, patrolling and harassing the enemy in mobile columns of up to battlegroup strength. On 12 September the Battalion inflicted significant losses on a German column conducting a reconnaissance in force.

Meanwhile, on 22 June 1941, Germany invaded the Soviet Union. The Mediterranean became a subsidiary front, with a lower priority for German supplies and reinforcements. On 5 July General Auchinleck replaced General Wavell as Commander-in-Chief, Middle East Command. General Cunningham became the commander of the new Eighth Army. In September, Gott assumed command of 7th Armoured Division.

Auchinleck's Offensive, November/December 1941

By November the Eighth Army was sufficiently strong for Auchinleck, under continual pressure from Churchill, to consider an offensive. Meanwhile Rommel was planning the capture of Tobruk. Auchinleck pre-empted this on 18 November by launching Operation Crusader, which involved 13 Corps tying down the Axis forces on the frontier, while 30 Corps outflanked the German positions to the south in order to defeat Rommel's armour and relieve Tobruk.

Sidi Rezegh, 21/22 November 1941
The 1st Battalion formed a part of 7th Armoured Division's Support Group in 30 Corps and by the evening of 20 November had reached the south side of Sidi Rezegh airfield, which was situated on flat ground above an escarpment overlooking the main road bypassing Tobruk. German and some Italian troops occupied the area north of the airfield where the escarpment lay. In the early hours of 21 November Lieutenant-Colonel De Salis issued orders to the Battalion to seize the ground occupied by the enemy so that gunner observation posts might be positioned to enable shelling of the bypass road. Despite conducting reconnaissance patrols during the night, the extent of the enemy position was not fully realised. There was no alternative to a frontal assault over 2,000 yards of flat, open ground, with three scout platoons in Bren carriers leading, and the motor platoons following dismounted. The Battalion was less one of its motor companies and had two batteries of 25-pounders under command, but no tanks in support.

*Rifleman John Beeley VC killed in action at Sidi Rezegh,
21 November 1941*

*HRH The Duke of Gloucester and Lieutenant-General Willoughby Norrie
at the grave of Rifleman Beeley VC, May 1942*

The attack, which was mounted at 8.30 a.m. with around 300 officers and Riflemen in the assaulting force, achieved remarkable success, over-running an enemy that was later assessed to have been 1,000 strong, including a German machine-gun company. 700 prisoners were taken. For much of the three hours that it took to capture the escarpment, it was a platoon and section commander's battle, with Riflemen skirmishing forward in pairs in the manner of their forebears in the Peninsula. Many acts of great gallantry were performed including an action for which Rifleman Beeley was subsequently awarded a posthumous Victoria Cross, the only Victoria Cross awarded to a member of the Regiment during the Second World War. The Battalion lost three officers and twenty-six other ranks killed and fifty wounded. Two of the three officers who died were Rhodesians.

During the remainder of 21 November the Battalion held the position it had occupied unmolested, but without armoured support it was extremely vulnerable against a German tank attack. Hence there was little it could do when, at 1.30 p.m. on 22 November, a huge force of about eighty tanks with supporting infantry and artillery assaulted the rear of the position and overwhelmed the companies and the commanding officer's tactical headquarters. Five officers and fifty other ranks escaped, but the majority were captured, including Lieutenant-Colonel De Salis. It was an unfortunate sequel to one of the finest actions fought by the Regiment during the War. Fortunately, one of the motor companies had survived, which, together with those who escaped, provided the nucleus around which the Battalion was quickly re-formed.

Meanwhile, the rest of 7th Armoured Division had been engaged in five days of hard and often confused tank battles, with the British failing to concentrate their armour in the manner of the Germans. Losses on both sides were heavy, but Rommel's mattered more as he lacked immediate replacements. After a 'dash to the wire' in an unsuccessful attempt to breach the frontier positions of 13 Corps, Rommel abandoned his plan to capture Tobruk and, by early January, had withdrawn his forces 700 miles to El Agheila from where, 8 months previously, he had come. By so doing, he shortened his lines of supply and once again extended those of the British.

General Ritchie succeeded General Cunningham in command of Eighth Army. Lieutenant-General Gott assumed command of 13 Corps. In December America entered the War.

Rommel's Second Desert Offensive, January/February 1942

At the end of December 1941, 7th Armoured Division was relieved in western Cyrenaica by the 1st Armoured Division, which had recently arrived from England. The Division included the 2nd Battalion (Lieutenant-Colonel O.N.D. Sismey), which disembarked on 2 December, spent three weeks equipping and training, and then moved forward 1,000 miles with 200 vehicles into the front line in early January. Meanwhile Rommel received a small number of additional tanks, with which he decided to launch an unexpected offensive against the British while they were off balance reorganizing after the battle of Sidi Rezegh.

British Withdrawal to the Gazala Line, 21 January to 5 February 1942

Rommel attacked on 21 January 1942, quickly precipitating a British withdrawal in some disarray over a distance of 350 miles to the Gazala line, west of Tobruk, which was reached on 5 February. The Germans by this time were running out of fuel. Both sides needed time to rebuild their strength. The 2nd Battalion had acted as a rearguard during much of the withdrawal, losing over 200 all ranks killed or captured and a large number of vehicles, including its echelon, which inadvertently drove straight into the middle of a German position. On 11 February the Battalion was withdrawn from the front line to recuperate.

1st, 2nd and 9th Battalions, March/April 1942

In March 1942 the 1st, 2nd and 9th Battalion were all in Egypt reconstituting. The 1st, which was at Cairo, was quickly brought up to strength after Sidi Rezegh. It was commanded by Lieutenant-Colonel G. de Bruyne and became the single motor battalion in 4th Armoured Brigade in 1st Armoured Division. It had four motor companies, each with two motor platoons, a scout platoon and an anti-tank platoon equipped with 2-pounder anti-tank guns, useful against soft-skinned vehicles but not main battle tanks. On 12 April the Battalion moved forward to the Gazala line.

The 2nd Battalion, which was also at Cairo, reorganized on similar lines to the 1st Battalion, but with the addition of a 3-inch mortar detachment with each motor company. It formed a part of the 7th Motor Brigade[9] in 7th Armoured Division. On 18 April the Battalion also moved forward to the Gazala line. The 9th Battalion, meanwhile, following its trials in Greece and Crete, had been brought up to strength and re-equipped by the end of 1941 and, under command of Lieutenant-Colonel C.M. Grenville-Grey, was carrying out various duties in the rear area. At the end of March it joined the 2nd Battalion in the 7th Motor Brigade. The 2nd Battalion, The Rifle Brigade, was the third motor battalion in the Brigade. By mid April the Brigade was complete on the Gazala line, contributing to the mobile (jock) columns operating forward of the main positions to observe and harass the enemy.

The Gazala Battles and Withdrawal to El Alamein, 26 May to 30 June 1942

The Gazala line stretched fifty miles southwards into the desert. It consisted of a number of defended localities or 'boxes' protected and linked by minefields, with the armoured brigades held in reserve to the rear of the forward positions. By May, both sides had built up their strength to a size greater than the previous November, but the Germans still had the qualitative edge in equipment.

On 26 May Rommel launched a major offensive, outflanking the British positions to the south and striking at the heart of the Eighth Army. In bitter, extremely hard-fought, and often frenetic battles over the next three weeks, the British were eventually forced to withdraw a further 350 miles to El Alamein, 60 miles west of Alexandria. The 1st and 2nd Battalions were constantly engaged in motoring across the desert to wherever they were needed to attack and delay the advancing Germans, while the 9th Battalion occupied one of the boxes. A number of losses were inflicted on the enemy by the anti-tank guns, the 1st Battalion having received some 6-pounders, but positions frequently had to be evacuated at short notice and were occasionally overrun. Lieutenant-Colonel de Bruyne of the 1st Battalion was captured and replaced by Lieutenant-Colonel C.d'A.P. Consett.

On 20/21 June the Germans succeeded in capturing Tobruk. On 25 June Auchinleck dismissed Ritchie and took personal command of Eighth Army. On 1 July the three 60th battalions, having fought numerous rearguard actions, reached the El Alamein line.

Ruweisat Battles (First Battle of Alamein), July 1942

The El Alamein line stretched thirty-eight miles south from the Mediterranean coast to the Qattara Depression. Although the German High Command originally wanted Rommel to pause at this point, the prize of achieving a rapid breakthrough to the Nile Delta was too tempting. During early July Rommel's forces tried time and again to breach the Eighth Army's incomplete positions, and time and again they were repulsed, with the three 60th battalions playing their part. On 7 July a company of the 9th Battalion carried out a particularly daring raid on Fuka aerodrome, eighty miles behind the German lines. By mid July, Allied forces were counter-attacking in strength, but by the end of July both sides were exhausted and an operational pause resulted.

Towards the end of July the lack of reinforcements from England necessitated the disbandment of the 9th Battalion, with the majority of the men being posted to the 1st and 2nd Battalion.[10] This was a sad end to the Battalion's service in the War since, in fighting spirit, the Battalion was in every respect the equal of others, as its members had shown during the rearguard actions in Greece, the defence of Crete and in the successful attack on Fuka aerodrome.

Lieutenant-General W.H.E. 'Strafer' Gott CB CBE DSO* MC

Lieutenant-General W.H.E. Gott

The death of General 'Strafer' Gott from injuries received when two German fighter aircraft (ME 109s) attacked the aeroplane in which he was flying to Cairo on 7 August 1942 deprived the Regiment of its most successful Second World War commander.

Commissioned into The King's Royal Rifle Corps in February 1915, he joined the 2nd Battalion in France where he quickly gained his nickname from the German prayer 'Gott Strafe England'. In July 1917 he was wounded and taken prisoner when his battalion was overwhelmed at Nieuport Bains. While a prisoner he spent his time trying to escape. On the third attempt he reached the Dutch frontier before being recaptured. He was awarded a Military Cross for his actions at Nieuport.

His rise to high rank during the Second World War was meteoric. He became commanding officer of the 1st Battalion in October 1938, handing over command on 1 February 1940, after which he was progressively commander of 7th Armoured Division's Support Group, 7th Armoured Division and 13 Corps. He had just been chosen for command of Eighth Army at the time of his death.

The loss of General Gott was deeply felt among the troops he had commanded and especially by all those who knew and admired him. He had all the attributes that make a great commander and leader: extreme determination, even ruthlessness if necessary, and yet great kindness; an almost boyish exuberance and yet great calmness in emergency; the human touch and yet a deep sense of duty. The confidence he reflected in his officers and men and his personal courage were outstanding. He shared the full hardship of desert life with his subordinates and never let his position in any way add to his own personal comforts. Everything he did he did thoroughly. A young officer in a letter to his father wrote: '"Strafer" has been killed. To most of us here if it had been the death of our own father it could hardly have come as a greater shock. ... Every Rifleman is broken hearted. And yet I don't know why we loved him so. He was so simple and concealed nothing, so clever and yet so full of common sense.'

He died at the age of 42 leaving a widow and two small children, one of whom he never saw. In a letter to his widow, the Prime Minister, Winston Churchill, said: 'He has left few or none his like behind him.'

Further sadness followed. In early August, General 'Strafer' Gott was chosen to take command of Eighth Army, but before he could do so, he was killed. General Montgomery was appointed in his place. At the same time, General Alexander replaced Auchinleck as Commander-in-Chief, Middle East Command.

Battle of Alam Halfa, 30 August to 7 September 1942

During August the Eighth Army strengthened its defences, while Rommel prepared to launch a major offensive against the El Alamein line. The renamed 4th Light Armoured Brigade, including the 1st Battalion, joined 7th Armoured Division, of which the 7th Motor Brigade,[11] with the 2nd Battalion, was already a part. The Division occupied positions in the south of the line where, late on 30 August, Rommel chose, as was expected, to pitch the main thrust of his attack, which he eventually directed towards seizure of the Alam Halfa ridge, some fifteen miles to the east.

On 31 August, the 1st and 2nd Battalion, the latter now under command of Lieutenant-Colonel W. Heathcoat-Amory, contributed significantly to delaying the enemy's advance through Eighth Army's minefields and during a fighting withdrawal to Alam Halfa, where the line held and the German attack was halted. Rommel's forces had reached their culminating point. He was short of tanks and running out of fuel. On 3 September Eighth Army counter-attacked pushing the Germans back towards the original El Alamein line, where, following a few days of further fighting, it stabilized.

During the remainder of September and October, the Eighth Army prepared for the battle that was to come. Meanwhile, in June 1942, the 11th Battalion, under command of Lieutenant-Colonel R.A.T. Eve, arrived in Egypt as a part of 24th Armoured Brigade in 10th Armoured Division. After three months training, the Battalion joined the rest of the Eighth Army in October in time to take part with the 1st and 2nd Battalion in the Battle of El Alamein.

Battle of El Alamein, 23 October to 3 November 1942

After Alam Halfa, Rommel's army strengthened their positions. In the north there were three belts of defended localities and minefields. In the south the defences were not so highly organized, but were sited to canalize any attempt to cross through them. In most places the minefields extended 5–9,000 yards in depth. Montgomery's intention was to breach the minefields and to defeat Rommel's army in place, with 30 Corps, supported by 10 Corps, attacking in the north and 13 Corps in the south. The main effort was in the north.

The Battle of El Alamein began during the evening of 23 October. The motor companies of the 11th Battalion were dispersed among the armoured regiments of 24th Armoured Brigade (10 Corps), which moved during the night of 23/24 October to exploit the minefield breaches in the north. Four days of heavy fighting followed, during which the Brigade was delayed among the minefields and often caught in exposed positions. Progress was slow and, despite the best efforts of the motor companies to seize ground and inflict casualties upon the enemy, tank losses were so great that the Brigade was withdrawn from the line. On 29 October the 11th Battalion was ordered to hand over its vehicles and equipment to the 2nd Battalion – a bitter pill – and was thus denied the exhilaration of participating in the forthcoming successes to which their early efforts had contributed. The Brigade and, with it, the 11th Battalion moved to Syria to refit.

The 1st Battalion with 4th Light Armoured Brigade (13 Corps) was in the vanguard of the attack in the south, moving forward during the night of 23 October to secure the ground on the far side of each minefield as it was breached. After four days of heavy fighting and casualties between the first and second minefields, the attack was abandoned.

The 2nd Battalion was not committed until 26 October when, with 7th Motor Brigade, it transferred to 1st Armoured Division (10 Corps) and together with 2nd Battalion, The Rifle Brigade, was ordered to attack a feature known as Kidney Ridge, where the Germans with anti-tank guns were preventing the British armour from advancing. The 2nd Battalion was directed to the north part of the feature, known as 'Woodcock', and the 2nd Battalion, The Rifle Brigade, to the south part, known as 'Snipe'.

Woodcock, 26/27 October 1942
The Battalion succeeded in capturing Woodcock during a night attack involving three companies advancing in their vehicles from a start line 3,000 yards from the objective. It was a difficult task and a splendid achievement, during which 100 prisoners and 6 anti-tank guns were seized. Fifteen members of the Battalion were killed and a further eighty wounded or posted missing. The position was subsequently held for a further 24 hours before relief. Meanwhile, the 2nd Battalion, The Rifle Brigade, succeeded in occupying Snipe and during 27 October repulsed repeated Italian and German tank attacks in a heroic action, for which its commanding officer, Lieutenant-Colonel V.B. Turner, was later awarded a Victoria Cross.

Operation Supercharge, 1 to 3 November 1942
On 1 November Montgomery launched Operation Supercharge, a major coordinated attempt to complete the breakthrough at Alamein. In the early hours of 3 November the 2nd Battalion launched another night attack, the second in a week, against a German anti-tank screen

overlooking the final minefield breaches in the north. Success was again achieved in difficult circumstances. Rommel's defences had at last been broken. The ground occupied by the Battalion subsequently became the point chosen for Eighth Army's breakout on the following morning.

Rommel suffered 13,500 casualties and lost 500 tanks during the Battle of El Alamein. A further 40,000 Italian troops, who were stranded without transport, were captured. The church bells were rung in England on Sunday, 15 November 1942, for the first time since 1940.

From Alamein to Tripoli, 4 November 1942 to 23 January 1943

On 4 November Rommel began the retreat, which was to end in the destruction of his army in Tunisia. General Montgomery set his whole force in pursuit. The 1st Battalion led the 4th Light Armoured Brigade through the minefields. Wherever the enemy stood he was attacked and the pursuit continued. However, mines, air attack, bad weather and extended lines of resupply all contrived to provide just enough opportunity for Rommel's forces to evade encirclement.

On 11 November the Battalion crossed the Egyptian frontier into Libya for the last time. By mid-December it was past El Agheila and into Tripolitania. On 24 December the 2nd Battalion, which had been in reserve, relieved the 1st. The advance continued. Increased air attacks and determined resistance by German rearguards inflicted a steady toll of casualties. On 23 January 1943 Tripoli was occupied. In the space of less than three months the Eighth Army had covered nearly 1,250 miles.

Battle of Mareth, February/March 1943

The Axis forces halted their withdrawal on the Mareth Line where they turned to face the Eighth Army. On 8 February the 2nd Battalion, which was still a part of 7th Armoured Division, now under command of Major-General G.W.E.J. Erskine (60th),[12] crossed into Tunisia and within 48 hours was probing the southern extremities of the Line. The terrain was now markedly different, with rugged foothills reaching up from the coastal plain, with narrow roads and readily defensible defiles, where the Battalion spent the next six weeks engaged in difficult fighting as it endeavoured to make progress with its long tail of vehicles.

Meanwhile, Montgomery, realizing that a frontal assault on the Mareth Line would be very costly, ordered the New Zealand Division together with 1st Armoured Division to make a wide detour to the south. The 1st Battalion, now under command of Lieutenant-Colonel J.L. Corbett-Winder, was assigned to the 7th Motor Brigade in 1st Armoured Division. The turning movement was successful and during the night of 27/28 March the enemy evacuated the Mareth Line.

After the Battle of Mareth the enemy occupied an extremely strong defensive position in the passes at Wadi Akrit, forty miles further north, from which they were evicted by the gallant actions of others. On 7 April, Eighth Army's advance continued until it was again held up by strong enemy positions some sixty miles short of Tunis.

The Final Act, 22 April to 13 May 1943

On 8 November 1942 Allied Forces under General Eisenhower landed in Morocco and Algeria. They then advanced into Tunisia from the west but met stiff German resistance. In April, General Alexander, Eisenhower's deputy, informed Montgomery that Eighth Army was to support 1st Army's advance on Tunis, which was to be the Allies' main effort. 1st Armoured Division, with the 7th Motor Brigade and the 1st Battalion, was placed under command of 1st Army. On 22 April 1st Army launched a major offensive to defeat the remaining Axis forces. The Hermann Göring Division opposed the battalions of the 7th Motor Brigade in mountainous terrain strongly favouring the defence. Patrolling was hazardous; to assault was even more so, with the Battalion suffering significant casualties during a successful night attack on the heights at Argoub el Megas[13] on 29/30 April. Meanwhile, the 2nd Battalion occupied the enemy by conducting limited offensive operations on Eighth Army's front. On 7 May Allied forces entered Tunis and by 13 May the last Germans and Italians surrendered. Some 250,000 prisoners were captured. The war in North Africa was over.

Quoting from the *Annals*:

> *The 2nd Battalion, a phoenix from the ashes of Calais … and the 1st Battalion which had been abroad so long … had paid off their debts to comrades in graves, prison camps and hospitals. … Holding key posts in each battalion were Riflemen from our 9th Battalion, the Rangers, who had endured successive misfortunes and had yet retained their own particular spirit, and were now particularly content to see over 200,000 Axis troops trapped against the sea as payment with a vengeance for Greece and Crete. Far away in Syria our 11th Battalion, who had assisted in the beginnings of this victory through their role at Alamein, although denied their part in the last act, took pride in its glorious outcome.[14]*

In North Africa, Greece and Crete the Regiment's total losses were 73 officers and 440 other ranks killed in action or died. The wounded probably numbered over 2,000.

After a victory parade in Tunis, the 1st and 2nd Battalion moved to a concentration area near Tripoli, where a Regimental parade was held on 10 June and where, on 21 June, both battalions lined a route out of Tripoli to salute and cheer their Colonel-in-Chief, King George VI. The

HM King George VI, Colonel in Chief, shaking hands with the commanding officer of the 1st Battalion, Tripoli, 21 June 1943

1st Battalion joined the 2nd Armoured Brigade in 1st Armoured Division. In July Lieutenant-Colonel W.D. Keown-Boyd assumed command. The 2nd Battalion remained in the re-titled and now independent 4th Armoured Brigade.

Italy, 1943–5 (*see map on page 159*)

During the night of 9/10 July 1943 the Allies invaded Sicily. On 25 July Mussolini was overthrown. On 3 September Eighth Army crossed the Messina Straits and started to advance up the toe of Italy. On 9 September the Allies landed at Salerno, thirty-five miles south of Naples. On 1 October the Allies entered Naples. The Germans, meanwhile, were reinforcing their army in Italy and preparing to occupy strongly defended positions on the Gustav Line, including the monastery at Monte Cassino, which overlooked the main road to Rome, eighty miles to the north-west.

2nd Battalion, September 1943 to January 1944

The 2nd Battalion was the first of three 60th battalions to fight in Italy, disembarking at Taranto on the Adriatic coast on 28 September 1943. After a month of duties in the rear area, the Battalion was involved in appalling weather in the advance upon, and crossing of, the River Sangro. Movement on and off the main coastal road was extremely difficult, with the Germans conducting a very effective fighting withdrawal. By the end of November, after much hard work, some lively engagements and a number of casualties, the Battalion occupied positions on the far side of the river. Two months later it returned to England with 4th Armoured Brigade in readiness for the invasion of Normandy.

11th Battalion, October 1943 to May 1944

The 11th Battalion spent the first nine months of 1943 training in Syria, the last two under a new commanding officer, Lieutenant-Colonel C.d'A.P. Consett, who had previously commanded the 1st Battalion. In September it moved to Egypt and on 22 October arrived in Italy where, within a week, it occupied positions on the Tyrrhenian coast. Six months of constant patrolling and probing of the Gustav Line followed. This period is well summarized in an account in the *Annals* which, although it relates to the 11th Battalion, fits exactly the experience of others:

> *Mention 'Italy' to a Rifleman of the 11th Battalion and what will the name conjure up? A picture of bare hillsides, with no vestige of cover against the weather; of low cloud and driving rain; of mules loaded with 'compo' rations, and the Indian muleteers who seemed to be even more obstinate than the mules; of 'stand-to' in a slit trench with a foot of water in the bottom; of bad 'vino' and worse cognac and above all of patrols – night after night slithering into unexpected ditches, waiting in ambush for the Boche, who seldom turned up, coming back with the occasional prisoner or the occasional casualty. It was a static, sticky, slimy war with more casualties than kudos and more mud than was good for morale. There were no spectacular advances, no daring jock-columns; just sitting and waiting, and getting wet.*[15]

On 15 February Lieutenant-Colonel H.C.J. Hunt (of Everest fame) assumed command of the Battalion, which, on 29 March, as part of a larger reorganization, crossed to the Adriatic side of the Apennines, where operations continued much as before, with success heavily dependent upon the skill and courage frequently demonstrated by junior commanders at platoon and section level. Gradually the Battalion forced the enemy in its sector on to the defensive as plans were laid by higher commanders to launch yet another attempt to breach the Gustav Line. On 11 May a grand offensive began and a week later Monte Cassino was taken. The German defence gave way and on 4 June, two days before D-Day, Rome was in Allied hands. Meanwhile, on 28 May, the 11th Battalion was relieved and on 10 June departed for Egypt, where it remained until sent to Greece in October.

1st Battalion, May 1944 to March 1945

On 27 May, just prior to the 11th Battalion's departure, the 1st Battalion arrived in Italy after spending nine months training with the 1st Armoured Division in Algeria. Lieutenant-Colonel E.A.W. Williams, a Calais escapee, was in command.[16] After a month of readjustment and continuation training, the Battalion moved forward to the front line, some sixty miles south-east of Florence, where the Germans were withdrawing to the Gothic Line, a fortified line across Italy similar in intent and strength to the Gustav Line. Operations followed much the same pattern as those previously conducted by the 2nd and 11th Battalion. The terrain continued to favour the defender and progress was slow.

On 25 August the Eighth Army launched a major offensive against the Gothic Line, which by the end of September had begun to crumble. The Germans, though, continued to contest every river, defile and ridge, which offered opportunity to delay the Allies' advance. The 1st Battalion suffered, not just from constant contact with the enemy but from being frequently regrouped and sometimes poorly tasked. On 25/26 October, when ordered to cross the River Ronco at night in a manner contrary to the commanding officer's better judgement, two companies, without tanks or anti-tank guns in support, were overrun in a German counter-attack that drove them back on a river which had suddenly flooded and was impassable. Nearly 120 all ranks were lost. However, within a month the Battalion had made up its numbers and was back in the line, enjoying success on 7 December when B Company, sixty strong, seized a particularly important feature, inflicting more casualties on the enemy than its own strength. Soon afterwards the Allied advance halted in preparation for a major spring offensive.

The Winter Line, 28 December 1944 to 26 February 1945

After some pre-Christmas rest and recreation, on 28 December the Battalion started an unbroken spell of sixty-two days occupying an extended frontage of 6,000 yards at Mezanno, east of Bologna. In bitter winter conditions both sides patrolled aggressively, leading to a number of sharp encounters, in which the initiative and gallantry of junior commanders and individual Riflemen often saved the day. On 4 January an attack by a brigade of élite troops from 16 SS Reichsführer Division was repulsed, resulting in the enemy suffering at least 70 killed or wounded as well as over 130 taken prisoner. Recording this period in the *Annals*, the author who was the Intelligence Officer and acting Adjutant at the time, wrote:

The 1st Battalion endured eight weeks and six days and nights of snow, mud and lack of sleep, beat off major attacks and dominated the winter darkness so close to the enemy that none of the 400 Riflemen of F Echelon, including Battalion HQ, were ever out of shell, and often machine-gun, range.[17]

After relief in the line on 26 February, Lieutenant-Colonel J.C. Hope assumed command of the Battalion. At the same time the Battalion joined 61 Brigade, commanded by Brigadier A.C. Gore (Rifle Brigade), with the 2nd and 7th Battalion, The Rifle Brigade. A period of training took place. Since arrival in Italy in May 1944, the Battalion had lost 62 killed, 188 wounded and 137 missing or prisoners, the latter mostly at the crossing of the Ronco in October.

The Final Offensive, 14 April to 3 May 1945

On 14 April the Allied offensive began. The 1st Battalion was grouped with the 16th/5th Lancers in a combined infantry/armoured battlegroup. Initially in reserve, on 20 October the battlegroup successfully forced a way through the Traghetto Gap, north-east of Bologna. On 23 April, as it pressed hard on the heels of the withdrawing Germans, the commanding officer, Lieutenant-Colonel Hope, was mortally wounded by a sniper, who was soon after given short shrift by his pursuers. On 2 May the German surrender in Italy was announced. On the same day the Allies entered Trieste. 61 Brigade was ordered to move swiftly into Austria, which the 1st Battalion reached on 9 May amid chaotic scenes and clashes between surrendering Germans, Cossacks and Titoists.

The Liberation of Greece, 1944–5

In August and September 1944, first, Romania, and then, Bulgaria, capitulated as Soviet forces headed towards Hungary and Austria. The German army of occupation in Greece, fearing for its position, abandoned the country, withdrawing through Yugoslavia. In mid-October an Allied Liberation Force entered Athens and set about establishing order in the country. The force included the 11th Battalion, commanded by Lieutenant-Colonel C.F.G. Henshaw, which, since June, had been resting and retraining in Egypt.

The situation in Greece was unpromising. The country was large, while the forces available were small. The Greek Communists, with whom the Battalion had to deal, were devious, truculent and unscrupulous and, in December, staged a *coup d'état* to overthrow George Papendreou's new government of national unity. Fighting began in Athens on 7 December and for the next four weeks civil war reigned, as the Allies supported the Government in its attempts to defeat the Communists. Meanwhile reinforcements were rapidly despatched from Italy.

The 11th Battalion, which initially occupied towns north of Athens, withdrew into the city. It was soon engaged defending its positions against sniping and bombing attacks, and in street fighting and house-to-house searches to dislodge the rebels. Some nasty situations were averted, thanks once again to the courage and initiative of junior commanders and individual Riflemen, although some isolated posts

11th Battalion waiting to leave HMS Black Prince *to land in Greece,*
October 1944

were overrun. By the beginning of January the situation was close to
being restored and soon afterwards the Communists agreed to disarm
and demobilize. Over 200 British lives were lost. The 11th Battalion
suffered seventeen all ranks killed, forty-five wounded and eighty taken
prisoner, although all the prisoners were returned by the end of January.

Once the coup was overcome, the situation eased and the Battalion
reverted to training in expectation of being required in another theatre.
But it was not to be. The War ended, with the 11th Battalion remaining
in Greece until its disbandment at the end of 1946 (see page 191).

North-West Europe, 1944–5

Normandy, June to August 1944

The plan was for three 60th battalions to take part in the invasion of
Normandy – the 2nd, 8th and 12th Battalion. The 8th (Queen Victoria's
Rifles) and the 12th (The Queen's Westminsters) had both been in
England since the start of the War. During 1939/40 much of their time

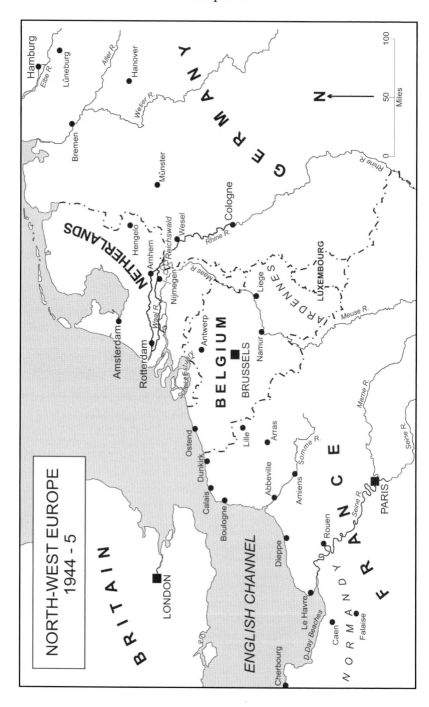

NORTH-WEST EUROPE
1944 - 5

was spent on Home Defence and it was not until 1940/41 that they were able to focus on conversion to the motor battalion role. Thereafter a great deal of training took place in England in readiness for D-Day. In February 1944 the 2nd Battalion returned from Italy to join the invasion force. The tempo of preparation increased and on 6 June 1944 (D-Day) the invasion was launched.

The leading elements of the 2nd Battalion, still under command of Lieutenant-Colonel W. Heathcoat-Amory, landed in France on 7 June (D+1), followed by the 12th Battalion, under command of Lieutenant-Colonel R.G.R. Oxley, on 16 June (D+10). However, in early July the departure of the 8th Battalion was halted as it was about to embark, and its members dispersed to provide battle casualty replacements for the Green Jacket battalions already in Normandy. One complete company was despatched to the 8th Battalion, The Rifle Brigade, and the majority of the others to the 2nd and 12th Battalion. It was an act of war but desperately hard to swallow, not least for the commanding officer, Lieutenant-Colonel C.T. Mitford-Slade, who had spent eighteen months training the Battalion for a role which was now denied him.

The 2nd and 12th Battalion were the single motor battalions in the 4th and 8th Armoured Brigade respectively. Both were independent brigades, each with three armoured regiments. A motor company was placed under command of each regiment. Spells spent in reserve were mixed with periods of intense activity during which the regiments supported various infantry brigades and divisions in turn, including 49th Infantry Division, commanded by Major-General E.H. Barker (60th).[18] On 26 June both battalions provided flank protection to 8 Corps during Operation Epsom, a major attack launched by General Montgomery to cross the River Odon and envelop Caen from the south. The Germans, however, fought hard and the attack was unsuccessful, with the advancing troops finding it difficult to make progress in the bocage of Normandy. Breaking out from the Normandy bridgehead was proving difficult and costly. By the end of July the 2nd Battalion had lost nearly ninety all ranks killed or wounded.

On 25/26 July the Americans launched the major offensive (Operation Cobra) that achieved the decisive breakthrough. By the end of July the 2nd and 12th Battalion were on the move. On 1 August the 12th was involved in the first of many actions to dislodge stubborn German troops barring their advance. Both battalions subsequently took part in the fighting near Falaise where, between 17 and 20 August, much of the German Seventh Army was annihilated. The battle for Normandy was over and a pursuit began. Meanwhile, Lieutenant-Colonel the Hon. M.G. Edwardes (Rifle Brigade) assumed command of the 12th Battalion.

Advance into the Low Countries, August/September 1944

Falaise opened the floodgates. The German back was temporarily broken as the Allies swept through northern France and into Belgium.

2nd Battalion coming ashore, Normandy, June 1944

2nd Battalion going into action near Caen, July 1944

Armour played a prominent part and the 2nd and 12th Battalion, with their respective armoured brigades, were well to the fore. On 28 August both battalions crossed the Seine to the north-west of Paris. On 1 September a stiff pocket of enemy resistance was encountered at Airaines, a village south of the River Somme between Amiens and Abbeville, where the new commanding officer of the 2nd Battalion, Lieutenant-Colonel R.B. Littledale, a Colditz escapee, was killed.[19] Further opposition was either sharply dealt with or bypassed for others to deal with later. On 3 September the 12th Battalion advanced over the First World War battlefields of Arras, through Lille and on to Brussels, which it reached on 7 September. The 2nd Battalion, on the left flank of the advance, was close to Antwerp when it halted on 10 September. On 14 September Lieutenant-Colonel R.H.W.S. Hastings (Rifle Brigade) assumed command of the 2nd.

The speed of the advance into Belgium was unparalleled and, although the battalions had suffered unwanted casualties en route, the level of success was exhilarating. However, the lines of communication reaching back to Normandy were overstretched. Clearing the Germans from the Scheldt estuary giving access to Antwerp was a strategic priority. Meanwhile the Germans were regrouping and preparing defensive positions forward of the Rhine.

Operation Market Garden, 17 to 26 September 1944

In an effort to maintain the momentum of the advance, on 17 September Montgomery launched Operation Market Garden, an attempt using airborne forces to capture the bridges over the River Waal at Nijmegen and the River Rhine at Arnhem. The 12th Battalion with a squadron of tanks followed behind the Guards Armoured Division, as British ground troops successfully linked up with the Americans at the captured bridge at Nijmegen, but failed to reach the British paratroops at Arnhem.

Operations, October 1944 to February 1945

Operation Market Garden created a salient of occupied territory north of Nijmegen, where the two 60th battalions spent much of their time over the coming months. To quote from the *Annals*:

The principal role [of the battalions] *was to hold a wide front, usually backed by armour, to protect the West or East flanks of the salient. This relieved infantry brigades to take part in the deliberate tidying up operations, which successively cleared South Holland and the Antwerp approaches and later the area between the Maas and the Rhine, an essential preliminary to the March 1945 assault crossing over the latter.*[20]

Battalion frontages were often 6–8,000 yards wide, requiring aggressive patrolling to keep the enemy on the defensive. Numerous encounters took place, with intermittent shelling and mortaring occasionally inflicting casualties. The pressure, however, was on the Germans as the battalions periodically undertook offensive operations to dislodge the enemy from their front and to advance closer to the Rhine. The 2nd Battalion was involved in a series of attacks between 26 and 28 October. On 25 November the 12th Battalion crossed the border into Germany for the first time in a brief sally south, before returning to its former area of operations.

On 16 December 1944 the Germans launched a counter-offensive in the Ardennes (Battle of the Bulge), which preoccupied the Allied High Command. However, operations in the battalion areas, with spells out of the line, continued much as before. During this period lasting through until early February 1945, many patrols were carried out with great success earning high praise for 'the keenness, energy and offensive spirit of all ranks'.

On 13 January Lieutenant-Colonel C.d'A.P. Consett, who had already commanded the 1st and 11th Battalions during the War, assumed command of the 2nd Battalion.

The Reichswald Forest, February/March 1945

After some preliminary operations in January in which the 12th Battalion was involved, on 8 February Montgomery launched Operation Veritable to drive the Germans back across the Rhine, prior to a subsequent crossing and advance deep into Germany. Both battalions were engaged in passing through the Reichswald and clearing the enemy from the Schlieffen Line, the last line of German defences before the Rhine. Poor weather, saturated ground and determined resistance by German paratroops made this a lengthy, difficult and dangerous task.

The 12th Battalion was the first of the 60th battalions through the Reichswald, linking up with American forces advancing from the south on 3 March. The 2nd Battalion had the tougher time in three days of continuous fighting from 1–3 March, during which it was issued with Kangaroos (Sherman tanks with the turrets removed for troop carrying) and mounted a battalion attack against the Schlieffen line. At least 50 Germans were killed and a further 150 taken prisoner before the remainder withdrew east across the Rhine. The Battalion suffered 50 casualties, representing some 20% of the dismounted strength of the motor companies. But success was achieved and the Rhine reached. The Battalion was relieved by the Regina Rifles of Canada, an allied regiment, and withdrew to regroup in preparation for the next phase.

In mid-March Lieutenant-Colonel G.W. White assumed command of the 12th Battalion, which exchanged its twelve 6-pounder anti-tank guns for six self-propelled 17-pounders and a platoon of 4.2-inch mortars.

Crossing the Rhine, 23/24 March 1945

On 23/24 March Montgomery's 21st Army Group crossed the Rhine near Wesel by assault boat and with airborne forces. The 2nd Battalion was the first of the 60th battalions to cross by raft and ferry on 25 March, followed by the 12th by bridge on 27 March.

Advance into Germany, March to May 1945

The advance into Germany bore similarities with the advance from Falaise into Belgium eight months earlier, but the enemy, fulfilling a German soldier's duty to die well, often resisted tenaciously and progress was sometimes slow. With victory imminent, every additional casualty on the Allied side became a cause of regret. Attacking or bypassing the enemy as they were encountered, the battalions were soon burdened with prisoners. On 2 April B Company[21] of the 12th Battalion suffered a nasty reverse when an unseen enemy repulsed a gallant attempt to cross the Twente Canal near Hengelo. But for the most part it was success. By 16 April the Battalion was close to Bremen.

The 2nd Battalion initially encountered less opposition than the 12th and on 10 April was rested for 72 hours in preparation for the breakout from crossings over the River Weser and River Aller. On 14 April the Battalion crossed both rivers and was soon engaged with the enemy who were still fighting stubbornly, requiring a series of company and battalion attacks to be launched over the next five days. Progress thereafter was easier.

The War was now close to being over. When the 'cease fire' sounded on 5 May, the 2nd Battalion had reached Hamburg and the 12th, Bremervörde, north-west of Bremen. The inevitable business of rounding up prisoners and attending to the aftermath of war began. During the eleven months since landing in Normandy, the 12th Battalion lost 105 all ranks killed, 246 wounded and 10 missing.

The Home Front

During the War the battalions, when in England, served on the Home Front carrying out Home Defence duties, especially during the early years when invasion was feared. The Regimental training and administrative system also worked flat out to meet the demands of the battalions. In particular, the Ladies Guild performed great work despatching 85,000 comforts such as gloves, socks and scarves to the battalions, as well as blankets to returning prisoners. Nearly 6,000 families of Riflemen were on its register, receiving 18,000 garments. Toys from Canada and America were directed to the children of casualties or prisoners of war. The Guild also ran a Hospital Visiting Scheme with 118 visitors covering nearly 400 hospitals; the needs of our Riflemen in hospital were thus rapidly met. Behind all this the

Riflemen's Aid Society provided funds for the Guild and dealt with 4,500 applications from past and present Riflemen and their families. Commenting in a letter, one recipient wrote: 'The Riflemen are convinced that their "Home Front" in the war was certainly the best and most efficient organisation of its kind.'[22]

After the loss of the battalions at Calais, Lieutenant-Colonel R.A.T. Eve, commanding The Rifle Depot, formed a Green Jacket Prisoner of War Parcel Depot Committee, with Mrs Eve as Honorary Secretary. Thanks to the efforts of its Honorary Treasurer, Brigadier F.G. Willan, £35,000 was raised to fund the organization and the despatch of parcels via the Red Cross to 2,000 Green Jacket prisoners of war.

Prisoner of War Escapes

The survivors of Calais constituted the largest group of Regimental prisoners of war (POW). Soon after capture, Captain E.A.W. Williams, Adjutant of the 2nd Battalion, managed to escape and to cross the Channel in a motorboat. Second Lieutenant T.S. Lucas of Queen Victoria's Rifles (QVR), rowed across in a dinghy. Lance Corporal R. Illingworth, a commission candidate with the QVR, used his knowledge of French to cross France and eventually reach Portugal. Captain Williams and Second Lieutenant Lucas were both awarded a Military Cross.

Escape, however, was not easy, especially from the German POW camps deep in Poland. Officers, who under the Geneva Convention were not allowed to work, had more time to plan escapes than the other ranks, who were required to provide labour in factories, fields and mines. On 28 May 1941 Major R.B. Littledale, with Lieutenants A.M. Sinclair and E.G.B. Davies-Scourfield, escaped from Stalag XXID at Posen in Poland. Littledale and Sinclair were subsequently recaptured in Bulgaria, while Davies-Scourfield was at large for nine months with the Polish underground before being caught on his way through Austria to Switzerland. All three were sent to Colditz where the 60th provided a hard core of inmates.[23] In his final attempt to escape, the most persistent of all, Lieutenant Sinclair, whom the Germans called 'The Red Fox', scaled a barbed wire fence in full view of two sentries and was shot. He was later awarded a posthumous Distinguished Service Order. A part of his citation reads:

> *From the moment he was taken prisoner at Calais in 1940 until he was shot in attempting to escape in daylight on the 25th September 1944, Lieutenant Sinclair devoted the whole of his energies to the task of escaping and so returning to continue the fight. He never deviated from this set purpose and, in spite of setbacks, and the hardest of luck, his courage and determination never wavered.*
>
> *In all, he made no fewer than seven great attempts to escape, each one having been planned to the smallest detail, entailing*

months of preparation and careful calculation. Even after being wounded in September 1943, during one of these magnificent efforts, he never gave up, but began to prepare for his next attempt almost before he had recovered from his wound.

Others were luckier. Major R.B. Littledale eventually made it, escaping from Colditz to Switzerland in October 1942, only to be killed in command of the 2nd Battalion during the advance from Normandy to the Low Countries (see page 183). Rifleman Hossington, captured with the 2nd Battalion at Calais, achieved 'a home run', escaping from Stalag XXIB in Poland in October 1940, reaching safety six months later. He was awarded a Distinguished Conduct Medal for his escape.

In Italy, Lieutenant-Colonel S.C.F. De Salis and Major H.A. Hope, both captured at Sidi Rezegh in November 1941, escaped during the brief period after the Italians collapsed in 1943 and before the Germans took over their POW camps. Lieutenant-Colonel G. de Bruyne, captured in the desert in 1942, and Rifleman Chapman also used this period to make good their escapes. Colonel de Bruyne subsequently operated with Italian partisans for over year before transiting the Gothic Line to freedom. Rifleman Chapman operated with the partisans but, in January 1945, was betrayed and shot by the Fascists, later being recorded as 'killed in action, while at large in enemy-occupied Italy'.

The Regiment's Contribution

During the War six out of the Regiment's eight battalions served in operational theatres overseas. Forty-three Battle Honours were awarded.

One hundred and fifty-nine officers and 986 other ranks were killed or died, almost half in North Africa, Greece and Crete. Their names are recorded in the Roll of Honour in Winchester Cathedral, and on war memorials and the headstones of their graves in this Country and in the theatres where they fell, including at Calais. The number of wounded and missing probably exceeded 8,000.

One member of the Regiment was awarded a Victoria Cross. Other awards included:

Distinguished Service Order	22
Military Cross	73
Distinguished Conduct Medal	13
Military Medal	106

Countless others performed acts of great bravery for which, as is the way in war, no award was made. In addition, and to quote from the *Annals*: 'no group did more to tie down German manpower and resources by escape and the threat of escape than Green Jacket officers.'[24]

For the most part, the battalions of the Regiment were able to fight in a manner and style in keeping with the tenets of Bouquet and de

Rottenburg: as motor battalions 'swift and bold in the old traditional role, skirmishing in the forefront of the battle, protecting the flanks, guarding a retreat, scattered wide in small groups, yet acting in combination',[25] with commanders operating on their own initiative and leading by example from the front. That they and their subordinates did so with such enormous courage, skill and distinction, and so selflessly and at such cost, has been a huge source of great pride and inspiration to Green Jackets ever since.

American Officers in the Second World War

In the winter of 1940/41 a Boston lawyer named J.K. Howard visited England, where he met Major-General Sir John Davidson, one of the Regiment's two Colonels-Commandant, who said 'I think it's time we had some Americans in the Regiment again'. Both decided to pursue the idea, which presented difficulties, as America had not yet entered the War and had laws in place to deter its citizens from becoming involved in the wars of others. However, in spring 1941, Sir Anthony Eden, the Foreign Secretary, who served in the Regiment with distinction in the First World War, and Mr John Winant, the American Ambassador in London, agreed that a limited number of American volunteers should be offered temporary British nationality and allowed to join the Regiment. An appropriate form of words was used in lieu of the usual oath of allegiance on attestation.

On 10 July 1941 the first five Americans, chosen out of many candidates to join the Regiment, left New York. On arrival they underwent recruit training at the 60th depot at Bushfield (Winchester) before attending officer training and receiving commissions in The King's Royal Rifle Corps on 18 April 1942. Another American, on transfer from a Canadian regiment, joined them and all six departed for North Africa, where they were all wounded serving with either the 1st or 2nd Battalions during the Battle of El Alamein.

In total, eighteen Americans were commissioned into the Regiment in 1942–43. They all served on active duty. Four, including one of those wounded at El Alamein, were killed in action: two in Tunisia, one in Italy and one with the French commandos in France. After America's entry into the War some left the Regiment to serve with the US Forces. Others remained. The last to leave did not depart until summer 1946.

American officers at the head of their platoon during recruit training at Bushfield Camp, November 1941

Chapter 9

1946–65: The Concluding Years

Adjusting to Peace, 1945–50

1st Battalion – Austria and Italy, 1945–7

The 1st Battalion spent the first four months after the Second World War striving to maintain law and order in Austria, where displaced soldiers and partisans, often armed, from various groups who had fought on different sides and sometimes on the same side, sought either to flee the area or to settle old scores. Members of the Battalion frequently found themselves interposing in highly volatile situations, where their lives were potentially at great risk. It was a task calling for a blend of courage, initiative, tact and good humour, for which the Battalion was well suited. Some aspects were distasteful, including the unattractive behaviour of the Yugoslav communists and the disarmament of the Cossacks, who had fought on the German side and were handed over to the Russians in questionable circumstances that took little account of the fate that most likely awaited them.

In August 1945 Lieutenant-Colonel S.C.F. De Salis resumed command, his previous tenure having been interrupted by his capture at Sidi Rezegh in November 1941. A month later the Battalion returned to the Po Valley in Italy, and to the little town of Linogio within striking distance of Venice. There followed a period of much turbulence as members of the Battalion returned to England at the end of their engagements without compensating drafts to replace them. It required considerable imagination and good leadership to ensure that the Riflemen were properly administered in post-War conditions of discomfort and shortage.

In March 1946, Lieutenant-Colonel T.L. Timpson, a Calais veteran, assumed command. In mid-year the Battalion moved to Naples to oversee elections, where a 'battle against the most expert thieves of the peninsula started'. But it did not last long for at the end of August the Battalion returned north to police the provisional boundary between Italy and Yugoslavia, known as the Morgan Line, in an area bedevilled by the unresolved problems of two World Wars. In November, after a period of rest and training, the Battalion occupied positions in the Allied zone adjoining the Morgan Line in weather that, during the winter, became appallingly cold. Occasional clashes generated international incidents, with patrol members on more than one occasion being abducted, poorly treated and eventually handed back, days or even weeks later, by the unrepentant Yugoslavs occupying the other side of the Line.

In February 1947 the Italian Peace Treaty was signed, giving over some territory in the disputed area to the Yugoslavs and creating a new border in place of the Morgan Line. Transition, however, had to await ratification of the Peace Treaty, which did not occur until September. By then, the Battalion, after spells in and out of the line, was back on duty and, on 16 September 1947, supervised the handover arrangements between the Italians and Yugoslavs. This was followed by a rapid departure from Italy, with the 1st Battalion returning to England by train and across the North Sea in early October.

Meanwhile, the introduction of the National Service Act in 1947 presaged a reorganization of the Infantry, with the 1st Battalion on its return to England designated an Army basic training unit and the 2nd required to disband. Thus, after spending four months at Aldershot, in February 1948 the 1st moved to Barton Stacey to assume responsibility for the training of all Green Jacket Regular and National Service recruits.

2nd Battalion – Denmark, Libya and Palestine, 1945–8

Immediately the War ended, the 2nd Battalion moved within days to Denmark, where it received a warm welcome. Its duties were not especially exacting and consisted of arranging the exodus of some 250,000 German troops. There was plenty of time for liaison in the evenings, with companies changing their locations several times and most spending a period in Copenhagen. However, after two months well-earned rest, the Battalion was warned for service as a reconnaissance unit in the Far East where the War with Japan continued. It was made up to full strength, with Lieutenant-Colonel E.G. Northey assuming command as the Battalion returned to England at the end of July for a spell of pre-embarkation leave.

On 15 August 1945, while the Battalion was on leave, the war with Japan ended and its tour in the Far East was cancelled. Instead, it was redirected to Libya where it arrived at Tripoli at the end of October. A week later, on 4 November, the Arabs in the Old City unexpectedly rose and attacked, not their old masters, the Italians, but the Jews with whom they had lived in peace for 500 years. Unfortunately the Battalion was called out too late to avert an appalling massacre of 124 unarmed Jews, mostly women and children. A period of 'keeping the peace' followed, interspersed with recreation and training.

8th Battalion

After preparing to participate in the invasion of Normandy, the 8th Battalion was not required but used to provide battle casualty replacements for others. Under command of Lieutenant-Colonel W. Heathcoat-Amory, a former commanding officer of the 2nd Battalion, it became a holding and training battalion for drafts destined for Green

Jacket battalions in North-West Europe, and for rehabilitating and retraining wounded Riflemen. It continued to perform this role until the end of the War, before demobilizing in autumn 1945.

10th Battalion

Having assumed the role of the Regiment's motor training battalion in 1943, the 10th Battalion ceased the task at the end of 1945 and demobilized.

11th Battalion – Greece, 1945–6

Following the nasty street-fighting and casualties suffered by the 11th Battalion during the failed coup attempt by the Greek Communists in December 1944 (see page 178), the period after the War, although quieter, was not devoid of incident as the weak coalition government sought to suppress opposition. Fortunately the Battalion was largely able to stand back from such matters, retaining cordial relations with the Greek National Guard, for which it provided training assistance. It was also able to move around the country relatively freely, keeping an ear to the ground in an effort to pre-empt trouble. Later in 1945, as Communist régimes took root on Greece's northern border, the British deployed to the area to ensure that the Country's territorial integrity was maintained while the Greek National Guard was properly established. Companies of the Battalion carried out patrols in the same area near the Florina Gap where the 9th Battalion had defended so gallantly in 1941, and in similarly cold weather.

On 31 March 1946 elections were held which passed off peacefully. Meanwhile, the Battalion was suffering from a loss of manpower as men departed on demobilisation, making it difficult to fulfil the unremitting round of guards and duties. In June, Lieutenant-Colonel D.R.C. Boileau, who had been captured in 1941 when in command of the 9th Battalion on Crete, became commanding officer. On 1 September 1946 the Battalion performed its last duty, standing by in case of trouble during the plebiscite when the Greek people voted for the return of the King. In October it was placed in suspended animation and its manpower dispersed.

12th Battalion – Germany, 1945

After concluding its advance through North-West Europe near Bremen, the 12th Battalion became locked into the duties of an army of occupation, soon to be known as the British Army of the Rhine (BAOR). It moved to Hanover where patrols were mounted to ensure observance of the night curfew and to arrest German troops who had evaded capture. There were also prison camps, factories and other vulnerable points to guard. In July the Battalion started to lose men on demobilization. The Battalion, however, was never destined to remain in the Army's post-War order of battle and in January 1946 its active service ceased and it was disbanded.

TA Battalions

In July 1947, as part of the wider post-War reorganization of the Army, the TA was re-formed. The three TA regiments, whose six battalions provided such valuable service during the War, reverted to the position in which they were before 1939, each fielding a single battalion. The history of these regiments is covered at Appendix D.

Palestine, 1946–8

In mid-1946 the Battalion was warned for service in Palestine as the only motor battalion in the Middle East. Travelling in October from Libya to Egypt to collect its vehicles and equipment, it departed for Palestine at the end of November. On its previous tour in 1936/7:

> *...the task had usually consisted of trying to prevent Arabs raiding the Jewish settlements. Now the Jewish population was constantly rising, many being illegal immigrants from Europe, whose treatment under Hitler had convinced them that never again would passive resistance be enough. Terrorist organisations, such as the Stern Gang and the Irgun Zvei Leumi (IZL), sought by many hostile actions, usually against the British, to impose their policies on the Administration. These actions included kidnapping, whipping, stealing arms, ammunition and military stores, mining roads and railways, and murder. The British task was difficult and onerous.*[1]

The Battalion was initially based near Tel Aviv where, in January 1947, Lieutenant-Colonel C.H. Gurney assumed command. From 1–17 March, in response to increased terrorist outrages, it took part in a major operation to cordon off Tel Aviv from the rest of Palestine, giving rise to some casualties from grenades. The spring and summer were then spent in necessary but unspectacular tasks, including protection of a 7-mile stretch of the Haifa–Cairo railway. In August there was a move to another camp thirty miles south of Tel Aviv where duties were lighter and there was time to train. This was followed in October by a move to El Bureij, six miles south of Gaza. In December, after a 2-month interregnum under Lieutenant-Colonel C.T. Mitford-Slade, former commanding officer of the 8th Battalion, command passed to Lieutenant-Colonel J.L. Corbett-Winder, a previous commanding officer of the 1st Battalion.

The Gaza area was predominantly Arab with scattered Jewish settlements, in which the key task was to maintain law and order. However, on 29 November 1947, the United Nations, to whom the

British Government had said that it would hand over its Mandate on 15 May 1948, announced that it intended to partition Palestine into an Arab and a Jewish state. This immediately prompted the stoning of Battalion vehicles, attacks on Riflemen and theft of weapons. It also soon prompted Arab attacks on Jews. By February 1948 British troops had started to thin out, leaving the Battalion, trying hard to remain impartial, responsible for the whole of Palestine south of the Gaza-Beersheba road. This area, through which the British would have to withdraw to the Canal Zone, had to be held to the last if the lines of communication were to be kept open.

The final days in Palestine were marked by numerous incidents and plenty of examples of junior commanders displaying considerable courage and initiative to prevent difficult situations becoming worse, with them sometimes threatening to open fire and sometimes having to do so. On 15 May 1948, as the evacuation was underway, an additional dimension was added when an Egyptian Air Force Spitfire attacked the 2nd Battalion's camp with bombs and machine gun fire, killing two Riflemen. In all other respects the evacuation was accomplished successfully, leading the commander in the area to comment that: 'It required a Regiment of great worth to carry out a task which had previously taxed the resources of a brigade. That the Regiment should have carried out this mission for nearly three months in the face of overwhelming difficulties with complete success was a measure of your quality.'[2]

2nd Battalion road block, Palestine, 1947

On reaching Egypt on 16 May, the reorganization of the Infantry ordered during the previous year took effect, as the Battalion began the process of dispersing its members and preparing for disbandment. After handing in its vehicles and equipment, 300 men returned to England in June. On 11 September 1948 the 2nd Battalion was placed in suspended animation.

The Training Organization, 1945–50

In November 1945 the Regiment's training organization, which had been centred at York since the autumn of 1942, returned to the south of England, with the functions of 27 Primary Training Centre divided. A new unit, 27 Green Jackets Holding Battalion, was temporarily established at Ogbourne St George, near Chiseldon, Wiltshire, to deal with the large number of holdees of both Green Jacket regiments, while recruit training resumed at Winchester. Towards the end of 1946 the function was re-absorbed by the re-titled 27 Infantry, later Green Jackets, Training Centre, with training companies at Bushfield and holding companies at the Rifle Depot. Pressure on accommodation then led to recruit training being moved to Barton Stacey, where, in February 1948, the 1st Battalion arrived to take over the Training Centre's role, which, in October 1948, reverted to Bushfield.

Although recruit training seemed a dreary task to give to a battalion with an outstanding fighting record, it was to stand the Regiment in good stead in the future. It was also a task well done under the guiding hand of Lieutenant-Colonel C.T. Mitford-Slade, with Captain E.N.W. Bramall in charge of the OCTU Platoon, which had replaced the Green Jacket OCTU formerly at York. Recreation, sport and rifle shooting all took on a new lease of life as the Battalion found that it had time to pursue activities, which the War had curtailed.

Elsewhere in the world dark clouds were forming. To quote from the *Annals*: 'In Summer 1950 the communist invasion of South Korea finally persuaded all but the most naïve admirers of our former Soviet ally that nothing except the nuclear deterrent was keeping them out of Western Europe. With the rise of the North Atlantic Organisation (NATO), so our commitments built up; the threat was from Soviet armour, so British armoured divisions were called for in BAOR, and they in turn would need motor battalions.'[3] Thus, after an interval of three years, expansion followed contraction, when it was announced that the 1st and 2nd Battalion would re-form as motor battalions, the 1st in BAOR and the 2nd in England.

To enable this to happen, the 1st Battalion handed over the task of recruit training to The Rifle Depot, which, in 1951, was re-titled The Green Jackets Depot, commanded by Colonel D.R.C. Boileau, the former commanding officer of the 11th Battalion. The permanent staff became fully integrated, drawing upon the resources of both Green Jacket regiments.

On 10 January 1951 the 1st Battalion marched through Winchester on its way to Germany. Before it departed, on 3 November 1950, King George VI, the Regiment's Colonel-in-Chief, visited the Regiment at Winchester, inspecting the Battalion at Bushfield and lunching at the Depot.

England and Germany, 1951–7

The 1st Battalion, commanded by Lieutenant-Colonel K.H. Collen, was stationed at Dempsey Barracks, Sennelager, as a part of 33 Armoured Brigade in the 11th Armoured Division. Its arrival coincided with the start of the annual training cycle for which BAOR is best remembered, commencing with individual training at the beginning of the year and ending with large-scale manoeuvres in the autumn. It soon became a desperate race to draw up half-tracks, carriers, wirelesses and other equipment, and to run cadres to train all the specialists before the exercise season began.

Other commitments were added to complicate; indeed, all it needed was 'a ruthless and over-ambitious Commanding Officer to make a nightmare of the "Rhine Army" rat race. Fortunately, our successive Commanding Officers, in true Rifle style, protected their battalions and saw that there was always some light-hearted venture afoot in which kindred spirits could join. Although the continual training and replacement of young National Service officers and Riflemen placed a heavy burden on Regulars, ... the reward was the stimulating and irreverent company of a splendid section of the nation's youth.'[4]

As soon as the 1st Battalion was up and running, priority switched to re-forming the 2nd, which the authorities decreed should be manned by individuals from both Green Jacket regiments, but bear the title of The King's Royal Rifle Corps. Thus, the commanding officer, Lieutenant-Colonel the Hon. M.F. Douglas-Pennant, was 60th, while his Adjutant was from The Rifle Brigade. By 1 March 1951 they had gathered a sufficient nucleus around them at the Depot to put in place the necessary plans for the Battalion to occupy Assaye Barracks, Tidworth, and to be operational by October. It was a tall order. However, after much hard work and training, the objective was met, with the Battalion successfully participating with 6th Armoured Division in the last large-scale manoeuvres to be held in England, other than on training areas.

In March 1952 the Battalion moved to Germany and to Oxford Barracks, Münster, where it was soon swept up in the same pattern of events as the 1st at Sennelager. Oxford Barracks was a former Luftwaffe barracks, nicely planted with trees and well laid out, while Dempsey Barracks dated from the Kaiser's time, with iron rings on the walls for the horses. Both battalions were on the old establishment of scout and motor platoons, without medium machine guns or anti-tank guns, an arrangement that gave little cause for comfort in the light of the perceived Soviet armoured threat.

1st Battalion carriers and half-tracks at Sennelager, Germany, 1952

A motor platoon on exercise in Germany, 1952

During the 1950s the Cold War between East and West, accentuated by the conflict in Korea, was at its height, with much time and effort devoted to study of the nuclear and conventional threat posed by the Soviet Union, and how best to deal with it; indeed, assessment of the threat and preparing a response to it was the dominant feature of service in BAOR at the time. The real fear that Soviet forces might cross

2nd Battalion Riflemen by a US Army 280mm howitzer
capable of firing atomic munitions, Germany, 1954

the Inner German Border at any time permeated daily life, on and off duty, with the battalions constantly called upon to practise their alarm schemes, including the rapid call-out of personnel and the loading of vehicles and equipment. While some might, quite understandably, have doubted the extent of the Army's preparedness and their chances of survival in a nuclear environment, many found the repetitive nature of the training cycle tedious. The constant turnover of National Servicemen was also wearing on the Regulars. It required considerable leadership on the part of commanders at every level to ensure standards did not slip. In October 1953 Lieutenant-Colonel R.F.L. Chance assumed command of the 1st Battalion and Lieutenant-Colonel E.A.W. Williams assumed command of the 2nd, the latter being replaced by Lieutenant-Colonel J.F.C. Mellor in October 1955.

But it was not all work and no play. While in Germany, both battalions continued the Regimental tradition of excelling at rifle shooting. In 1951 the 1st Battalion won the KRRC Cup, the major units championship at Bisley, an achievement repeated in 1952. In 1956 the 2nd won the Queen Victoria Trophy, the equivalent non-central championship, for the third year running. Many other individual and team shooting trophies were won.

Sport, too, played a prominent part in the lives of the battalions. Success at Army level was not easy to achieve, with some regiments and corps packing their teams with National Servicemen recruited for no reason other than their excellence at a particular sport. Thus, no infantry battalion since the War had won the Army inter-unit boxing championship until the 2nd Battalion managed it in 1956, with Rifleman Maynard going on to become the Army bantamweight champion. Other notable successes at Army level were achieved on the racquets court and the ski slopes, while at BAOR level the 2nd Battalion won the inter-unit cricket, boxing and golf championships.

The early 1950s were also marked by sadness and celebration. In 1952 the Regiment's Colonel-in-Chief, King George VI, died, with members of the Regiment included in the funeral cortège and lining the streets. In 1953, Coronation Year, Queen Elizabeth II consented to assume her father's place as Colonel-in-Chief, with the Regiment well represented during the procession on Coronation Day. On the same day the momentous news was received of the ascent of Everest by a team led by the former commanding officer of the 11th Battalion, Brigadier H.C.J. (John) Hunt.[5]

On 25 July 1955, on what was a glorious summer day, the Regiment celebrated its Bicentenary at Winchester in the presence of its new Colonel-in-Chief, whose Private Secretary, Lieutenant-Colonel the Rt. Hon. Sir Martin (later Lord) Charteris, was second-in-command of the 11th Battalion in Greece. At the same time, Lieutenant-Colonel Sir Martin Gilliat, a former company commander in the 2nd Battalion, was Private Secretary to Her Majesty Queen Elizabeth, The Queen Mother.

Meanwhile, in BAOR, '1955 was the year that mixed battle groups of armoured squadrons and lorried infantry companies began to appear, and some of the rest of the Army began to realise what the Green Jackets had long known – that only a motor battalion or something like it could hope to survive alongside the efficient Centurions [tanks] in an adverse air, armoured and artillery situation.'[6] It was, therefore, extremely galling for the 2nd Battalion, which was more experienced than most in such matters, when it was announced in the same year that it was to be disbanded for the second time in a decade. After spending a final year in Germany, the Battalion returned in October 1956 to Assaye Barracks, Tidworth, where its disbandment was postponed pending a resolution of the Suez crisis. Once that had occurred, the earlier decision was endorsed. On 31 December 1957, less than six years after its re-formation, the Battalion exited the Army's order of battle for the last time on a sad but appropriately high note, crowning all former glories by again winning the KRRC Cup at Bisley.

North Africa, 1955–8

By the time the 2nd Battalion left Germany, the 1st had already been gone a year. Departing from BAOR in June 1955, it stopped over briefly at Tidworth to take part in the Bicentenary celebrations at Winchester in July, before moving to Derna, a small seaside town in Libya, in September. It was not an ideal posting, especially for the Riflemen, with the Battalion split between two barracks either side of the town, which had poor facilities and were only made bearable through improvisation and the ingenuity of all ranks. Derna was also a long way from anywhere, with few attractions in town, although the weather, the sea and, for some, the desert, provided a degree of compensation.

The 1st Battalion's role, besides that of motor infantry, was 'fire brigade' battalion in 10th Armoured Division, whose area of operations stretched from the Persian Gulf to the western end of the Mediterranean. Very soon after arrival, C Company, commanded by Major N.J. Warry, was despatched 2,000 miles to Sharjah (now part of the United Arab Emirates), where efforts were being made to dissuade the Saudi Arabian Government from occupying the potentially oil-rich Buraimi Oasis. By the time the Company arrived, the worst was over. Nevertheless, it remained in place until relieved in January 1956 by D Company, commanded by Major R.C. Gibbs,[7] a future Chief of the General Staff. In March, the Company moved at one hour's notice to Bahrain where it was required to support the police in quelling political demonstrations and where A Company joined it. Both companies were back at Derna by June.

In July 1956 President Nasser nationalized the Suez Canal, with the Battalion, reinforced by the arrival of 300 Regular reservists, held at 24 hours notice to move for many months. By the time the allied invasion of Suez took place in November, anti-British feeling was running high, with the Officers Mess and some vehicles damaged by bombing and stoning. D Company was despatched to Tobruk to keep the peace. The Battalion, however, was not used during the invasion as it was considered politically unacceptable to deploy from Libya into Egypt. The reservists returned to the United Kingdom, some openly expressing a sense of grievance that their time had been wasted. Meanwhile, in September, Lieutenant-Colonel H.A. Hope assumed command.

In 1957 it was announced that 10th Armoured Division would be disbanded and that the Battalion would cease to be a motor battalion. In October it moved to Gialo Barracks, Tripoli, which the 2nd Battalion had occupied in 1945. The last months in Derna had been marked by a number of exercises and expeditions, including to the Kufra Oasis in the Sahara.

The Battalion spent just over a year in Tripoli, training, exercising, shooting and, during one 6-week period, conducting a trial during which sufficient Land Rovers and trailers were issued for the whole battalion to be mobile. However, just as the final 200-mile sortie into the desert to prove the concept was about to take place, on 14 July 1958 King Faisal of Iraq was assassinated and all the vehicles were hurriedly withdrawn as British garrisons all over the Middle East moved on to high alert. Meanwhile, the general lack of facilities and the isolation were having their impact and it proved difficult to persuade the Regulars to prolong their service. The Battalion suffered from acute under-manning and required time in England to make up its numbers. Instead, it was sent to Ballykinler in Northern Ireland.

Formation of the Green Jackets Brigade, 1958

On 6 November 1958 a parade was held at the Depot at Winchester to mark the inauguration of the Green Jackets Brigade, an administrative grouping of the two Rifle regiments, The King's Royal Rifle Corps and The Rifle Brigade, with The Oxfordshire and Buckinghamshire Light Infantry (43rd and 52nd). Whilst mergers and amalgamations in the British Army normally generate more heat than light, this was a natural union born out of the regiments' close association with each other on numerous battlefields, including Quebec in 1759, and in Sir John Moore's Light Brigade (Division) during the Peninsular War.

Regimental titles proclaimed the unity of the Brigade, the 1st Battalion becoming 2nd Green Jackets, The King's Royal Rifle Corps. The new cap badge, a silver Maltese cross within a wreath under the crown and the Battle Honour 'Peninsula' common to all the regiments, was not unlike the 60th cross-belt badge worn when it was The Duke of York's Rifle Corps. All wore a 'Green Jacket' shoulder flash in battle dress. Drill with the new 7.62 mm self-loading rifle was standardized. While some idiosyncratic customs and dress distinctions persisted, they were of little matter when measured against the sum of the whole. Sharing, exchange and learning from each other, to which the 60th and The Rifle Brigade had been accustomed for many years, was extended to the 43rd and 52nd, and soon became commonplace. On 1 January 1959 The Green Jackets Depot was renamed The Green Jackets Brigade Depot. The scene was set for what was logically to follow on 1 January 1966 when the three regiments merged to become The Royal Green Jackets.

Northern Ireland, 1959–60

On leaving Tripoli at the end of 1958, the 1st Battalion staged over Christmas and the New Year at a freezing hutted camp at Piddlehinton in Dorset before moving on to Abercorn Barracks, Ballykinler, in January 1959. Lieutenant-Colonel T.H. Acton (Rifle Brigade),[8] the new commanding officer, then set about the task of rebuilding it as a Regular battalion. Although 50% of the Riflemen were still National Servicemen, conscription was coming to an end. There were no more than two corporals in a rifle company. The first step, therefore, was to establish a strong complement of well-qualified junior NCOs. Additional priorities were to achieve high standards of training at individual, platoon and company level, and better amenities for the Riflemen and the increasing number of families that accompanied them. The security situation in Ulster at the time also meant that the Battalion was faced with a heavy toll of guards and duties, with a company on call at short notice to deploy to wherever it might be needed.

During 1959 the Battalion was equipped with the self-loading rifle (SLR) and in the following year carried out trials on the General Purpose Machine Gun (GPMG), which later replaced the Bren light machine gun and the Vickers medium machine gun. Meanwhile the .303 Bren was converted to the same calibre as the 7.62 mm SLR. New green shower-proof combat clothing was issued together with 1958 pattern webbing equipment. For the first time the Battalion had the opportunity to use helicopters during training. The proximity of good ranges meant that the Battalion was able to continue its focus on rifle shooting, finishing runner-up for the KRRC Cup in 1959 and 1960. Sport, too, had its place, with a number of individuals excelling at athletics, hockey and boxing, including Rifleman Webster who represented the Army at featherweight. Extra-mural activities, such as go-karting, water-skiing, golf, fishing and field sports, provided further opportunity for those with a will to take advantage of the opportunities on offer.

Much was achieved at Ballykinler. The Battalion was happy and more efficient, thanks to greater continuity and less equipment, than for some time. A move from the bracing air on the east coast of Northern Ireland to the claustrophobic environment of Berlin beckoned.

Berlin, 1960–2

Berlin was on the front-line of the Cold War, with the nuclear and conventional threat posed by the Soviet Union, and feared by the West, magnified in the minds of those living there by the proximity to the city of Soviet and Warsaw Pact forces. Following agreement at Potsdam in 1945, it was divided into four sectors, the Soviet zone being in East Berlin, while in West Berlin, the French were in the north, the British in the centre and the Americans in the south. Although the access routes into West Berlin by air, road and rail through Soviet-controlled East Germany were guaranteed by treaty, concern that the Soviet Union might close them, and that West Berlin would be isolated from the rest of the free world, greatly heightened the sense of insecurity and vulnerability felt by its citizens. The Garrison, therefore, was kept at a high state of readiness to counter any Soviet surprises, with the movement of troops out of West Berlin, on or off duty, strictly controlled to ensure that numbers did not drop below required levels. Alarm schemes had to be constantly honed and practised, often under the eagle eye of senior commanders and staff. Laxity, too, was frowned upon in a situation where Guardsmen predominated among the senior ranks. Standards of dress, drill and discipline had to be impeccable if black marks were to be avoided. The need to get the Battalion off to a good start was imperative. The appearance of the Brigadier and a posse of Royal Military Police awaiting the Battalion on its arrival at Charlottenburg Station did not augur well.

The Battalion's move to Berlin in December 1960 was its last before the introduction of air trooping and took 36 hours, by bus, boat and train. The commanding officer had conducted a preliminary reconnaissance and knew what was in store. His aim was to strike a balance between the demands of the chain of command and the need

Wiring off the Soviet War Memorial, Berlin, August 1961

Brandenburg Gate, Berlin, 1961

to give free rein to the natural exuberance, spirit and wit of the Riflemen. This was successfully achieved, although not without its moments. Grudgingly, those accustomed to looking for fault proffered praise as the Battalion maximized the limited opportunities for training in the Grünewald; continued to demonstrate its skill on the range, winning the KRRC Cup in 1961; and stole the show with its marching and music at the annual Queen's Birthday Parades. Even duties, such as those guarding the three Nazis, Hess, Speer and Schirach, at Spandau Prison, were performed to a standard above that by which Riflemen are generally judged. Trouble, however, never lurked far away, especially in the nightclubs and bars of Berlin, and it required constant alertness and much effort to ensure that good order was maintained.

In March 1961 Lieutenant-Colonel J.H.P. Curtis assumed command. He brought with him fresh tactical thinking which he soon set out to inculcate within the Battalion, which at this point had a headquarter company, three rifle companies and a support company, the last with an anti-tank platoon (120 mm Mobat recoilless guns), a mortar platoon and a reconnaissance and assault pioneer platoon. During the year a support platoon of a section of anti-tank guns and a section of mortars was posted to each rifle company. The Battalion also received a new range of Larkspur combat radio sets, enabling vehicle and man-pack sets to operate on the same net and with improved range. Whenever opportunity arose, small groups of officers and Riflemen disappeared into West Germany and beyond to undertake adventurous training.

The Berlin Crisis, August to November 1961

By 1961 the Soviet and East German authorities had become extremely concerned about the flood of refugees escaping into West Berlin from the east. They decided to stop it. On Saturday, 12 August 1961, Soviet forces supported by troops from East Germany surrounded Berlin, ringing West Berlin with single coils of wire. The move was unexpected and it was not until 16 August that the Battalion was instructed to wire off the Soviet War Memorial just west of the Brandenburg Gate, using the pretext that it was necessary to protect the Soviet Guard from the enraged actions of the Berliners. Border patrols along the boundaries of the British sector were initiated and observation posts manned, including one at the top of the old Reichstag building. Gradually the situation calmed as politicians sought to resolve matters, with the infamous Berlin Wall being built in November.

In March 1962 the Battalion was the first to leave Berlin after the Wall was erected to take part in a period of field firing on the ranges at Sennelager, near Paderborn. By now, too, it knew of its next posting. To summarize from the *Annals*: 'The period in Berlin had been useful to the Battalion. It had learnt to hold its own in a Brigade, exposed to the glare of publicity, and it had developed a professional attention to detail at all levels, which had not been a pronounced characteristic during the rapid turnover of the National Service period. ... The Battalion [however] was not sorry to leave, this time by air, for Colchester in the first week of July 1962.'[9]

Colchester (1), 1962–3

On arrival at Roman Barracks, Colchester, the Battalion became an airportable battalion in 19 Brigade, a part of the Army's Strategic Reserve held at varying degrees of notice for service abroad. It was equipped with Land Rovers and trailers to enable carriage in long-range RAF transport planes. To be ready for this, air movement regulations had to be carefully studied and detailed loading plans prepared. A fleet of 3-ton trucks was held in case the Battalion was required to fulfil its alternative NATO reinforcement role.

Roman Barracks was brand new, with good living accommodation, but lacking critical storage and garage space. The Battalion, however, had over 600 Regulars for the first time since 1939, and a busy programme lay ahead. Within weeks it was on exercise at Otterburn in Northumberland and on return immediately started preparing for Exercise Sandstorm in Libya, to which the Battalion flew in January 1963, practising its loading and emplacement drills on the way.

Training in the desert was a new experience for most of the younger members of the Battalion, who quickly had to learn the skills at which their predecessors had excelled during previous tours of duty in North Africa. They were also subject to enormous variations in weather conditions and temperature. The exercises were well planned and rewarding, with opportunity for adventurous training and relaxation by the Mediterranean. On return to England in March, Lieutenant-Colonel G.H. Mills assumed command.[10]

With many soldiers now enlisting on 6 and 9-year engagements, the new commanding officer was determined to provide all young officers, NCOs and Riflemen with progressive rather than repetitive training, which, from a broad base, increasingly focused on developing their professional and specialist skills, and encouraging them to pursue a full career in the Army. All sorts of expedients were put in place to ensure that this happened. The Battalion also carried out its first spell on the Strategic Reserve 'Spearhead' roster with the leading company at 24 hours notice to fly overseas, and the rest at 72 hours. Time spent in preparing for Spearhead was soon to be regarded as time well spent, because in July 1963 the Battalion was ordered back on to the roster at short notice and, after much uncertainty, despatched on what was later to turn into a 6-month emergency tour of duty in British Guiana. Fortunately, the last instructions of the commanding officer before departure were to leave the shooting team at Bisley, where the coveted KRRC Cup was won.

Lieutenant C.J.P. Miers briefing a patrol in British Guiana, 1963

British Guiana, 1963

The problem in British Guiana, a British colony on the north-east coast of tropical South America, was inter-communal. For years the Africans had dominated, but the Indian population was now in the majority, with both sides voting on racial lines. Feeling threatened by the policies of the Indian-led government under Mr Cheddi Jagan, the Prime Minister, the African opposition, under their leader, Mr Forbes Burnham, fomented a general strike. Violence erupted, which was beyond the capacity of the police and the single resident battalion – 1st Battalion, Coldstream Guards – to handle. The Prime Minister asked the Governor, Sir Ralph Grey, for help. By the time the Battalion arrived, the general strike had already lasted eleven weeks.

The leading company, D Company, under Major R.K. Guy,[11] a future Adjutant General, arrived on 5 July and was immediately despatched to patrol a troublesome district east of the capital, Georgetown, in a temperature of 90° Fahrenheit and about 95% humidity. Swords (bayonets) were fixed because, although both communities were mainly friendly towards the British, no one wanted to risk being carved up by a long razor-sharp machete used for cane cutting, should its owner decide to resist arrest. The despatch of the Battalion, however, quickly served its purpose. Within 48 hours the African opposition party, realizing that the British Government meant business, ended the strike. The situation, however, was expected to remain volatile for some time as tempers cooled, and so the Battalion was ordered to remain for six months.

For the first two months the Battalion occupied a number of platoon and company bases on sugar estates and in Georgetown, in order to prevent a recurrence of violence. In early September it handed over these bases to the 1st Battalion, Grenadier Guards, which had relieved the 1st Battalion, Coldstream Guards, and concentrated at the Country's main airport, Atkinson Field. Good use was then made of the remaining time in the Country to train, exercise and to despatch expeditions into the hinterland, before returning to Colchester in January 1964.

Colchester (2), 1964

Before the Battalion left British Guiana warning was received of its next posting to Penang, Malaysia, in early 1965. Planning began, although a further year of exercises and training in England and abroad lay ahead. In March 1964 the Battalion was unexpectedly committed to the Allied Mobile Force (Land), a formation with a role on the flanks of NATO. Three months later it flew to Bardufoss, 70 miles north of Narvik in Norway and within the Arctic Circle, to take part in an AMF(L) exercise alongside Norwegian, Italian and Belgian troops. It was a challenging exercise and a good test of fitness in mountainous terrain with plenty of variety to create interest. It also marked the beginning and the end of the Battalion's training with the AMF(L) as an exercise in Turkey later in the year was cancelled.

1964 was a vintage year at Bisley. The shooting team not only won the KRRC Cup for the last time in the Regiment's history, but Sergeant R.V. Smith won the Queen's Medal as Army Champion. Victory was also achieved in the Army Racquets Inter-Regimental Doubles Championships and the Army Squash Championships.

Sergeant R.V. Smith, Winner, Queen's Medal, Bisley, 1964

Captain P.M. Welsh, Runner-up, Queen's Medal, Bisley, 1957 and 1962

In the autumn the Battalion participated in a 19 Brigade exercise on Salisbury Plain and at Otterburn and Stanford training areas. The Battalion's focus, however, was rapidly shifting towards preparation for its forthcoming tour in Malaysia. On 20 November 1964 the advance party departed, with the main body following in January.

Malaysia, 1965

On arrival at Minden Barracks, Penang, command of the Battalion passed to Lieutenant-Colonel E.N.W. Bramall,[12] a future Chief of the General Staff and Chief of the Defence Staff. A smooth handover took place with 1st Green Jackets, 43rd and 52nd, commanded by Lieutenant-Colonel D.G. House (60th).[13]

The island of Penang lies five miles off the west coast of the Malay Peninsula and sixty miles south of the border with Thailand. The barracks, on the side of a hill, were spacious and airy, and a relatively short distance from Georgetown, the main centre of population. The inhabitants were friendly, the recreation facilities were good and there were very pleasant sandy beaches on the north coast.

A few weeks after arrival the company officers and NCOs, who had been training at the Jungle Warfare School in Johore since early January, rejoined. An intense period of jungle training then started in preparation for a four and a half month operational tour in Borneo, which began at the end of April.

Borneo, 1965

The Battalion was deployed in the 1st Division of Sarawak, a former British-administered territory adjoining Sabah (formerly North Borneo). The two territories together constituted East Malaysia. The independent Sultanate of Brunei, previously a British protectorate, lay in the middle.

British and Commonwealth forces were despatched to East Malaysia at the request of the Malaysian Government. The threats were both internal and external. The creation of the newly-independent state of Malaysia in 1963 had not been universally welcomed, especially by the Chinese, some of whom, it was assessed, might try to initiate a communist insurrection similar to the Malayan emergency in the 1950s. Indonesia, whose territory in Kalimantan bordered East Malaysia, provided the external threat, laying claim to Sarawak and Sabah and deploying forces along the border in a manner considered to be confrontational; hence the expression 'Indonesian Confrontation' used to describe the campaign.

The Battalion was structured with a headquarter company and three rifle companies, each with a 81 mm mortar section, and a support company with an assault pioneer and a tracker/reconnaissance platoon. Anti-tank guns were not deployed. Additionally, there was an Air Platoon,

Forward patrol base, Borneo, 1965

Patrol preparing to leave its base

On patrol, Borneo, 1965

Lieutenant C.B.Q. Wallace with the Village Headman of Kampong Tringgus

209

known as 'Rifle Green Airways', with two 3-seat Sioux helicopters, *Celer* and *Audax*, piloted by regimental officers. A rear party remained in Penang to care for the families.

The Battalion's area of operations covered a frontage of 20 miles, and in depth stretched to the coastline in the north and, in particular, to Kuching, the capital of Sarawak, which was only 25 miles from the border. Companies and platoons were deployed either in strongly-fortified forward bases close to border villages or held in reserve at Semengo Camp, 7 miles south of Kuching, close to the airport. 105 mm pack howitzers manned by the Royal Artillery and 81 mm mortars were distributed either singly or in pairs to the forward bases.

The primary task of the Battalion was 'to deter, by active patrolling, any would be [Indonesian] infiltration across the border and, should this fail, to get the maximum information of the enemy's movements so that he could be cut off and destroyed by helicopter-borne reserves.'[14]

Although at the strategic level British and Commonwealth forces were engaged defensively, at the tactical level the Battalion very soon wrested the initiative from the Indonesians, patrolling aggressively across the border, interdicting their movement and attacking their camps. This involved a great deal of 'jungle bashing' in hostile, hilly terrain, criss-crossed by water courses, where the only reliable means of navigation were by compass and grid-lined air photograph, since ordnance survey mapping did not extend to the border areas. Royal Navy and RAF helicopters provided some mobility but not if their use prejudiced surprise. Stealth and the indirect approach, as practised by Bouquet and his Royal Americans 200 years previously in forests not too dissimilar to those in Sarawak, were the preferred ways. Great emphasis was also placed on winning the 'hearts and minds' of the Iban tribesmen living in the border areas, since they might otherwise have been susceptible to Indonesian or terrorist influence.

This Brief History does not provide space for a detailed account of the Battalion's actions, which are admirably covered in the *Annals*, with descriptions of a number of operations mounted against the Indonesians and, on one significant occasion, to suppress the activities of communist terrorists in the bazaars near Kuching. Reflecting at the end of the tour, the commanding officer modestly stated that it was a 'very satisfactory campaign'. In fact it was more than that; it was extremely successful, for as he reflected in a post-tour report:

There was a clear-cut and worthy aim, for we were helping friends who had asked for help. The physical challenges were tough and demanding, and the successful surmounting of them correspondingly rewarding. There was plenty of opportunity for young men to prove their nerve and endurance in contact with a tough and brave enemy, and there was considerable scope for initiative and intelligence as well. There were short moments of high excitement, and even when there were no contacts the business of patrolling and living in forward bases was never dull. Above all, although the risks and hazards were real enough, not too many soldiers got hurt, and fewer still lost their lives.[15]

By the end of the tour, the Battalion had killed forty-four Indonesians and wounded many more for the loss of one Rifleman killed and three wounded. Two Military Crosses were awarded. In September the Battalion returned to Penang, knowing that it was shortly to take on a new identity and that its next tour was due to start in Sabah in January.

Transition to Royal Green Jackets

The Battalion was first told on 28 May 1965 that the three regiments in The Green Jackets Brigade would merge into one large regiment on 1 January 1966. While the announcement elicited some sadness, it can hardly have come as a total surprise. The three regiments, after all, were already titled Green Jackets and were functioning corporately to good effect. Old regimental titles were also to be retained in brackets after the new, albeit as it turned out only temporarily, thus taking some of the sting out of the tail which the immediate loss of regimental identity might have engendered.

Thus, after a period of leave and training on return from Borneo, the Battalion paraded at Minden Barracks during the evening of 31 December 1965 to listen to the Band and Bugles sound Retreat. At the end of the performance the commanding officer delivered an inspiring speech with words that speak for themselves and bring this Brief History to a fitting close.

In five hours time as we enter 1966 our Regiment, the 2nd Green Jackets, The King's Royal Rifle Corps, which has been in existence for 210 years, will cease to exist as a separate regiment of the British Army and instead we will become the 2nd Battalion of a new and larger regiment, The Royal Green Jackets, whose Colonel-in-Chief will be Her Majesty The Queen.

In this life, if you are sensible and particularly if you are young, you look forward and not back; and indeed it is the tradition of Riflemen that they are progressive and move with the times. But we would not be human if we did not feel very considerable sadness at the passing of a regiment with such a proud and wonderful history, and one in which so many of us have had such splendid times and such great comradeship, some, for close on a quarter of a century. The name of The King's Royal Rifle Corps, the 60th Rifles as it has often been known, the K.R.R.'s, as it has sometimes affectionately been called, will always have a very special place in our hearts and that is exactly as it should be.

Field Marshal Lord Bramall
KG GCB OBE MC

*Field Marshal Lord Bramall, the last commanding officer of The King's
Royal Rifle Corps. Painting by, and courtesy of, June Mendoza.*

Lord Bramall was commissioned into the Regiment in 1943 and served in
Normandy and North-West Europe in 1944-5, being awarded a Military
Cross for his actions. After numerous appointments at a senior level, he
was Chief of the General Staff (1979-82) and the only member of The
King's Royal Rifle Corps ever to have been Chief of the Defence
Staff (1982-5). He was created a Life Peer in 1987 and became a Knight
of the Garter in 1990.

Lord Bramall's ideas on leadership, encapsulated in a pamphlet entitled
Leadership the Green Jacket Way (1966), published while he was in
command of the 2nd Battalion, The Royal Green Jackets (The King's
Royal Rifle Corps), have since provided enduring guidance and direction
to Green Jackets and a legacy equivalent in kind to that left in their time
by Bouquet and de Rottenburg. Long regarded as the 'Godfather of the
Regiment', Lord Bramall's total commitment to The King's Royal Rifle
Corps and its well-being during his 43 years of military service, and
subsequently, have been, and continue to be, hugely appreciated and an
absolute inspiration and example to others.

However, I want you all to appreciate this, that, although the name will go, the spirit and the ideals which made the Regiment what it was - the fighting qualities, the pride in professional skill, the intelligent and humane discipline, the sympathy and understanding between all ranks, and the concern for the individual, for his welfare and for those of his dependants, all these will remain and will be equally conspicuous in the new Regiment as they were in the old.

The motto 'Swift and Bold' given to us by General Wolfe at the battle of Quebec must and will continue to apply, and those who serve in the new Regiment can still expect things to happen, whether it be operational or other business, in an intelligent, efficient yet economical and, I hope, unpompous way. You can rest assured that The Royal Green Jackets will continue to enjoy the same extremely high reputation that The King's Royal Rifle Corps always had in the eyes of the Army, and quite honestly one cannot say better than that.

So, as the Regimental flag comes down for the last time to the familiar tune of Auld Lang Syne, in which I hope you will join, let us remember with great pride the great and glorious past of our old Regiment, The King's Royal Rifle Corps, the comradeship and good times we have had, and the men who lived alongside us, have fought with us and in some cases have died in the service of the Regiment; and let us be grateful that we have been lucky enough to be included in such company.'[16]

Epilogue

On 1 January 1966 the title, heritage and traditions of The King's Royal Rifle Corps (60th Rifles), together with those of The Oxfordshire and Buckinghamshire Light Infantry (43rd and 52nd) and The Rifle Brigade, were absorbed into, and became a part of, the history of The Royal Green Jackets. With the consent of Her Majesty Queen Elizabeth II, the Royal title transferred to the new Regiment and she became its Colonel-in-Chief. The only surviving battalion of the 60th was re-designated the 2nd Battalion, The Royal Green Jackets (The King's Royal Rifle Corps). On 15 June 1968, in anticipation of a reduction in the number of Royal Green Jacket battalions from three to two, the subsidiary title in brackets was dropped. Since that date, only the 1st Cadet Battalion, The King's Royal Rifle Corps, has continued to bear the name of the Regiment in its title and to wear its cap badge. After 210 years of unbroken service from 1755–1965, the Regiment ceased to form a part of the Regular Army's order of battle.

Since 1966 surviving members of the Regiment have met regularly to renew old friendships and to reminisce at events organized by The King's Royal Rifle Corps Association, which despite the passing years continues to flourish. The officers of the *Celer et Audax* Club still hold an annual dinner, a custom initiated nearly 150 years ago. Each year, too, heads are bowed as the Regiment remembers its dead on Remembrance Day and other occasions. In these and many other ways, those who proudly served in the Regiment continue to uphold and cherish its memory and to enjoy the bonds of comradeship first experienced when they joined The King's Royal Rifle Corps.

The unique circumstances of the Regiment's birth in North America not only set it apart from others in origin, but created the conditions that shaped its future. Learning from the mistakes of General Braddock on the banks of the Monongahela River in 1755 required the Royal Americans to do things differently to the rest of the British Army if the French and their Indian allies were to be defeated. However, doing things differently, as the Royal Americans did so effectively, was never a facet which the Regiment, throughout its history, pursued as an end in itself but always for a purpose: to do better and more imaginatively, with greater efficiency, fewer casualties and without fuss, what needed to be done. To succeed required leaders ready to cast aside conventional wisdom and to adopt tactics, dress and procedures, which were innovative in concept and ahead of the thinking of others. The Regiment was fortunate to have had such leaders to hand when they were most needed, in particular, Bouquet, de Rottenburg and Hawley, and in more recent times, Gott and Bramall. It was the ideas that they fostered which led the Regiment to appreciate the importance of independence and agility of mind; of self-reliance and self-discipline; and of being proficient at battle-winning skills, such as marksmanship, fieldcraft and manoeuvre. Commanders also learned to go about their business with real concern for the welfare of their subordinates, and with a lightness of touch and professionalism, which focused on the essentials, derided pretentiousness and engendered mutual trust and respect between officers and men.

This Brief History has included many examples of the Regiment's pioneering ways and of its readiness to adopt practices, which contributed significantly to the British Army's success in war; for example, at the forefront of Wellington's army during the Peninsular War, as mounted infantry in South Africa and in the motor battalion role during the Second World War. Success was often achieved in company with The Rifle Brigade. Both shared the characteristics and tenets of Rifle regiments, including a touch of style and an element of élitism born out of doing things differently, at a faster pace and often (but not always) more successfully than others. Meanwhile, competition between them spurred both to heights of greater excellence. Both, too, recognized the importance of recruiting able officers and preparing them for high command, and of fostering the talents of Riflemen quick-witted enough to think for themselves and act on their own.

Ultimately, however, the Regiment's record of service, its achievements, its losses, and the many acts of gallantry performed by its members, must speak for themselves. The future, moreover, does not lie in the past. The King's Royal Rifle Corps (60th Rifles) no longer exists in body, but its spirit lives on and endures within The Royal Green Jackets, which draws its strength from perpetuating the common ancestry, history, traditions and ethos of its forebears. In particular, and appropriately, The Royal Green Jackets adopted the Regiment's motto, 'Swift and Bold', which summarizes exactly how a Rifleman today is expected to act – just as his predecessors did at Quebec in 1759 and on countless occasions thereafter.

Appendix A
Battalion Locations: 1755–1965

Note: For Postings during the First and Second World War, see Chapters 6 and 8.

1st Battalion		2nd Battalion		3rd Battalion		4th Battalion	
1756–67	North America	1756–8	North America	1756–8	North America	1756–9	North America
1767–86	West Indies	1758–65	Canada	1758–61	Canada	1760–63	Canada
1786–97	Canada	1765–72	North America	1762–3	West Indies	1763	Disbanded
1797–9	Guernsey	1772–87	West Indies	1764	Disbanded		
1800–10	West Indies	1787–1800	Canada				
1810–11	England	1800–7	West Indies	1775	Re-formed	1775	Re-formed
1811–19	South Africa	1807–8	Jersey	1776–82	North America	1776–82	North America
1820–4	Canada	1808–9	Spain	1783	Disbanded	1783	Disbanded
1824–6	England	1809–17	West Indies				
1827–8	Portugal	1817–24	Canada	1787	Re-formed	1787	Re-formed
1828–30	Ireland	1824–30	West Indies	1788–93	West Indies	1788–96	West Indies
1830–4	Gibraltar	1830–1	England	1794	Guernsey	1796–7	Guernsey
1834–6	Malta	1832–4	Ireland	1795–1806	West Indies	1797–1805	West Indies
1836–40	Ionian Islands	1834–7	Gibraltar	1806–7	Guernsey	1805–6	England
1840–3	England	1837–41	Ionian Islands	1807–16	West Indies	1806–8	South Africa
1843–5	Ireland	1841–4	West Indies	1816–19	Canada	1808–10	West Indies
1845–60	India	1844–7	Canada	1819	Disbanded	1810–2	England
1860–3	England	1847–8	England			1812–19	West Indies
1863–6	Ireland	1848–51	Ireland			1819	Disbanded
1866–7	Malta	1851–8	South Africa	1855	Re-formed		
1867–76	Canada	1858–60	India	1855–7	Ireland	1857	Re-formed
1877–80	England	1860–1	China	1857–61	India	1857–60	England
1880–6	Ireland	1862–6	England	1861–5	Burma	1860–1	Ireland
1886–90	England	1866–7	Ireland	1865–71	India	1861–9	Canada
1891–5	India	1867–81	India	1871–2	Aden	1869–75	England
1897–9	Mauritius	1881	South Africa	1872–9	England	1875–6	Ireland
				1879–82	South Africa		

1st Battalion

1899–1902	South Africa
1902–6	Egypt & Crete
1906–8	Egypt & Sudan
1909–14	England
1914–19	First World War
1919–20	England
1920–2	Ireland
1922–34	India
1934–8	Burma
1938–9	Egypt
1939–45	Second World War
1945–7	Italy
1948–50	England
1951–5	Germany (BAOR)
1955–8	Libya
1959–60	Northern Ireland
1960–2	Germany (Berlin)
1962–3	England
1963	British Guiana
1964	England
1965	Malaysia (Borneo)

2nd Battalion

1882–8	England
1888–91	Ireland
1892–5	Gibraltar
1895–6	Malta
1896–9	South Africa
1899	India
1899–1901	South Africa
1901–9	India
1910–14	England
1914–19	First World War
1920	England
1921–2	Ireland
1922–4	Germany
1925–32	England
1932–5	Northern Ireland
1935–6	England
1936–7	Palestine
1938–9	England
1939–45	Second World War
1945–6	Libya
1946–8	Palestine
1948	Disbanded
1951	Re-formed
1951–2	England
1952–6	Germany (BAOR)
1956–7	England
1957	Disbanded

3rd Battalion

1882	Malta
1883–4	Egypt
1884–6	Cyprus
1886–91	Gibraltar
1892–8	England
1898–9	Ireland
1900–3	South Africa
1903–4	Ireland
1904–5	Bermuda
1905–7	England
1908–10	Malta & Crete
1910–14	India
1914–19	First World War
1919–22	India
1923	Disbanded

4th Battalion

1876–91	India
1891–2	Burma
1893–8	England
1898–1901	Ireland
1902–4	South Africa
1904–9	England
1909–14	India
1914–19	First World War
1919–22	India
1923	Disbanded

5th Battalion

1797–8	England
1798–9	Ireland
1799–1803	West Indies
1803–5	Canada
1805–7	England
1807–8	Ireland
1808–14	Peninsular War
1814–16	Ireland
1816–18	Gibraltar
1818	Disbanded

6th Battalion

1799–1800	England
1801–18	West Indies
1818	Disbanded

7th Battalion

1813–14	Guernsey
1814–17	Canada
1817	Disbanded

8th Battalion

1813–16	Portugal & Gibraltar
1816	Disbanded

Appendix B
The Origin of the Regimental Motto

Regimental records state that Major-General James Wolfe was so impressed with the alertness, intrepidity and spirited conduct of the grenadier companies of the 2nd and 3rd Battalion of the 60th Royal Americans before Quebec that he conferred on them the motto *Celer et Audax* (Swift and Bold). The exact occasion of this 'spirited conduct' is not certain. An analysis of the possibilities is included in the *Annals, Volume I, Appendix 1*. Most probably it was on 9 August 1759 when it is believed that the grenadier companies, who were escorting Wolfe at the time, had a sharp encounter with the enemy and that he was extremely pleased with the outcome.

The relevance and significance of General Wolfe's gesture seems to have attracted little attention thereafter until, sixty-five years later, permission was sought to resume use of the Motto. The reply, dated 11 October 1824 and addressed to the Regiment's commanding officers from the Deputy Adjutant General at Horse Guards, stated:

> *I have the honour to acquaint you, by direction of the Commander-in-Chief, that His Majesty has been pleased to permit the 60th Regiment, 'The Duke of York's Own Rifle Corps', to resume the motto 'Celer at Audax', which was formerly worn by the Regiment in commemoration of its distinguished bravery whilst employed with the British Army in North America, under Major-General Wolfe, in the year 1759.*

The Motto subsequently played a central role in underpinning the Regimental approach to soldiering, occupying pride of place on the Regiment's cap badge and accoutrements. On 1 January 1966 the English translation 'Swift and Bold' was adopted as the Regimental Motto of The Royal Green Jackets.

Appendix C

Citations of Regimental Recipients of the Victoria Cross

e = elected by ballot † = posthumous award

Notes:
1. Ranks and decorations were those held at the time of the act of gallantry for which the Victoria Cross was awarded.
2. Privates were known as Riflemen, although the rank was not formally approved until 1923.

INDIAN MUTINY, 1857–9

Eight members of the 1st Battalion, 60th Rifles, were awarded a Victoria Cross for actions during the relief of Delhi in 1857, five as the result of a ballot. In accordance with the terms of the Royal Warrant of 29 January 1856, such ballots were permitted in circumstances when units performed collective acts of gallantry where all were deemed to be equally brave, the number of awards being dictated by the size of the unit involved. This was the first instance in the history of the Victoria Cross of awards being decided in this way.

RIFLEMAN S. TURNER
1st Battalion, 60th Rifles
Citation: 'For having, at Delhi, on the night of the 19th of June, 1857, during a severe conflict with the enemy who attacked the rear of the camp, carried off on his shoulders under a heavy fire, a mortally wounded officer, Lieutenant Humphreys, of the Indian Service. During this service Private Turner was wounded by a sabre-cut in the right arm. His gallant conduct saved the above named officer from the fate of others, whose mangled remains were not recovered until the following day.' (*London Gazette*, 20 March 1860)

COLOUR SERGEANT S. GARVIN
1st Battalion, 60th Rifles
Citation: 'For daring and gallant conduct before Delhi on the 23rdJune, 1857, in volunteering to lead a small party of men, under a heavy fire, to the "Sammy House" for the purpose of dislodging a number of the enemy in position there, who kept up a destructive fire on the advanced battery of heavy guns, in which, after a sharp contest, he succeeded. Also recommended for gallant conduct throughout the operations before Delhi.' (*London Gazette*, 20 January 1860)

LIEUTENANT A.E. HEATHCOTE[e]
1st Battalion, 60th Rifles

Citation: 'For highly gallant and daring conduct at Delhi throughout the siege, from June to September 1857, during which he was wounded. He volunteered for services of extreme danger, especially during the six days of severe fighting in the streets after the assault. Elected by the officers of his regiment.' (*London Gazette*, 20 January 1860)

COLOUR SERGEANT G. WALLER[e]
1st Battalion, 60th Rifles

Citation: 'For conspicuous bravery at Delhi, on 14th September, 1857, in charging and capturing the enemy's guns near the Cabul Gate; and again, on the 18th of September, 1857, in the repulse of a sudden attack made by the enemy on a gun near the Chandney Chouk. Elected by the non-commissioned officers of the regiment.' (*London Gazette*, 20 January 1860)

RIFLEMAN J. THOMPSON[e]
1st Battalion, 60th Rifles

Citation: 'For gallant conduct in saving the life of his Captain (Captain Wilmot) at Delhi on the 9th of July 1857, by dashing forward to his relief when that officer was surrounded by a party of Ghazis who made a sudden rush on him from a serai. He killed two of them before further assistance arrived. Also recommended for Conspicuous Conduct throughout the siege. Wounded. Elected by the Privates of the regiment.' (*London Gazette*, 20 January 1860)

RIFLEMAN J. DIVANE[e]
1st Battalion, 60th Rifles

Citation: 'For distinguished gallantry in heading a successful charge made by the Baluchi and Sikh troops on one of the enemy's trenches before Delhi, on the 10th September, 1857. He leaped out of our trenches, closely followed by the native troops, and was shot down from the top of the enemy's breastworks. Elected by the privates of the regiment.' (*London Gazette*, 20 January 1860)

BUGLER W. SUTTON[e]
1st Battalion, 60th Rifles

Citation: 'For gallant conduct at Delhi on the 13th September, 1857, the night previous to the assault, in volunteering to reconnoitre the breach. This soldier's conduct was conspicuous throughout the operations, especially on the 2nd August, 1857, on which occasion, during an attack by the enemy in force, he rushed forward over the trenches and killed one of the enemy buglers who was in the act of sounding. Elected by the Privates of the regiment.' (*London Gazette*, 20 January 1860)

ENSIGN E.A. LISLE PHILLIPPS†
1st Battalion, 60th Rifles

Citation: 'Ensign Everard Aloysius Lisle Phillipps, of the 11th Regiment of Bengal Native Infantry, would have been recommended to Her Majesty for the decoration of the Victoria Cross, had he survived, for many gallant deeds which he performed during the siege of Delhi, during which he was wounded three times. At the assault of that city he captured the Water Bastion with a small party of men and was finally killed in the streets of Delhi on the 18th of September.' (Memorandum to *The London Gazette*, 21 October 1859)

Ensign Lisle Phillipps was ineligible for a Victoria Cross in 1857 because posthumous awards were not then permitted. Fifty years later, it was announced that:

> *The King had been graciously pleased to approve of the* [retrospective] *Decoration of the Victoria Cross being delivered to the representatives of the Officers and men who fell in the performance of acts of valour, and with reference to whom it was notified in the London Gazette that they would have been recommended to Her late Majesty for the Victoria Cross had they survived.* (London Gazette, *15 January 1907*)

The Memorandum of 21 October 1859 refers to Ensign Lisle Phillipps as a member of the 11th Regiment of Bengal Native Infantry. However, on 18 September 1857, the following entry appeared in the London Gazette: '60th Foot, Everard Lisle Phillipps, Gent., to be Ensign, without purchase, vice W. H. Napier, died of wounds. Dated 5 June 1857.' In the light of this entry, the Ministry of Defence acknowledged in a Memorandum appended to the Victoria Cross Register dated 31 May 2001 that 'it would be appropriate and honourable for The Royal Green Jackets to regard Ensign Phillipps as having held a commission in their forebears, the 60th Rifles, at the time of his death in the action for which he was subsequently awarded the Victoria Cross'.

Although the Memorandum in the *London Gazette* of 21 October 1859 refers to Ensign Lisle Philips as having been killed on 18 September 1857, it is known that he died from a gunshot wound to the head on the streets of Delhi on 17 September.

RIFLEMAN V. BAMBRICK
1st Battalion, 60th Rifles

Citation: 'For conspicuous bravery at Bareilly, on the 6th May, 1858, when in a serai he was attacked by three Ghazees, one of whom he cut down. He was wounded twice on this occasion.' (*London Gazette*, 24 December 1858)

ZULU WAR, 1879

BREVET LIEUTENANT-COLONEL R.H. BULLER
(Later General Sir Redvers Buller VC GCB GCMG)
60th Rifles

Citation: 'For his gallant conduct [in command of the Frontier Light Force] at the retreat at Inhlobana, Zululand, on the 28th March 1879, in having assisted, whilst hotly pursued by Zulus, in rescuing Captain C D'Arcy, of the Frontier Light Horse, who was retiring on foot, and carrying him on his horse until he overtook the rearguard. Also for having on the same date and under the same circumstances conveyed Lieutenant C Everitt, of the Frontier Light Horse, whose horse had been killed under him, to a place of safety. Later on Colonel Buller, in the same manner, saved a trooper of the Frontier Light Horse, whose horse was completely exhausted, and who otherwise would have been killed by the Zulus, who were within 80 yards of him.' (*London Gazette*, 17 June 1879)

EGYPT, 1882

RIFLEMAN F. CORBETT
3rd Battalion, The King's Royal Rifle Corps

Citation: 'During the reconnaissance upon Kafr Dowar, Egypt, on the 5th August, 1882, the Mounted Infantry, with which Private Corbett was serving, came under a hot fire from the enemy and suffered some loss, including Lieutenant Howard Vyse, mortally wounded. This officer fell in the open, and there being then no time to move him, Private Corbett asked and obtained permission to remain by him, and though under a constant fire, he sat down and endeavoured to stop the bleeding of this officer's wounds, until the Mounted Infantry received orders to retire, when he rendered valuable assistance in carrying him off the field.' (*London Gazette*, 16 February 1883)

SUDAN, 1884

LIEUTENANT P.S. MARLING
(Later Colonel Sir Percival Marling VC CB Bt)
3rd Battalion, The King's Royal Rifle Corps

Citation: 'For his conspicuous bravery [in command of a detachment of Mounted Infantry] at the Battle of Tamaii, Sudan, on the 13th March, 1884, in risking his life to save that of Private Morley, Royal Sussex Regiment, who having been shot was lifted and placed in front of Lieutenant Marling on his horse. He fell off almost immediately, when Lieutenant Marling dismounted and gave up his horse for the purpose of carrying off Private Morley, the enemy pressing close on to them until they succeeded in carrying him about 80 yards to a place of comparative safety.' (*London Gazette*, 21 May 1884)

SOUTH AFRICAN WAR, 1899–1902

LIEUTENANT THE HON. F.H.S. ROBERTS†
The King's Royal Rifle Corps

Citation: 'At Colenso, South Africa, on 15th December, 1899, the detachments serving the guns of the 14th and 66th Batteries, Royal Field Artillery, had all been either killed, wounded, or driven from their guns by infantry fire at close range, and the guns were deserted. About 500 yards behind the guns was a donga, in which some of the few horses and drivers left alive were sheltered. The intervening space was swept with shell and rifle fire. Lieutenant Roberts and Captain Congreve, Rifle Brigade, who were in the donga, assisted to hook a team into a limber, went out, and assisted to limber up a gun. Captain Congreve was shot through the leg and his horse shot in three places. Lieutenant Roberts assisted Captain Congreve. He was wounded in three places and died of his wounds.' (*London Gazette*, 2 February 1900)

Lieutenant Roberts was on General Sir Redvers Buller's staff and one of six people, including Captain W.N. Congreve of The Rifle Brigade, to be awarded a Victoria Cross during the Battle of Colenso. He and his Father, Field Marshal Lord Roberts VC, are one of only three 'fathers and sons' to have been awarded Victoria Crosses.

LIEUTENANT L.A.E. PRICE-DAVIES DSO
(Later Major-General L.A.E. Price-Davies VC CB CMG DSO)
The King's Royal Rifle Corps

Citation: 'At Blood River Poort, South Africa, on the 17th September, 1901, when the Boers had overwhelmed the right of the British column, and some four hundred of them were galloping round the flank and rear of the guns, riding up to the drivers (who were trying to get the guns away) and calling upon them to surrender, Lieutenant Price-Davies [serving with the Mounted Infantry], hearing an order to fire upon the charging Boers, at once drew his revolver and dashed upon them, firing at them in a most gallant and desperate attempt to rescue the guns. He was immediately shot and knocked off his horse, but was not mortally wounded, although he had ridden to what seemed to be almost certain death without a moment's hesitation.' (*London Gazette*, 29 November 1901)

The guns were captured and Lieutenant Price-Davies was taken prisoner.

FIRST WORLD WAR, 1914–18

LIEUTENANT J.H.S. DIMMER
(Later Lieutenant-Colonel J.H.S. Dimmer VC MC)
2nd Battalion, The King's Royal Rifle Corps

Citation: 'On November 12th, 1914, the 2nd Battalion was holding a section of trenches at Klein Zillebeke [Belgium]. Lieutenant Dimmer was in charge of the machine gun section. About noon there was a very heavy artillery bombardment followed by an attack in mass by the Prussian Guard supported by violent machine gun fire. Almost all of the machine gun section were hit, and Lieutenant Dimmer continued firing one gun single-handed. Twice he had to leave his emplacement to remedy stoppages, which he did successfully but each time he was wounded. He was wounded a third time by shrapnel, but continued firing his gun and inflicting enormous casualties on the serried German masses who continued to advance to within 50 yards of our trenches. Then they suddenly broke and ran, but Lieutenant Dimmer was wounded again by the German artillery covering the retreat. However, he insisted, in spite of his wounds, in reporting personally to brigade headquarters.' (*London Gazette*, 19 November 1914)

Lieutenant Dimmer was later promoted to lieutenant-colonel and killed in action on 21 March 1918 while commanding the 2nd/4th Battalion, The Royal Berkshire Regiment.

LIEUTENANT J.F.P. BUTLER
(Later Captain J.F.P. Butler VC DSO)
The King's Royal Rifle Corps

Citation: 'For most conspicuous bravery in the Cameroons, West Africa. On the 17th November, 1914, with a party of thirteen men, he went into the thick bush and at once attacked the enemy, in strength about one hundred, including several Europeans, defeated them, and captured their machine gun and many loads of ammunition. On the 27th December 1914, when on patrol duty with a few men, he swam the Ekam River, which was held by the enemy, alone and in the face of a brisk fire completed his reconnaissance on the further bank, and returned in safety. Two of his men were wounded while he was actually in the water.' (*London Gazette*, 23 August 1915)

SECOND LIEUTENANT G.H. WOOLLEY
(Later the Reverend G.H. Woolley VC OBE MC)
1/9th (County of London) Battalion, The London Regiment
(Queen Victoria's Rifles)

Citation: 'For most conspicuous bravery on Hill 60 [near Ypres, Belgium] during the night of 20–21 April, 1915. Although the only officer on the hill at the time, and with very few men, he successfully resisted all attacks on his trench, and continued throwing bombs and encouraging his men till relieved. His trench during all this time was being heavily shelled and bombed, and was subjected to heavy machine-gun fire by the enemy.' (*London Gazette*, 22 May 1915)

RIFLEMAN W. MARINER
2nd Battalion, The King's Royal Rifle Corps

Citation: 'During a violent thunderstorm on the night of the 22nd May, 1915, he left his trench near Cambrin, France, and crept out through the German wire entanglements till he reached the emplacement of a German machine gun which had been damaging our parapets and hindering our working parties. After climbing on the top of the German parapet he threw a bomb in under the roof of the gun emplacement and heard some groaning and the enemy running away. After about a quarter of an hour he heard some of them coming back again and climbed up on the other side of the emplacement and threw another bomb among them left-handed. He then lay still while the Germans opened a heavy fire on the wire entanglements behind him, and it was only after about an hour that he was able to crawl back to his own trench. Before starting out he had requested a sergeant to open fire on the enemy's trenches as soon as he had thrown his bombs. Rifleman Mariner was out alone for one and a half hours carrying out this gallant work.' (*London Gazette*, 23 June 1915)

Rifleman Mariner was subsequently killed in action on 30 June 1916.

RIFLEMAN G.S. PEACHMENT
2nd Battalion, The King's Royal Rifle Corps

Citation: 'For most conspicuous bravery near Hulluch [France] on the 25th September, 1915. During very heavy fighting when our front line was compelled to retire in order to reorganize, Private Peachment, seeing his Company Commander, Captain Dubs, lying wounded, crawled to assist him. The enemy's fire was intense, but though there was a shell-hole quite close, in which a few men had taken cover, Private Peachment never thought of saving himself. He knelt in the open by his officer and tried to help him, but while doing this he was first wounded by a bomb and a minute later mortally wounded by a rifle bullet. He was one of the youngest men in his battalion, and gave this splendid example of courage and self-sacrifice.' (*London Gazette*, 18 November 1915)

Rifleman Peachment was one of eight First World War recipients aged 18.

SERGEANT A. GILL[†]
2nd Battalion, The King's Royal Rifle Corps

Citation: 'For most conspicuous bravery. On the 27th July, 1916, at Delville Wood [France] the enemy made a very strong counter-attack on the right flank of the battalion, and rushed the bombing post after killing all the company bombers. Sergeant Gill at once rallied the remnants of his platoon, none of whom were skilled bombers, and reorganized his defences, a most difficult and dangerous task, the trench being very shallow and much damaged. Soon afterwards the enemy nearly surrounded his men by creeping up through the thick undergrowth and commenced sniping at about twenty yards' range. Although it was almost certain death, Sergeant Gill stood boldly up in order to direct the fire of his men. He was killed almost at once, but not before he had shown his men where the enemy were and thus enabled them to hold up their advance. By his supreme devotion to duty and self-sacrifice he saved a very dangerous situation.' (*London Gazette*, 26 October 1916)

One third of the fifty-one Victoria Crosses awarded during the Battle of the Somme were posthumous.

SERGEANT E. COOPER
(Later Major E. Cooper VC)
12th (Service) Battalion, The King's Royal Rifle Corps
Citation: 'For most conspicuous bravery and initiative in attack on the 16th August, 1917, at Langemarck, Flanders [Belgium]. Enemy machine guns from a concrete blockhouse, 250 yards away, were holding up the advance of the battalion on his left, and were also causing heavy casualties to his own battalion. Sergeant Cooper, with four men, immediately rushed the blockhouse though heavily fired on. About 100 yards distant he ordered his men to lie down and fire at the blockhouse. Finding this did not silence the machine guns he immediately rushed forward straight at them and fired his revolver into an opening in the blockhouse. The machine guns ceased firing and the garrison surrendered. Seven machine guns and forty-five prisoners were captured in this blockhouse. By this magnificent act of courage he undoubtedly saved what might have been a serious check to the whole advance, at the same time saving a great number of lives.' (*London Gazette*, 14 September 1917)

RIFLEMAN A.E. SHEPHERD
(Later Corporal A.E. Shepherd)
12th (Service) Battalion, The King's Royal Rifle Corps
Citation: 'For most conspicuous bravery as a company runner on 20th November, 1917, at Cambrai [France]. When his company was held up by a machine gun at point-blank range he volunteered to rush the gun and, though ordered not to, rushed forward and threw a Mills bomb, killing two gunners and capturing the gun. The company, on continuing its advance, came under heavy enfilade machine gun fire. When the last officer and the last non-commissioned officer had become casualties he took command of the company, ordered the men to lie down, and himself went back some 70 yards under severe fire to obtain the help of a tank. He then returned to his company and finally led them to their last objective. He showed throughout conspicuous determination and resource.' (*London Gazette*, 13 February 1918)

LANCE-CORPORAL J.A. CHRISTIE
1/11th (County of London) Battalion, The London Regiment
(Finsbury Rifles)

Citation: 'For most conspicuous bravery [at Fejja, Palestine on 21/22 December 1917] when, after a position had been captured, the enemy immediately made counter and bombing attacks up communication trenches. Lance-Corporal Christie, realising the position, took a supply of bombs over the top, proceeding alone about fifty yards in the open along the communication trench and bombed the enemy. He continued to do this alone in spite of very heavy opposition until a block had been established. Returning towards our lines he heard voices behind him; he at once turned back and bombed another party moving up the trench, entirely breaking up a further bombing attack. By his prompt and effective action he undoubtedly cleared a difficult position at a most critical time and saved many lives. Throughout he was subjected to heavy machine-gun fire and shell fire. He showed the greatest coolness and a total disregard for his own safety.' (*London Gazette*, 27 February 1918)

SECOND WORLD WAR, 1939–45

RIFLEMAN J. BEELEY†
1st Battalion, The King's Royal Rifle Corps

Citation: 'On the 21st November, 1941, during the attack at Sidi Rezegh, North Africa, against a strong enemy position, the company to which Rifleman Beeley belonged was pinned down by heavy fire at point-blank range from the front and flank on the flat, open ground of the aerodrome. All the officers but one of the company and many of the other ranks had been either killed or wounded. On his own initiative, and when there was no sort of cover, Rifleman Beeley got to his feet carrying a Bren gun and ran forward towards a strong enemy post containing an anti-tank gun. He ran thirty yards and discharged a complete magazine at the post from a range of twenty yards, killing or wounding the entire crew of the anti-tank gun. The post was silenced and Rifleman Beeley's platoon was enabled to advance, but Rifleman Beeley fell dead across his gun, hit in at least four places. Rifleman Beeley went to certain death in a gallant and successful attempt to carry the day. His courage and self-sacrifice were a glorious example to his comrades and inspired them to further efforts to reach their objective, which was eventually captured by them, together with 700 prisoners.' (*London Gazette*, 21 April 1942)

Appendix D

Territorials, Militia and Cadets[1]

Territorial Battalions and Regiments
Origins and Organization

The origins and genealogy of the Territorial battalions of The King's Royal Rifle Corps in the 19th Century are complex and beyond the scope of this Brief History to relate. Most trace their descent back to the era of the French Revolutionary Wars and to the formation of volunteer groups, usually of company size and often made up of men pursuing the same trade or profession, who wanted to take up arms in defence of their Country (Home Defence). After 1815 many of the groups were disbanded, although a number survived in the guise of self-funding rifle clubs. In 1851, fearing invasion by France, the Militia was revived. The threat then receded, only to reappear in 1858. Aware of the Country's lack of preparedness for war, the British people demanded the right to train in their own defence and, although the Government was reluctant and the War Office was opposed, on 12 May 1859 the raising of Rifle Volunteer Corps as auxiliaries to the Regular Army was officially authorized. In 1871 the control of these Corps passed from the Lord Lieutenant of each county to the Crown. Up to the outbreak of the South African War in 1899, the Volunteer Corps cost the Government very little. They were maintained by voluntary contributions; they purchased their own, often resplendent, uniforms, as well as items of clothing and equipment; and the officers and men were unpaid.

In 1881, as part of the Cardwell Reforms, twelve Rifle Volunteer Corps in London were designated volunteer battalions of The King's Royal Rifle Corps. By 1904 the number had reduced to ten. On 1 April 1908, as a result of Haldane's Territorial and Reserve Forces Act, 1907, a new Territorial Force was created, with money provided from the Exchequer for clothing, equipment and pay, into which the Rifle Volunteer Corps were absorbed. In the case of those in London, they were all grouped into a new regiment, The London Regiment, with The King's Royal Rifle Corps ceasing to have any formal connection with them. However, eight years later, in July 1916, the majority of the previous affiliations were restored, with six battalions of The London Regiment linked to The King's Royal Rifle Corps:[2]

6th (City of London) Battalion (City of London Rifles)[3]
9th (County of London) Battalion (Queen Victoria's Rifles)
11th (County of London) Battalion (Finsbury Rifles)
12th (County of London) Battalion (The Rangers)
15th (County of London) Battalion (Prince of Wales's Own Civil Service Rifles)
16th (County of London) Battalion (Queen's Westminster Rifles)

In 1920 the Territorial Force was renamed the Territorial Army (TA) and, in 1922, each of The London Regiment's battalions was re-titled as a regiment. In the same year the Civil Service Rifles and The Queen's Westminster Rifles merged to become the 16th London Regiment (Queen's Westminster and Civil Service Rifles). In 1935 the City of London Rifles and the Finsbury Rifles ceased to be TA regiments of The King's Royal Rifle Corps on becoming anti-aircraft regiments.

In 1939 each of The King's Royal Rifle Corps TA regiments added a second battalion and in 1941 they were re-titled:

7th and 8th Battalion (Queen Victoria's Rifles), The King's Royal Rifle Corps
9th and 10th Battalion, The King's Royal Rifle Corps (The Rangers)
11th and 12th Battalion (The Queen's Westminsters), The King's Royal Rifle Corps

After the Second World War, in July 1947, the TA was re-formed, occasioning the first of a succession of post-War reorganizations, with The Rangers transferring to The Rifle Brigade and in 1950 merging with The London Rifle Brigade to become The London Rifle Brigade Rangers. Queen Victoria's Rifles, commanded by Lieutenant-Colonel P.J. Bradford, and The Queen's Westminsters, commanded by Lieutenant-Colonel C.F.G. Henshaw, remained a part of The King's Royal Rifle Corps, each with a single battalion.

On re-formation, the Regiment's two TA battalions formed a part of 56 (London) Armoured Division, with Queen Victoria's Rifles designated a motor battalion in 22 Armoured Brigade and The Queen's Westminsters in 168 Lorried Infantry Brigade. The links with Regular battalions became closer, with Riflemen of all ranks, on completion of their National Service (introduced in 1947), required to spend time with the TA attending evening and weekend training and an annual two-week camp. In 1954, at the height of the Cold War, the Division carried out a major divisional exercise on Salisbury Plain with the battalions brought up to full establishment with the recall of reservists. The Division, however, soon ceased to be an armoured formation reducing in size to an armoured brigade.

In 1956 the armoured brigade was disbanded and the TA battalions re-roled as dismounted infantry. A new brigade, 169 (Green Jackets) Brigade TA, comprising Queen Victoria's Rifles, The Queen's

Westminsters and The London Rifle Brigade Rangers, was formed within 56 (London) Division. Brigadier G.W. White (60th) was the brigade commander. He handed over to Brigadier J.F.C. Mellor (60th) in 1959. Part-time service for National Servicemen ceased.

In 1961 Queen Victoria's Rifles and The Queen's Westminsters merged to become The Queen's Royal Rifles, under the command of Lieutenant-Colonel J.N. Butterwick, who served with the 12th Battalion during the Second World War and was the last commanding officer of The Queen's Westminsters. In 1962, Lieutenant-Colonel K.N. Loudoun-Shand, formerly of Queen Victoria's Rifles, succeeded him. To quote from the *Annals*: 'The Queen's Royal Rifles rightly gave first emphasis to recruiting, never easy in the West End of London, and successfully used the challenge of tough training to draw in young men, who in the light of abolished National Service sought a greater challenge than routine life at work and home. ... A contingent of "Ever Readies", with higher call-out and training commitments and consequent bounties, was formed, prepared to fly anywhere at short notice.'[4] A platoon of "Ever Readies" subsequently exercised with 2nd Green Jackets, The King's Royal Rifle Corps, in Libya in 1963, and with the Queen's Own Rifles of Canada in minus 95° of frost in 1965. In February of the same year, Lieutenant-Colonel Viscount (Nick) Eden assumed command. His father, Anthony Eden, the Earl of Avon, a former 60th officer and Prime Minister from 1955-7, was the Regiment's first Honorary Colonel, being succeeded by Richard Wood, later Lord Holderness, in August 1962.[5]

In 1967 the TA was replaced by the Territorial and Volunteer Reserve (TAVR) and reduced in strength from 110,000 to 50,000. As a result, on 1 April, after a brief six years of distinguished service, The Queen's Royal Rifles, The London Rifle Brigade Rangers and the TA battalion of The Oxfordshire and Buckinghamshire Light Infantry reorganised into two separate battalions taking components and men from each. The 4th (Volunteer) Battalion, The Royal Green Jackets, was sponsored by The Queen's Royal Rifles and based at 56 Davies Street, Mayfair, London; as a 'Volunteer' battalion its members had increased commitments and regular rates of pay. The 5th (Territorial) Battalion, The Royal Green Jackets, was sponsored by The London Rifle Brigade Rangers and based at Sun Street, London; as a 'Territorial' battalion its members had a lesser Home Defence commitment and did much of their training unpaid. These arrangements, however, did not last long as further reorganizations took place that lie outside the time period of this Brief History and fall to historians of The Royal Green Jackets to record.

Reorganization, though, matched by inadequate funding, were part of a pattern with which those who served in the Militia and Territorial battalions of the Regiment during the previous 100 years will have been familiar. Remarkably, it diminished neither their spirit nor their loyalty, and when their support was most needed, in war, it was readily forthcoming.

Record of Service, 1899–1965

The Rifle Volunteer Corps did not serve in the South African War of 1899-1902 as units, but did furnish considerable numbers of volunteers to join the Regular battalions and to serve either individually or in groups with the City (of London) Imperial Volunteers (CIV) or its mounted equivalent, the Imperial Yeomanry. The CIV was formed especially for service in South Africa on the initiative of the Lord Mayor, Sir Alfred Newton. Each volunteer who joined was enrolled as a Freeman of the City of London. The CIV ultimately consisted of over 1,700 officers and men. One group was known as Special Service Company (No.1) of The King's Royal Rifle Corps, comprising detachments from four Volunteer battalions. All the Corps who provided volunteers for service in South Africa were awarded the Battle Honour 'South Africa, 1900-02'.

The six battalions of The London Regiment associated with The King's Royal Rifle Corps all increased in size to three battalions during the First World War, two for service overseas and one as a Home battalion. The 1st Battalion of Queen Victoria's Rifles and The Queen's Westminster Rifles both deployed to France in November 1914 and the 1st Battalion of The Rangers in the following month. The distinguished record of the battalions during the First World War is not covered in this Brief History but may be found in the many well-documented histories of The London Regiment. Members of two of the Regiment's affiliated Territorial battalions, Second Lieutenant G.H. Woolley (Queen Victoria's Rifles) and Lance Corporal J.A. Christie (Finsbury Rifles), were awarded a Victoria Cross. Brief details of their awards are at Appendix C.

Between the two World Wars, the TA was occasionally called upon to deal with civil unrest, including during the Coal Strike in 1921 and the General Strike in 1926. The Government's emphasis on disarmament, together with financial crises affecting expenditure on the TA, inevitably resulted in a decline in recruiting. Commanding officers had to struggle and to improvise to sustain their regiments. The Rangers, for example, were fortunate to be closely associated with the Gas Light and Coke Company, who loaned their vans to take the Battalion to camp in 1937. The efforts of the commanding officers, however, paid off handsomely as when the call to arms came in 1939, the TA regiments of The King's Royal Rifle Corps were as well, if not better, prepared than any others. The Rangers and The Queen's Westminsters were organized as infantry battalions transported on mobilization in troop-carrying vehicles driven by the Royal Army Service Corps, while Queen Victoria's Rifles, the first Green Jacket battalion to arrive in Calais in 1940, was a reconnaissance battalion equipped with motor cycles and side cars. Their service during the Second World War as motor battalions is covered in Chapter 8.

In the period after 1945, individual members of the TA frequently volunteered for service with the Regular Army or were called up as

Queen Victoria's Rifles at Beaulieu, 1939

reservists. The TA regiments also showed the way in marksmanship at Bisley. In 1935 Rifleman W.H. Hodder of The Queen's Westminsters won the inaugural King's Medal for Champion Territorial shot, the first of many shooting trophies won by the regiments. The regiments, too, played their part in civic and ceremonial duties in London, often impressing the crowds with their smart uniforms, fast marching pace and the stirring sound of silver bugles. Above all, the loyalty and commitment to the Regiment of the Territorial battalions and regiments of The King's Royal Rifle Corps, and their pride in being Green Jackets, were always second to none. Although inadequate recognition may occasionally have been accorded to their achievements, their record of service in peace and war is one of which all today may and should be justifiably proud.

Premises

Over the years the Territorial elements of the Regiment occupied numerous premises in London. In 1886 The Queen's Westminster Volunteers occupied 58 Buckingham Gate as their headquarters, the building being paid for by public subscription. In 1890 the antecedent Rifle Volunteer Corps of Queen Victoria's Rifles established their headquarters at 56 Davies Street, Mayfair, entirely at their own expense, on land made available by the generosity of the Duke of Westminster. The building was bombed in the Second World War, with rebuilding not complete until 1952. The Civil Service Rifles, up to the time of their

Kaiser Wilhelm II

The portrait presented to The Queen's Westminsters

In July 1891 Kaiser Wilhelm II, Emperor of Germany and King of Prussia, was in the middle of a State visit to London when he asked to inspect a unit of the Rifle Volunteer Corps. There were only 48 hours in which to organise and assemble the men, and it seemed that it might not be possible, when the Duke of Westminster intervened and said that his Regiment would do it. Urgent messages were then despatched to all the members of The Queen's Westminster Volunteers and at 8 a.m. on Friday, 10 July 1891, 30 officers, 54 sergeants and 700 other ranks, out of a total regimental strength of 1,100, paraded before the Kaiser in the grounds of Buckingham Palace. The Kaiser was so impressed with the speed with which the Volunteers responded to his request, and with the excellence of their drill and turnout, that he commissioned a portrait of himself, which he presented to the Regiment in token of his appreciation. He also told Queen Victoria that he much liked the Regiment's field grey uniform and on return to Berlin he gave orders that his army was to be clothed in a uniform of similar design and colour.

On receipt, the Kaiser's portrait was hung on a wall at the Regiment's headquarters at 58 Buckingham Gate, London. During the First World War it was placed in storage. During the Second World War it was turned to face the wall. On the Regiment's merger with Queen Victoria's Rifles in 1961, the portrait was moved to 56 Davies Street, London, where it now hangs in the Officers Mess.

Seventh Regiment of the New York National Guard

The Regiment's links with New York and Governor's Island (see page 18) extend back to 1756, prior to the creation of the Seventh Regiment of the New York National Guard, a famous National Guard regiment with a history dating back to 1806. It was from the Seventh Regiment that the name 'National Guard' was derived and adopted by volunteer units across the United States of America.

At some date lost in the past, links were forged between the Seventh Regiment and The Queen's Westminsters, which, in 1904, Sir Howard Vincent, Colonel Commandant of The Queen's Westminsters, cemented by presenting a challenge shield as a guarantee of perpetual friendship between the two regiments. This shield, known as the Howard Vincent Shield, was competed for in shoulder-to-shoulder rifle shooting matches between teams from the two regiments.

Due to the difficulties caused by distance and the intervention of two World Wars, only four matches took place prior to The Queen's Westminsters merger with Queen Victoria's Rifles in 1961. The Queen's Westminsters won the first at Bisley in 1905, while the Seventh Regiment won the other three in America in 1906, and at Bisley in 1926 and 1957.

Although The Queen's Westminsters are no longer in a position to recover the Shield, the record stands, with the friendship perpetuated by its successors.

---

amalgamation, had their headquarters at Somerset House. The Rangers headquarters was in Chenies Street, off the Tottenham Court Road.

City Links

The close links established by the Regiment's Territorials with the City of London, the City of Westminster and other institutions, municipal authorities and businesses in London, were central to ensuring that support for recruiting and other activities was forthcoming when needed. Much-valued special relationships existed with Lloyds of London and some City Livery companies, including the Goldsmiths, Haberdashers and Salters.

Militia

In addition to acquiring twelve Rifle Volunteer Corps battalions as a result of the Cardwell Reforms of 1881, the Regiment acquired five Militia battalions, which were designated battalions of the Regiment as follows:

5th Battalion – The Huntingdonshire Militia (Rifles)

6th Battalion – The Royal Denbigh and Flint Militia (Rifles)

7th Battalion – 2nd or Edmonton Royal Rifle Regiment of Middlesex Militia

8th Battalion – The Carlow Militia (Rifles)

9th Battalion – North Cork Militia (Rifles)

The Royal Denbigh and Flint Militia were disbanded in 1889, and the Carlow and North Cork Militia in 1908. The two surviving Militia battalions then became the 5th Battalion (Huntingdon Militia) and the 6th Battalion (Royal 2nd Middlesex Militia). Each was given the role of a Special Reserve battalion, supplying reservists as reinforcements in times of need. They were disbanded in 1953.

The North Cork Militia (9th Battalion) volunteered for service during the South African War. Arriving at Capetown on 1 February 1900, it protected the lines of communication in the rear of Lord Roberts's advancing army. It later undertook blockhouse duty on the railway line near Vereeniging, before returning to Ireland in August 1901 with the Battle Honour 'South Africa, 1900–01'.

Cadets
1st Cadet Battalion, The King's Royal Rifle Corps

The 1st Cadet Battalion owes its foundation to the Reverend Freeman Wills, who was commissioned into the Volunteer Army in the rank of Captain on 26 July 1890.[6] He was also Vicar of St Agatha's just behind Sun Street, Finsbury Square. On receiving his commission he decided to form a cadet company within the 1st Cadet Battalion, The Royal West Surrey Regiment. The Company quickly expanded to become the 2nd Cadet Battalion, The Royal West Surrey Regiment, at which point he moved the Battalion Headquarters to No. 2 Finsbury Square (and in 1904 to 42 Sun Street, which he had specially built for the purpose). In 1894 he applied to HRH Prince George, Duke of Cambridge, Colonel-in-Chief, to affiliate to the Regiment, with the title of 1st Cadet Battalion, The King's Royal Rifle Corps. Consent was granted on 8 November 1894 and the Battalion has remained a part of the Regiment ever since.

In the days of its foundation Cadet battalions were privately organized and funded. On becoming a part of The King's Royal Rifle Corps subscriptions began to flow in and after the commanding officer had spent nearly £1,000, the Battalion was placed on a financial basis, which many Volunteer Corps would have envied. There were to be many ups and down in later years, especially when recognition of the Cadet Force was withdrawn between the two World Wars, but fortunately the enthusiasm and commitment of those involved consistently triumphed over the parsimony of Governments.

This Brief History does not provide space for a detailed coverage of the Battalion's record, which may be found elsewhere – see Endnote 1. Remarkably, however, in 1900, when volunteers were urgently needed for the South African War, the Reverend Wills persuaded the War Office to accept a company of the older cadets, principally NCOs, to enrol in the City Imperial Volunteers. Over 100 did so, with others joining other units. Four were killed. As a result, the Battalion was awarded the Battle Honour 'South Africa, 1900-02', the only Cadet battalion ever to receive a battle honour.[7] It was also permitted to call its cadets 'Riflemen'.

At the outbreak of the First World War, nearly all the cadets over 18 years old enlisted immediately, with 400 enrolling in the City of London Rifles. In total, over 8,000 former members of the 1st Cadet Battalion served during the course of the War, three of whom were awarded a Victoria Cross, including Lieutenant J.H.S. Dimmer, serving with the 2nd Battalion in Belgium in 1914.[8] Former cadets also served with distinction during the Second World War, including with the battalions of the Regiment in North Africa, Italy and North West Europe.

2nd Cadet Battalion, The King's Royal Rifle Corps

In 1942 a Home Guard instruction was issued ordering each Home Guard battalion to raise a cadet unit. Lieutenant-Colonel R.L. Clark of Queen Victoria's Rifles was given the task and on 15 May the Queen Victoria's Rifles Cadet Corps was born. Over the next three years the unit expanded to five companies, which in April 1945 led to it being re-titled the 2nd Cadet Battalion, The King's Royal Rifle Corps. In 1951 the 1st and 2nd Cadet Battalion were amalgamated. This resulted in the disposal of the Headquarters of the 1st Cadet Battalion at 42 Sun Street. In 1954 the Battalion office of the 'new' 1st Cadet Battalion was established at 56 Davies Street, where it remains to this day.

Over the years large numbers of cadets have been associated with the Regiment, some through membership of the 1st and 2nd Cadet Battalion and others through membership of army or school cadet forces affiliated to the Regiment. Many subsequently joined the Regular and Territorial Army, and especially the battalions of The King's Royal Rifle Corps. The link with public school cadet forces was especially important in ensuring a steady stream of able officers, while the others provided some of the Regiment's best NCOs, a good proportion of whom were subsequently commissioned. An especially close liaison was established with Eton College by which a 60th officer alternated with a Guardsman as Adjutant of the Officer Training Corps.

However, of all the Regiment's cadet units, the 1st Cadet Battalion is the one that has most jealously guarded, through thick and thin, its links with its parent Regiment. Since 1894 it has proudly promoted and upheld the history, heritage and traditions of the Regiment amongst its members. It has often excelled on the range and at sport. Its record of service and the dedication of its instructors have long been an inspiration and an example to others. Today, forty years after the Regiment became a part of The Royal Green Jackets, the 1st Cadet Battalion continues to flourish as the last in the line, retaining its title and proudly wearing the cap badge of The King's Royal Rifle Corps.

Allied and Affiliated Regiments

Canada
The Queen's Own Rifles of Canada

The Brockville Rifles	The Regina Rifle Regiment
The King's Own Rifles of Canada	The Dufferin and Haldimand
The Halifax Rifles	Rifles of Canada
The Victoria Rifles of Canada	The Royal Rifles of Canada

Australia	**South Africa**
Sydney University Regiment	The Kaffrarian Rifles

Rhodesia	**Fiji**
The Royal Rhodesia Regiment	The Fiji Infantry Regiment

Kenya
The Kenya Regiment

Affiliated
2nd King Edward VII's Own Goorkha Rifles (The Sirmoor Rifles)
1st and 2nd Cadet Battalion, The King's Royal Rifle Corps
A number of Combined and Army Cadet Force units

Alliances and affiliations differ. Within the British Army, an alliance describes a formal link established with a Service unit of another country. An affiliation describes a formal link established between two units in Britain's Armed Forces, including its Reserves and Cadets.

The exact circumstances giving rise to some of the Regiment's alliances, in particular, with Canada's Militia units, are not recorded in the Annals. Alliances, too, almost always followed many years after the first links were established. Evidence of this is often reflected in the adoption of shared customs and dress, such as the wearing of cross-belts and black buttons, long before the date of the alliance or affiliation. In some instances, the Regiment's alliances and affiliations were born out of shared danger and the support given to the Regiment during time of war. In all cases, the alliance or affiliation was greatly valued and reciprocated whenever opportunity permitted. Some are now perpetuated by The Royal Green Jackets.

Alliances

Canada

It is unsurprising, given the Regiment's service in Canada between 1758 and its departure as the last British Army unit to leave Canada in 1871, and the service of so many of Canada's Militia units during the First World War, that a number of alliances should have resulted. A synopsis of the history of the regiments concerned may be found in *The King's Royal Rifle Corps Chronicle* of 1949. Sadly, a number, for example, the alliance with The King's Own Rifles of Canada, formerly the 60th Rifles of Canada, did not survive various reorganizations of the Canadian Army Militia between 1956 and 1965. The alliances with The Queen's Own Rifles of Canada, The Brockville Rifles and The Regina Rifle Regiment did survive and were adopted by The Royal Green Jackets in 1966.

The Queen's Own Rifles of Canada (Toronto)
The Queen's Own Rifles of Canada, a Regular infantry regiment at the time of the alliance, traces its origins to the Militia of 1860, a detachment of which served alongside the 1st Battalion, 60th Rifles, during the Red River Expedition in 1870. The alliance, however, did not come into being until 1959 and was shared with The Buffs. In 1968 the 2nd Battalion was disbanded and in 1969 the 1st was re-designated the 3rd Battalion, Princess Patricia's Canadian Light Infantry. The Queen's Own Rifles of Canada became a Militia unit.

The Brockville Rifles (Brockville, Ontario)
The Brockville Rifles was formed in 1866 at the time of the Fenian Raids. It was initially titled the '41st Brockville Battalion of Rifles', being re-titled 'The Brockville Rifles' in 1920. It became an artillery unit in 1946 and remains a Militia unit. The alliance dates back to 1928.

The Regina Rifle Regiment (Regina, Saskatchewan)
The Regina Rifle Regiment was formed in the early 1900s as the '95th Regiment'. Soon afterwards it was re-designated the '95th Saskatchewan Rifles', becoming 'The Regina Rifle Regiment' in 1924. The Regiment is now 'The Royal Regina Rifles' and remains a Militia unit. The alliance dates back to 1914.

Australia

The Sydney University Regiment
In 1900 the Sydney University Rifle Corps was formed. It was re-designated The Sydney University Regiment (SUR) in 1927. Royal assent to an alliance with The King's Royal Rifle Corps was given in 1929. Over the years a number of officers and officer cadets from the SUR have spent time with the Regiment, including service with the TA regiments in London. The alliance was adopted by The Royal Green Jackets in 1966 and continues to flourish.

South Africa

The Kaffrarian Rifles
The links with The Kaffrarian Rifles date back to the service of the 3rd Battalion in South Africa in the early 1880s, although there was not an alliance until 1927. It was suspended in 1961, when South Africa quit the Commonwealth, and was resurrected by The Royal Green Jackets in 1995, after South Africa rejoined. The Kaffrarian Rifles was re-designated 'The Buffalo Volunteer Rifles' in 1999, the title by which the Regiment was known from its creation in 1876 to 1883.

Rhodesia

The Royal Rhodesia Regiment
The alliance with The Royal Rhodesia Regiment originated after the service of significant numbers of Rhodesians in the battalions of The King's Royal Rifle Corps during the First World War. The *Annals* refer particularly to the arrival of a draft in the 2nd Battalion, where they were formed into a section of especially accomplished snipers. The number of Rhodesians in the Battalion later increased, resulting in the establishment of No 8 (Rhodesia) Platoon.

Even larger numbers of Rhodesians served with the Regiment in the Second World War, resulting in a motor company of Rhodesians being formed in the 1st Battalion, which was widely considered one of the finest companies in the Regiment. In November 1941, two out of the three officers killed at Sidi Rezegh were Rhodesian. A year later Major O.H. Newton, a Rhodesian commanding D Company in the 1st Battalion, was killed. He was the only officer in the Regiment awarded a Military Cross and two bars during the Second World War.

The alliance lapsed after 1965.

Fiji

The Fiji Infantry Regiment
The alliance with The Fiji Infantry Regiment was established in 1950 in recognition of the service of 250 volunteers who served in the 4th Battalion during the First World War and were awarded two Distinguished Conduct Medals, five Military Crosses and five Military Medals. In the early 1960s a small number of Fijians joined 2nd Green Jackets, The King's Royal Rifle Corps; one, Second Lieutenant M.M.K. Yasa, became an officer in the Regiment.

The alliance was adopted by The Royal Green Jackets in 1966.

Kenya

The Kenya Regiment
The Kenya Regiment was formed in 1937 and disbanded in 1963 prior to Kenyan Independence. Its roles were to provide aid to the civil power in emergency and to supply officers of European origin for the King's African Rifles in time of war. From 1950 the Green Jackets supplied the permanent staff, including during the Mau Mau Emergency from 1952–6. Three out of five commanding officers, ten officers and thirty-four warrant officers and senior NCOs from the 60th served with the Regiment between 1950 and 1963.

Because of the strong 60th connection, an alliance was approved in 1956. Following the Regiment's disbandment, the alliance ended but the links continue, with the Regiment's Colours laid up in The Light Division Chapel at Sir John Moore Barracks, Winchester, and its silver in the Officers Mess.

Affiliations

2nd King Edward VII's Own Goorkha Rifles (The Sirmoor Rifles)
Reference was made in Chapter 3 to the friendship established between the 60th, the Sirmoor Rifles and the Guides during the relief of Delhi in 1857. This friendship has since been perpetuated in many different ways and on numerous occasions. Following the partition of India in 1947, the 2nd King Edward VII's Own Goorkha Rifles (The Sirmoor Rifles) became a regiment of the British Army (rather than the Indian Army) and an affiliation was approved. This has now been subsumed within the affiliation that exists between The Royal Green Jackets and The Royal Gurkha Rifles.

Although no alliance ever existed between the Guides and The King's Royal Rifle Corps, one was established in 1994 between The Royal Green Jackets and the 2nd Battalion, The Frontier Force (Guides), a regiment in the Pakistan Army.

Cadets
See Appendix D.

Appendix F

The Depot and Links with Winchester

Winchester, to all Riflemen, has always meant, and does mean, Home, the place from which we have set forth on many military adventures; the place about which we have thought with pleasure and longing in our absences overseas; the place to which we have returned with thanksgiving at the end of our appointed tasks.

(Acceptance Speech at City of Winchester Freedom Ceremony, 18 July 1946)

Winchester became 'Home' to the Regiment when The Rifle Depot was established in the Upper Barracks (now Peninsula Barracks) in 1858. Before that the site was used as a Royal castle (1067–1645), as Charles II's intended Royal Palace (1682–5), and as a barracks for prisoners of war. During the Napoleonic Wars, from 2–3,000 troops were housed on the site, with various regiments in occupation at different times, including the 60th.

In 1756, when the Regiment was in the act of being raised, a depot was established on Governor's Island, New York (see page 18). In 1763, a home depot was also established on the Isle of Wight, where battalions overseas based one or more companies for recruiting and administrative purposes, including the despatch and receipt of drafts. The Isle of Wight remained the depot until 1823, after which battalions based their depot wherever it was most convenient; thus, at various times, depots were established, for example, at Chatham, Plymouth, Portsmouth, Dublin and Jersey. A more permanent arrangement was clearly desirable. This was achieved in 1858 when the home base and training centres of the two Rifle regiments, the 60th and The Rifle Brigade, were collocated at The Rifle Depot, Winchester. Each regiment, however, while sharing facilities, retained its independence, running parallel organisations, each with its own commanding officer. Integration of the recruit training and administrative functions under a single commander did not occur until The Rifle Depot became The Green Jackets Depot in 1951. It changed its name again in 1958, when it became The Green Jackets Brigade Depot.

On 19 December 1894 disaster struck when the main barrack block, the King's House, was destroyed by fire, requiring The Rifle Depot to move briefly to the Portsdown Forts, Portsmouth, and then into barracks at Gosport. On 8 June 1899 HRH The Prince of Wales laid the foundation stone for the Upper Barracks at Winchester to be rebuilt. The new barracks was occupied in 1904.

*The march-past after receiving the Freedom of the City of Winchester,
18 July 1946*

*HRH The Duke of Gloucester at Peninsula Barracks, Winchester,
28 May 1965*

At the outbreak of the Second World War, there was insufficient space at The Rifle Depot to accommodate all the recruits in training, and so the 60th element moved to Bushfield Camp, two miles outside Winchester. A number of further moves followed over the next twelve years (see Chapters 8 and 9) before recruit training reverted to Upper Barracks after the creation of The Green Jackets Depot in 1951. A final move to Bushfield to permit modernization of the Depot took place between 1961 and 1964. It was only after modernization that the barracks was named 'Peninsula Barracks'. Between 1942–4, prior to D-Day, the 60th Infantry Regiment of the 9th Division of the United States Army occupied the barracks, requiring all but a small rear party to move elsewhere.

During the course of the Regiment's 107 years at The Rifle Depot extremely close links were established with the City of Winchester. These remain in place and have been adopted, and are perpetuated, by The Royal Green Jackets, with Regimental Headquarters, The Royal Green Jackets, and The Royal Green Jackets Museum located at Peninsula Barracks. On 18 July 1946 The King's Royal Rifle Corps and The Rifle Brigade were each awarded the Freedom of the City of Winchester in recognition, especially, of the gallantry and achievements of each regiment in the First and Second World Wars. The Freedom has been exercised on a number of occasions since.

Strong links also exist with the Cathedral, which houses the Rolls of Honour of the Regiment's war dead in the South African, First and Second World Wars. The Rolls include the names of many from Winchester College, the source of a large number of the Regiment's officers. There are other important memorials inside the Cathedral, including the South African War Memorial Window, while the First World War Memorial Statue outside the West Door serves as a memorial to all those who died in the service of the Regiment in both World Wars and other conflicts.

Elsewhere within the City's boundaries, the Regimental link with Winchester survives through unbroken occupation since 1904 of the Regiment's Memorial Cottages (now Green Jacket Close) and through use of the St Cross cricket ground, where Green Jacket cricket continues to be played. Many members of the Regiment in the past also chose to live in and around Winchester on retirement, and some still do.

Over the years the citizens of Winchester were, and continue to be, generous in their support to The King's Royal Rifle Corps, and its successor, The Royal Green Jackets. The fact, too, that so many members of the Regiment passed through the gates of The Rifle Depot at some point during their service meant that most had memories of the City and, while some may not have enjoyed their training, all had stories to tell. But as memories fade, it will be the memorials in the Cathedral that stand to last the longest, providing testament to future generations for centuries to come of the Regiment's presence in Winchester and of its service to the Country.

Further Reading

Further information about the Regiment may be found in the Regimental publications below, which are not easily obtainable by members of the general public. A copy of each is held in The Royal Green Jackets Museum Archives at Winchester (Tel: +44 (0)1962 828532 or +44 (0)1962 828549).

The Annals of The King's Royal Rifle Corps, 1755-1965 (Seven Volumes)

Volume I	*The Royal Americans*, by Lieutenant-Colonel Lewis Butler (1913)
Volume II	*The Green Jacket*, by Lieutenant-Colonel Lewis Butler (1923)
Volume III	*The 60th: The KRRC*, by Lieutenant-Colonel Lewis Butler (1926)
Volume IV	*The 60th: The KRRC*, by Major-General Sir Steuart Hare (1929)
Volume V	*The Great War*, by Major-General Sir Steuart Hare (1932)
Volume VI	*1921-1943*, by Brigadier G.H. Mills and Lieutenant-Colonel R.F. Nixon (1971)
Volume VII	*1943-1965*, by Major-General G.H. Mills (1979)
Appendix	*Uniform, Armament and Equipment*, by S.M. Milne and Major-General Astley Terry (1913)

The Chronicles of The King's Royal Rifle Corps published annually, 1901-65

A Regimental Chronicle and List of Officers, by Captain N.W. Wallace (1879), covering the period 1756-1878

Colonel Henry Bouquet: A Biographical Sketch, by Lieutenant-General Sir Edward Hutton (1911)

A Sketch of the Services of the Fifth Battalion Sixtieth Regiment (Rifles), by Major-General Gibbes Rigaud (1879)

The Battle Honours of The King's Royal Rifle Corps 1755-1918, by Captain T.N.F. Wilson (1927)

Swift and Bold: The Story of The King's Royal Rifle Corps in the Second World War 1939-1945, by Major-General Sir Hereward Wake and Major W.F. Deedes (1949)

A Tribute to Lieutenant-General W.H.E. Gott CB CBE DSO* MC, edited by Brigadier H.R.W. Vernon (1984)

Other Reading:

Famous Regiments: The King's Royal Rifle Corps, by Herbert Fairlie Wood (1967)

The Royal Americans, a 72-page booklet by Sir Philip Goodhart (2005)

Endnotes

Chapter 1 **1755–83: The Royal Americans**

¹ A number of variations of Braddock's last words have been published, including 'We shall learn better how to do it the next time' (Lewis Butler, *The Annals of The King's Royal Rifle Corps, Vol. I: The Royal Americans* (London: Smith Elder, 1913), 1) and 'Another time we shall know better how to deal with them' (The Hon. J.W. Fortescue, *A History of The British Army, Vol. II* (London: Macmillan, 1899), 279).

² The Thirteen Colonies were Connecticut, Delaware, Georgia, Maryland, Massachusetts, New Hampshire, New Jersey, New York, North Carolina, Pennsylvania, Rhode Island, South Carolina, Virginia. Their total population was more than one million. The population of French Canada (New France) was 70,000.

³ George Washington, later first President of the United States, was aged 23 at the time.

⁴ Fortescue, *A History of The British Army, Vol. II*, 281.

⁵ It was common practice in the 18th Century for European armies to recruit officers and soldiers from other countries.

⁶ William Pitt the Elder, first Earl of Chatham.

⁷ The purpose of the Colonel-in-Chief was to provide general superintendence over the Regiment, while the Colonels-Commandant were responsible for the more detailed administration of the battalions to which they were appointed. During the early years of the Regiment it was not unusual for Colonels-Commandant to exercise command of 'their battalion' in the field as well as in barracks.

⁸ Butler, *Annals, Vol. I*, 17–18.

⁹ Certain inducements were used to encourage service in America, including the promise of grants of land. For example, a field officer was entitled to 5,000 acres, a captain to 3,000, a subaltern to 2,000, an NCO to 200 and a private to 50. See Butler, *Annals, Vol. I*, 23.

¹⁰ Butler, *Annals, Vol. I*, 25.

¹¹ Recruiting later extended to Massachusets, New York, Maryland and North Carolina.

¹² Butler, *Annals, Vol. I*, 30.

¹³ Amherst's three Brigadiers at Louisbourg were Whitmore, Charles Lawrence, Colonel-Commandant of the 3rd Battalion, and Wolfe.

¹⁴ Butler, *Annals, Vol. I*, 47. The mention of the 'green jackets' worn by the light troops is frequently referred to as the first occasion on which the Regiment wore green.

¹⁵ Haldimand switched from command of the 2nd to the 4th Battalion in 1757.

¹⁶ Lord Howe was considered by General Wolfe to have been 'the best soldier in the British Army'.

¹⁷ Bradstreet joined the 60th on 8 March 1757 following the disbandment of the 51st Regiment of Foot.

¹⁸ Colonel George Washington, commanding a force of Virginian militia, was also a member of Forbes's expedition.

¹⁹ Fortescue, *A History of the British Army, Vol. II*, 334. Butler, *Annals, Vol. I*, 63–4.

²⁰ Forbes, aged 65, suffered from acute ill health and was heavily reliant on Bouquet's leadership. Forbes died, in March 1759, only 3 months after the expedition ended.

²¹ Butler, *Annals, Vol. I*, 82.

²² Wolfe's dying moments are portrayed in a number of paintings, in which different officers surround him. One, painted in 1764 by Edward Penny of the Royal Academy,

shows four officers surrounding Wolfe, one of whom is said to be Captain S.J. Hollandt, an engineer officer in the Royal Americans, who allegedly was about to give a report to the General. Others also aver that a Royal American officer was present, naming Lieutenant Brown of the grenadiers and Lieutenant Des Barres, an engineer officer. It is most unlikely that all were present. It is not absolutely certain that any were.

23 Quebec was the first occasion on which the 60th fought alongside one of the regiments – in this case the 43rd – with which it was to merge in 1966 to form The Royal Green Jackets.

24 35th (Dorsetshire), later Royal Sussex Regiment.

25 Haviland became Colonel-Commandant of the 3rd Battalion on 9 December 1760.

26 Haldimand remained Governor until September 1765. He was later knighted and became Governor-General of Canada from 1778–84.

27 The 42nd (Black Watch) was newly arrived from the West Indies and relatively inexperienced in forest warfare.

28 Although Amherst resigned as Commander-in-Chief, he remained Colonel-in-Chief of the 60th Royal Americans, with a two-month interval in 1768, until his death in August 1797.

29 Butler, *Annals, Vol. I*, 207.

30 A rule previously breached when the 3rd Battalion was deployed to the Caribbean in 1761–2.

31 Butler, *Annals, Vol. I*, 218.

32 Ibid., 224.

Chapter 2 **1784–1815: from Red Coats to Green Jackets**

1 51st (2nd Yorkshire, West Riding) Light Infantry.

2 Lewis Butler, *The Annals of The King's Royal Rifle Corps, Vol. I: The Royal Americans* (London: Smith Elder, 1913), 238.

3 Ibid., 252.

4 Ibid., 254.

5 Ibid., 257.

6 Ibid., 252.

7 Lord Amherst was appointed Field Marshal on his resignation as Commander-in-Chief in 1795.

8 Lewis Butler, *The Annals of The King's Royal Rifle Corps, Vol. II: The Green Jacket* (London: John Murray, 1923), 13.

9 Rifles were anything up to 18 inches shorter than the British Army musket and hence required much longer bayonets, known as 'swords', if the user were not to be placed at a disadvantage in any close encounter with a 'musketeer'. Rifles also took longer to reload which is why riflemen operated in pairs, one covering the other during reloading with 'swords' fixed, in case they were rushed by the enemy. As rifles with fixed 'swords' risked injury on the march, Rifle regiments never sloped arms but carried them at the trail.

10 Butler, *Annals, Vol. II*, 16.

11 General Moore's Brigade Major was Captain Paul Anderson of the 60th. During the rest of his life, Moore had Anderson at his side, giving Anderson his dying instructions after the Battle of Corunna.

12 General Abercromby, who became Commander-in-Chief in 1797, resigned in early 1798 after making some justified but injudicious comments about the inadequate state of military preparedness in Ireland.

13 Butler, *Annals, Vol. II*, 24. Hompesch's Riflemen, of course, would not have been British but mainly Germans, Austrians and Hungarians.

14 Although the term 'Rifleman' was commonly used to refer to private soldiers in the 60th, 'Rifleman' did not replace 'Private' as a recognised rank in the British Army until 1923.

15 Butler, *Annals, Vol. II*, 27.

16 Ibid., 29.

17 Ibid., 30.

[18] Whitelocke was granted a majority in the 4th Battalion on 2 October 1788, the year that John Moore briefly held a majority in the same Battalion. Whitelocke ceased to appear on the Regimental roll of officers after 1791. Moore was later a member of the court-martial which sentenced Whitelocke to be cashiered for his part in the failed expedition to Brazil. Robert Craufurd also took part in the expedition as a brigade commander, surrendering his brigade but being exonerated from blame.

[19] George Prevost was the son of Augustin Prevost and a former commanding officer of the 4th Battalion, who served in St Vincent in 1795-6.

[20] Butler, *Annals, Vol. I*, 274.

[21] The same General Baird who commanded the expeditionary force, including the 2nd Battalion, that sailed in 1808 to Corunna.

[22] Butler, *Annals, Vol. I*, 282.

[23] Davy may well have been the first of many Old Etonians who joined the Regiment. In 1808 he was aged 28, having presumably purchased his promotion.

[24] The Baker rifle was named after its designer, Ezekiel Baker. It weighed 9 lbs, was $2\frac{1}{2}$ feet in length, and had seven grooves, making a quarter turn in the length of the barrel. The bullet was spherical and encircled by a leaden band, which fitted into the grooves. The rifle was difficult to load and mallets were for a time used to force the 'rifle-balls' into the grooves of the bore. Difficulties were also encountered with the powder horns, which were ill adapted for service and wasteful of powder. The rifle, however, was accurate up to 200 yards, which was almost three times the effective range of a musket. The rate of fire was much slower, one aimed shot a minute, while four shots a minute were possible with a musket.

[25] Butler, *Annals, Vol. II*, 60.

[26] Burrard served in the 4th Battalion from 1776 to its disbandment in 1783.

[27] Butler, *Annals, Vol. II*, 78.

[28] 45th (Nottinghamshire), later The Sherwood Foresters.

[29] Butler, *Annals, Vol. II*, 95.

[30] Beresford, later General Viscount Beresford, was Colonel-in-Chief of the 60th from 1852-4.

[31] Butler, *Annals, Vol. II*, 104.

[32] Davy, who achieved the rank of General, was Colonel-Commandant of the 1st Battalion from 1842 until his death in 1856.

[33] In February 1810 Wellington created the famous Light Division, giving command to Craufurd. Rifle companies of the 60th had no cause to serve with the Light Division, which included within its ranks Riflemen from the 95th as well as soldiers from the 43rd and 52nd. No attempt is made in this Brief History to include an account of the origins, tenets and actions of the Light Division in the Peninsula, although they play a key role in inspiring and underpinning the ethos of The Light Infantry and The Royal Green Jackets, the two regiments which today constitute The Light Division.

[34] 81st (Loyal Lincoln Volunteers), later The Loyal North Lancashire Regiment.

[35] Butler, *Annals, Vol. II*, 114.

[36] This may explain, in whole or in part, why the Regiment was not granted the Battle Honour 'Bussaco' until 27 April 1879, fifty-four years after receipt of the last of the Regiment's other Peninsular War battle honours.

[37] Beresford, a British general, held the rank of Marshal in the Portuguese Army.

[38] A grandson of General Augustin Prevost, commander of the British at Savannah (1779).

[39] Woodgate commanded the 4th Battalion from 1814-17.

[40] Butler, *Annals, Vol. II*, 153.

[41] The capture of both Ciudad Rodrigo and Badajoz was followed, to the eternal shame of the British Army, by widespread looting, rape and pillage which, despite the brave attempts of some, they were unable to prevent.

[42] 13th (1st Somersetshire) Light Infantry.

[43] Losses on such a scale suggest that events in the Pyrenees in late July 1813, which are often overlooked, merit the same degree of consideration and approbation as Wellington's other victories.

[44] On discharge he unusually received full pay for life.

[45] On the day after Vic de Bigorre, the similarly little-known battle of Tarbes took place during which three battalions of the 95th Rifles greatly distinguished themselves.

[46] Butler, *Annals, Vol. II*, 241–2.

[47] 40th (2nd Somersetshire), later South Lancashire Regiment, and 45th (Nottinghamshire), later The Sherwood Foresters.

[48] The 95th Rifles were also awarded sixteen battle honours. The 43rd and 52nd together received fourteen.

[49] The spelling of place names reflects that used when the Honour was published.

[50] Butler, *Annals, Vol. II*, 246.

[51] Galiffe, Schoedde and a Lieutenant Muller embarked with the 5th Battalion at Cork in 1808 and were the only officers to serve continuously with the Battalion throughout the Peninsular War and to return to Cork with the Battalion in 1814.

[52] Schoedde was promoted lieutenant-colonel in 1829, going on to command the 48th and 55th Regiments. In 1841–2 he served as a major-general in the First Chinese War. He was knighted and died at Lyndhurst in 1871.

[53] Galiffe and Loochstadt were present at all fifteen of the actions for which the Regiment received a Battle Honour. Major Schoedde was present at all except Albuera. Officers, however, did not receive Military General Service Medal clasps on the occasions when they received a Gold Medal/Cross.

[54] Butler, *Annals, Vol. II*, 289

[55] Ibid., 290.

Chapter 3 **1815–60: Peace and Imperial Wars**

[1] Lewis Butler, *The Annals of The King's Royal Rifle Corps, Vol. II* (London: John Murray, 1923), 302.

[2] Ibid., 311.

[3] Ibid., 311.

[4] Ibid., 316.

[5] Ibid., 322.

[6] Ibid., 312.

[7] 67th (South Hampshire) Regiment.

[8] The various Ionian Islands – Corfu, Cephelonia, Zante, Santa Maura, Ithaca, Cerigo and Paxo – at this time belonged to Great Britain either by conquest in the wars with France or by cession at the peace of 1814. They were handed over by Britain to Greece in 1864.

[9] Later Lieutenant-General Viscount Melville, a Colonel-Commandant from 1863–75. He is credited with instituting the annual Regimental Dinner for officers in 1859. See Lewis Butler, *The Annals of The King's Royal Rifle Corps, Vol. III: The 60th: The KRRC* (London: John Murray, 1926), 59 and 319.

[10] Butler, *Annals, Vol. II*, 319–20.

[11] Butler, *Annals, Vol. III*, 24.

[12] Ibid., 43.

[13] The spelling used in the Adjutant General's letter of notification dated 30 December 1852. See Butler, *Annals, Vol. III*, 58.

[14] Ibid., 57.

[15] In addition to the naming of Ladysmith, Harrismith, fifty miles west of Ladysmith, was named after Sir Harry Smith.

[16] Ibid., 66.

[17] Sir Harry Smith was replaced by Lieutenant-General the Hon. George Cathcart in April 1852.

[18] Butler, *Annals, Vol. III*, 75.

[19] Ibid., 79.

[20] Ibid., 86.

[21] The mutineers planned the mutiny to coincide with the start of the church service, which the soldiers attended without weapons. However, because the weather was so hot, the service was postponed 30 minutes. The Battalion, therefore, happened to be on parade in advance of the service, rather than in the church, and thus was able to respond immediately. After the Mutiny, soldiers in India were ordered to attend church with their weapons, which were stacked at the back of the church under guard.

[22] Butler, *Annals, Vol. III*, 111.

[23] Throughout the time that the Delhi Field Force occupied the ridge, the mutineers were able to enter and leave the city freely. It is incorrect, therefore, as often occurs, to refer to a 'siege' at Delhi.

[24] The close relationship of the 60th and the Guides at Delhi, second only to the 60th's relationship with the Sirmoor Battalion of Gurkhas, is reflected today in a formal Alliance linking The Royal Green Jackets and the 2nd Battalion, The Frontier Force (Guides), a regiment in the Pakistan Army.

[25] Butler, *Annals, Vol. III*, 123.

[26] Ibid., 129.

[27] Ibid., 141.

[28] Ibid., 156.

[29] Ibid., 152.

[30] The Victoria Cross was first awarded for acts of gallantry during the Crimean War.

[31] Sir Colin Campbell served in the 7th Battalion during its time in Canada (1814-15) and with the 5th Battalion in Gibraltar until its disbandment in 1818. He declared his service with the 5th Battalion to be the happiest time of his life. At the end of the Mutiny he was raised to the peerage under the title of Baron Clyde of Clydesdale (Lord Clyde) and in 1862 was appointed a Field Marshal. He died in 1863.

[32] Butler, *Annals, Vol. III*, 186.

[33] Assumed to be Brigadier Sutton, commander of the 2nd Brigade in which the 2nd Battalion was grouped.

[34] Butler, *Annals, Vol. III*, 197-8.

Chapter 4 1861–98: Peace and More Imperial Wars

[1] Lewis Butler, *The Annals of The King's Royal Rifle Corps, Vol. III: The 60th: The KRRC* (London: John Murray, 1926), 218.

[2] Ibid., 221.

[3] Canada was granted self-governing Dominion status in 1867.

[4] Because of its historic links with Canada, the Regiment later established alliances with a number of Canadian Militia regiments. See Appendix E.

[5] The Suez Canal was opened in November 1869.

[6] Steuart Hare, *The Annals of The King's Royal Rifle Corps, Vol. IV: The 60th: The KRRC* (London: John Murray, 1929), 37.

[7] Lewis Butler, *Annals, Vol. III*, 294.

[8] Ibid., 295.

[9] Steuart Hare, *Annals, Vol. IV*, 111.

[10] 58th (Rutlandshire), later The Northamptonshire Regiment.

[11] Steuart Hare, *Annals, Vol. IV*, 23-4.

[12] Ibid., 332.

[13] Colonel-Commandant, 1908-19

[14] The Camel Corps had four regiments, the others being the Heavy, Light and Guards Camel Regiments.

[15] Gordon was killed at Khartoum in January 1885.

[16] Steuart Hare, *Annals, Vol. IV*, 137-8.

[17] Ibid., 139.

[18] Ibid., 114.

[19] Ibid..

[20] Ibid., 351-2.

Chapter 5 1899–1913: The South African War and Subsequent Years

[1] The Boers used 7 mm Mauser rifles with smokeless powder and ammunition clips holding five rounds, all of which could be loaded at one time. The .303 Lee-Metford used by the British had a magazine of ten rounds, but these had to be loaded manually one at a time.

[2] The eight guns, which were critical to the defence of Ladysmith, consisted of two naval 4.7 inch, four naval 12-pounders and two 6.3 inch howitzers.

[3] Lieutenant-Colonel Gore-Browne exchanged to command the 2nd Battalion, when it departed for India, via Ceylon, in July 1900.

[4] Lieutenant Roberts was ADC to General Clery, commanding the 2nd Division. He was the son of Field Marshal Lord Roberts VC. Captain WN Congreve of The Rifle Brigade was one of the other four to be awarded a Victoria Cross.

[5] The impact of 'Black Week' led to many in the Rifle Volunteer Corps joining the Regiment, the City Imperial Volunteers (CIV) or the Imperial Yeomanry. A company of cadets from the 1st Cadet Battalion, The King's Royal Rifle Corps, joined the CIV. See Appendix D.

[6] Steuart Hare, *The Annals of The King's Royal Rifle Corps, Vol. IV: The 60th; The KRRC* (London: John Murray, 1929), 231.

[7] The Orange Free State was annexed and re-titled the Orange River Colony on 24 May 1900.

[8] The self-governing Dominion of South Africa was subsequently established on 31 May 1910.

[9] Crete was handed to Greece in 1908. The allied troops left in 1909.

[10] Steuart Hare, *Annals, Vol. IV*, 312.

[11] Ibid., 313.

[12] Ibid., 327.

[13] Field Marshal Lord Grenfell was gazetted as an Ensign in the 60th Rifles in August 1859. Promotion was slow and he did not become a captain until 1871. He joined the staff in South Africa in 1873 and did not serve at Regimental duty thereafter. In January 1899 he became Governor of Malta, where he made a great success of the job and was raised to the peerage. From 1904–8 he was Commander-in-Chief in Ireland, after which he was promoted Field Marshal. He became a Colonel-Commandant in 1898 and senior Colonel-Commandant from 1908 until his death in 1925.

[14] After the First World War the *Celer et Audax* Club, the KRRC Association, the Riflemen's Aid Association (Society) and the Chronicle were all administered from the Regiment's London office at 71 Eccleston Square. The office relocated to 32 Eccleston Square in 1927, where it remained until it moved to the Depot at Winchester in 1964.

Chapter 6 1914–18: The First World War

[1] During the course of the War, the United States, Italy, Greece, Romania, Portugal and Japan joined the Allies. Turkey and Bulgaria joined the Central Powers. Serbia was an ally from the outset.

[2] This number excludes Dominion and Colonial troops.

[3] A further Service battalion, 26 KRRC, was raised at Winchester in July 1919, but was disbanded two weeks later.

[4] The first Service drafting battalion, 14 KRRC, was not established until 31 October 1914.

[5] The 2nd Battalion, The Oxfordshire & Buckinghamshire Light Infantry, saved the day at Nonne Boschen by launching the critical counter-attack that halted the Germans.

[6] Lieutenant Dimmer was a former member of the 1st Cadet Battalion, The King's Royal Rifle Corps. He was killed in action on 21 March 1918 while commanding the 2nd/4th Battalion, The Royal Berkshire Regiment.

[7] Prince Maurice of Battenburg joined the 1st Battalion in 1911 and was killed on 27 October 1914. His brother, HH Prince Leopold of Battenburg, was also in the Regiment from 1914–21. He was with the 1st Battalion in France, but was invalided home as the result of a fall and was afterwards unfit for active service. He served on the staff in India and retired as a major. He died in 1922.

[8] Steuart Hare, *The Annals of The King's Royal Rifle Corps, Vol. V: The Great War* (London: John Murray, 1932), 9–10.

[9] Ibid., 99.

[10] Ibid.

[11] Rifleman Peachment was one of eight First World War soldiers aged 18 to be awarded a Victoria Cross.

[12] General Rawlinson joined the 4th Battalion in India in 1884, before transferring to the Coldstream Guards prior to attendance at the Staff College in 1892. He was a staff

officer in General White's Headquarters at Ladysmith during its defence in 1899–1900, was later Commandant of the Staff College, and during the First World War commanded 7th Division and IV Corps before taking over Fourth Army. From 1920 he was Commander-in-Chief in India, where he died in 1925.

[13] Tanks were used for the first time in the First World War during a major attack at Flers-Courcelette on 15 September 1916. The results were mixed. When the tanks worked, they worked well, but the majority of the forty-nine assigned to support the infantry suffered mechanical failure.

[14] The estimate of German casualties varies enormously but the number was probably about the same as the BEF (420,000).

[15] The other battalion holding the bridgehead was 1st Battalion, The Northamptonshire Regiment.

[16] Steuart Hare, *Annals, Vol. V*, 298.

[17] The Treaty of Versailles was subsequently signed on 28 June 1919.

[18] The breakdown of the total of 12,824 is 567 officers, 74 warrant officers, 2,174 non-commissioned officers, 23 buglers and 9,986 Riflemen. The Rifle Brigade's losses were 11,575 officers and men. On 22 July 1919 The King's Royal Rifle Corps and The Rifle Brigade held a joint Service of Remembrance at Westminster Abbey to honour their dead.

[19] The figure of 130,000 is an aggregate of casualty returns and does not take into account double, and probably triple, counting of those who were wounded more than once.

[20] Two former members of the Regiment were awarded a Victoria Cross for acts of gallantry during the First World War: Captain F.O. Grenfell of the 9th Lancers during a cavalry charge in Belgium in 1914 (killed in action in 1915) and Lieutenant-Colonel A.D. Borton, commanding officer of the 2/22nd (County of London) Battalion, The London Regiment (The Queen's), in Palestine in 1917.

[21] The list of awards included two Distinguished Conduct Medals, five Military Crosses and five Military Medals awarded to members of the Fijian contingent serving with the 4th Battalion.

[22] The Military Cross was instituted in 1914. Eligibility originally extended to officers of the rank of captain and below, and to warrant officers. In 1915 majors became eligible. In 1916 the Military Medal was instituted for other ranks, including warrant officers.

[23] Lieutenant-General Morland joined the 3rd Battalion in 1884, attending the Staff College in 1890. During the First World War he commanded 14th and 5th Divisions, before commanding X Corps during the Battle of the Somme and XIII Corps in 1918. He subsequently commanded the British Army of Occupation in the Rhineland and Aldershot Command as a General, before ill health forced his retirement. He died in 1925 shortly after becoming a Colonel-Commandant.

[24] Lieutenant-General Pitcairn Campbell spent most of his service prior to the South African War at Regimental duty. He commanded the 1st Battalion after the death of Lieutenant-Colonel Gunning at the Battle of Talana and was with the Battalion at Ladysmith. He later commanded the 3rd Battalion in Ireland. During the First World War he commanded Southern Command and then Western Command. He retired in 1920 and was Colonel Commandant of the 4th Battalion from 1918 until its disbandment in 1923. He died in 1933.

Chapter 7 1919–38: Between the Two World Wars

[1] The 20th Battalion shed its Pioneer role and served as an infantry battalion during the Occupation.

[2] Giles Mills and Roger Nixon, *The Annals of The King's Royal Rifle Corps, Vol. VI: 1921–1943* (London: Leo Cooper, 1971), 6–7.

[3] Ibid., 20.

[4] In the summer of 1919 the Coalition Government instructed Departments to plan on the assumption that Great Britain would not be involved in a major war during the next ten years, and that no expeditionary force would be required. Between 1923 and 1933 allocations for purchases or maintenance of Army weapons and warlike stores averaged

about £2 million per annum – under 9% of the already small sum spent on armament. In 1928, as the world moved towards the Wall Street crash and depression, the Rule was reaffirmed (ironically, by Winston Churchill) and applied more stringently than before. Unless an explicit rejection of the Rule was made at any point, it was applied on a continuous basis. It was rescinded in March 1932. It was not until 1934 that serious attempts were initiated to make good equipment deficiencies.

[5] Giles Mills and Roger Nixon, *Annals, Vol VI*, 23.

[6] Ibid., 29.

[7] Ibid., 40–1.

Chapter 8 1939–45: **The Second World War**

[1] The first American unit to occupy the Rifle Depot in readiness for the invasion of France was, coincidentally, the 60th Infantry Regiment of the 9th Division of the United States Army.

[2] Later Lieutenant-General Sir Euan Miller. He was awarded a DSO for his actions at Calais. He commanded 7th Armoured Division after the Second World War and became Military Secretary before retiring in 1954. He was a Colonel-Commandant from 1954–61.

[3] In total, 204 Green Jackets died at Calais. 1st Battalion, The Rifle Brigade, lost nearly eighty killed, including the commanding officer, Lieutenant-Colonel C.B.A. Hoskyns.

[4] Operation Barbarossa, the German invasion of the Soviet Union, was launched on 22 June 1941.

[5] Later Field Marshal Lord Wilson of Libya.

[6] The Brigade was a part of 2nd Armoured Division, which Churchill had earlier bravely ordered to North Africa at a time when Great Britain was still threatened by invasion.

[7] Major A.R.W. (Toby) Low, later Lord Aldington, commanded C Company. He was awarded a DSO for his actions on 13 April 1941.

[8] Giles Mills and Roger Nixon, *The Annals of The King's Royal Rifle Corps, Vol. VI: 1921-1943* (London: Leo Cooper, 1971), 136.

[9] Brigadier J.M.L. (Callum) Renton (Rifle Brigade) commanded the 7th Motor Brigade.

[10] The 9th Battalion, The Rifle Brigade, was disbanded at the same time for the same reason.

[11] Brigadier T.J.B. Bosville (Rifle Brigade) commanded 7th Motor Brigade on the promotion of Major-General Renton (Rifle Brigade) to command 7th Armoured Division.

[12] Later General Sir George Erskine. He commanded the 2nd Battalion from June 1940 to January 1941 and was Colonel-Commandant of the 2nd Battalion from 1955-8 and of 2nd Green Jackets, The King's Royal Rifle Corps, from 1961-5.

[13] Thirty-five miles south-west of Tunis.

[14] Giles Mills and Roger Nixon, *Annals, Vol. VI*, 373.

[15] Giles Mills, *The Annals of The King's Royal Rifle Corps, Vol. VII: 1943-65* (*Celer et Audax* Club, 1979), 13.

[16] Later Major-General E.A.W. Willams. He commanded 2nd Division in Germany from 1960-2. He was Colonel-Commandant of 2nd Green Jackets, The King's Royal Rifle Corps, in 1965, and Colonel-Commandant of The Royal Green Jackets from 1966-70.

[17] Giles Mills, *Annals, Vol. VII*, 149.

[18] Later General Sir Evelyn Barker. He commanded the 2nd Battalion from July 1936 to August 1938 and was Colonel-Commandant of the Battalion from 1946-55.

[19] He assumed command from Lieutenant-Colonel Heathcoat-Amory on 29 July 1944.

[20] Giles Mills, *Annals, Vol. VII*, 62.

[21] B Company was commanded by Major W.F. (Bill) Deedes, later Lord Deedes and the Editor of *The Daily Telegraph*.

[22] Giles Mills, *Annals, Vol. VII*, 35.

[23] Others included Lieutenants M.J. Gilliat (later Sir Martin Gilliat, Private Secretary to HM Queen Elizabeth, The Queen Mother), P. Pardoe and P.H. Parker.

[24] Giles Mills, *Annals, Vol. VII*, 31.

[25] *KRRC Chronicle*, 1943, p. 28.

Chapter 9 **1946–65: The Concluding Years**

1 Giles Mills, *The Annals of The King's Royal Rifle Corps, Vol. VII: 1943-65 (Celer et Audax* Club, 1979), 201.
2 Ibid., 207.
3 Ibid., 211.
4 Ibid., 216.
5 Brigadier Hunt, later Brigadier Lord Hunt, was still serving at the time of the Everest expedition. In 1929 he was awarded the King's Medal at Sandhurst. He joined the Regiment in 1930 and retired in 1956 after being Assistant Commandant at the Staff College, Camberley.
6 Mills, *Annals, Vol. VII,* 222.
7 Later Field Marshal Sir Roland Gibbs, Chief of the General Staff from 1976-9.
8 At the same time Lieutenant-Colonel (later Brigadier) E.G.B. Davies-Scourfield of the 60th commanded 3rd Green Jackets, The Rifle Brigade.
9 Mills, *Annals, Vol. VII,* 254.
10 Later Major-General G.H. Mills, author of Volumes VI and VII of the Regimental *Annals.*
11 Later General Sir Roland Guy.
12 Later Field Marshal Lord Bramall of Bushfield.
13 Later Lieutenant-General Sir David House.
14 Mills, *Annals, Vol. VII,* 288.
15 Ibid., 294.
16 Ibid., 312.

Appendix D **Territorials, Militia and Cadets**

1 In writing this Appendix, the author has drawn heavily on, and is grateful for, the information provided in Colonel A.R. Martin's *Historical Record of The London Regiment* and Captain R.L. Collett's *The History of 1st Cadet Battalion, The King's Royal Rifle Corps: Centenary 1894-1994,* both published in pamphlet form, seemingly undated.
2 In 1859, when Rifle Volunteer Corps were first raised, there was no County of London. London consisted solely of the City of London, with Surrey and Kent extending to the south bank of the Thames at Deptford and Greenwich, with Middlesex on the North bank. Consequently, units raised in what later became the County of London bore the old county names.
3 The 6th (City of London) Battalion was nicknamed the 'Cast Iron Sixth' because it wore a heavy black cap badge.
4 Giles Mills, *The Annals of The King's Royal Rifle Corps, Vol. VII: 1943-65 (Celer et Audax* Club, 1979), 239. During its existence The Queen's Royal Rifles ran a very successful Parachute Club initiated by Major J.R.T. Eve, which included a freefall display team performing at shows all over the south of England.
5 Major Anthony Eden served with the 21st (Service) Battalion, The King's Royal Rifle Corps (Yeoman Rifles), during the First World War and was awarded a Military Cross for distinguished services. He was Honorary Colonel of The Queen's Westminsters from 1952-61. His son, Nick, is well remembered for establishing the Green Jackets London Club at 56 Davies Street. Lieutenant the Hon. Richard Wood (Lord Holderness) was severely wounded in December 1942, losing both legs as the result of an air attack while serving with the 2nd Battalion in North Africa. He was Honorary Colonel of the 4th (Volunteer) Battalion, The Royal Green Jackets, from 1967-89.
6 By 1901 the Reverend Wills had risen to the rank of Colonel. He died in 1913.
7 Army Order 151 of 1905.
8 The others awarded a Victoria Cross were Lieutenant-Colonel Harry Greenwood VC, DSO and Bar, OBE, MC, of the 9th Battalion, The King's Own Yorkshire Light Infantry, for acts of gallantry in France in 1918, and Captain Albert Ball, VC, DSO and Two Bars, MC, of The Sherwood Foresters attached to the Royal Flying Corps, for repeated acts of gallantry over France in 1917.

Index

This index covers the content of the preliminary pages, the Endnotes and the Appendices, as well as the main Chapters of this book. It is as comprehensive as the limited availability of space has permitted.

Index

Index